SIX STOPS ON THE NATIONAL SECURITY TOUR

T0373554

The U.S. military economy incorporates hundreds of American communities. This is the first book to connect our national security apparatus to the local level via deeply reported portraits of six carefully selected locations, including military Meccas and out-of-the-way places. They are woven into the warfare economy by bases, nuclear weapons labs, and production sites. The book includes an invaluable overview of how the military is structured, how its budget is made, and what it costs. It also shows how the military economy perpetuates itself. In on-the-ground reporting, Pemberton traces the lines of connection between the tour stops presented here and our country's foreign policy, industrial policy, and budget priorities. She examines the meaning of national security in the current moment, as climate change becomes what the military itself calls "an urgent and growing threat." And she dramatically demonstrates how redirecting our militarized foreign and industrial policy toward climate security can help these communities become part of the solution. For students, scholars, public servants, and all concerned citizens, this book is essential reading.

Miriam Pemberton has studied the U.S. military economy and the means of shrinking it down to size for decades, first as Director of the National Commission for Economic Conversion and Disarmament and then as a Research Fellow at the Institute for Policy Studies. With Lawrence Korb, she headed the task force that for a decade produced the annual "Unified Security Budget of the United States." With William Hartung she edited *Lessons from Iraq: Avoiding the Next War* (Paradigm, 2008). She headed up the team that produced three successive versions of "Military vs. Climate Security: The Budgets Compared." Pemberton holds a PhD from the University of Michigan.

SIX STOPS ON THE NATIONAL SECURITY TOUR

Rethinking Warfare Economies

Miriam Pemberton

Routledge
Taylor & Francis Group

NEW YORK AND LONDON

Cover image: © Getty Images

First published 2023
by Routledge
605 Third Avenue, New York, NY 10158

and by Routledge
4 Park Square, Milton Park, Abingdon, Oxon, OX14 4RN

Routledge is an imprint of the Taylor & Francis Group, an informa business

© 2023 Taylor & Francis

The right of Miriam Pemberton to be identified as author of this work has been asserted in accordance with sections 77 and 78 of the Copyright, Designs and Patents Act 1988.

Library of Congress Cataloging-in-Publication Data
A catalog record for this title has been requested

ISBN: 978-1-032-27684-7 (hbk)
ISBN: 978-0-367-25767-5 (pbk)
ISBN: 978-1-003-29370-5 (ebk)

DOI: 10.4324/9781003293705

Typeset in Bembo
by Newgen Publishing UK

For my family, most of all

CONTENTS

FIGURES

ACKNOWLEDGMENTS

In gratitude

To those who gave me my early education in these topics, getting me started on the unpremeditated path that wound up here: especially Seymour Melman, Greg Bischak, Jeff Dumas, Christine Evans-Klock, Ann Markusen, Jim Raffel, and Joel Yudken. To my colleagues at the Institute for Policy Studies, especially its former director, John Cavanagh, who gave me the space, support, and fellowship to pursue this passion.

To my three most generous readers, editors and consultants: Bill Hartung, John Feffer, and Col. Lawrence Wilkerson (ret.).

It turned out that among all the people I talked to, one person at each stop on the tour did the most to bring the place alive. These were John Harrity, John Dubnansky, Don Nakamoto, Bryan Barnhouse, Minesh Bacrani, and Bob Devine. Thank you.

To Jennifer Knerr, who gracefully shepherded this project at Routledge, and Kanaga Thara Balaji, Stuart Murray, and Jacqueline Dorsey.

And last and most, to Alan, with love, for editing, advising, cheerleading, life-sharing and, not least, many bouts of technical assistance.

INTRODUCTION

We'll start the tour at the military's ground zero, in Washington, DC. Or, specifically, in its Virginia segment across the Potomac. While now and then you drive by military installations in DC and its Maryland suburbs (Walter Reed Army Medical Center, the Naval Surface Warfare Center, the National Defense University for example), you have a hard time avoiding them on the Virginia side of the river.

Begin where the tourists often do, at the Lee Mansion, overlooking Arlington National Cemetery. The military set its footprint here at the start of the Civil War, when General Lee abandoned his wife's estate and the Union moved in. Following its defeat at Bull Run, the Union army carved the western edge of the estate into a fortification to defend Washington. It's still there, now as an Army–Marines base called Joint Base Myer-Henderson Hall—270 acres, crooked like a protecting arm around the cemetery.

The process of dislodging this area's Confederate "heritage" from the landscape has begun. Lee Highway, a major artery that circles around the cemetery from the northwest, retains the name for the time being, but since 2019 its extension down the river no longer carries the name of Jefferson Davis. Between the river and the cemetery at its south end lies the ground zero epicenter itself, the Pentagon.

It too sits on the grounds of the original Lee Estate. Its five concentric rings, linked by 17.5 miles of corridors on the ground and second floors, were built during World War II in concrete, and low to the ground, to conserve steel for ships and weapons. The design carries its own Civil War echoes: Fort Sumter, site of the war's opening act, is also pentagonal.

Long before 9/11, the building actually acquired the nickname Ground Zero, a nod to its status as the likely target of a nuclear first strike. General Leslie Groves

DOI: 10.4324/9781003293705-1

of the Army Corps of Engineers oversaw its construction. In Chapter 6 we'll visit his other big wartime construction project, in Los Alamos.

At 6.5 million square feet, the Pentagon remains the largest office building in the world. Apart from his dislike of the building's aesthetics, Franklin Roosevelt's Uncle Fred Delano—Washington, DC's chief architectural planner at the time— wondered why such a gargantuan permanent building was needed for a temporary war emergency. (When, a few years later, the War Department became the Department of Defense (DoD), he got his answer.)

Its three above-ground stories sit on two more underground. While patronizing the food court down here, some 26,000 workers in the building (uniformed military, civilian and support personnel) can buy jewelry, a new suit, or chocolate (in the shape of the Hiroshima nuclear bomb, if desired) or get their hair done or their shoes repaired. Or hit the gym, the basketball court or the pool. Or see a dentist. This is all mostly a matter of convenience, removing the midday errand nightmare of navigating massive parking lots and traffic whizzing in all directions around the building. But touring this underground city also conjures an eerie feeling of a separate world where, in the event of a true national security emergency above ground, a lot of the routines of ordinary life could go on undisturbed.

Fanning out across town from this spot is an array of military satellite installations—for example, the Defense Advanced Research Projects Agency, the Defense Mapping Agency, the Defense Information Systems Agency, the U.S. Army National Guard Readiness Center and, upriver, the CIA. Up I-95 at Fort Meade, between Washington and Baltimore, is the National Security Agency (NSA), whose five million square feet is second only to the Pentagon.

And, finally, the ground in this area is saturated with defense contractors. The database governmentcontractswon.com lists more than a thousand of them in Arlington County alone, where the Pentagon sits. Since 2000 these Arlington contractors have signed more than 55,000 reported individual military contracts totaling more than $54 billion.

Little manufacturing is done here—the fighter jets get assembled far away from Washington, in places like Texas and California. The bulk of these DC contractors populate sleek, corporate-bland office high-rises, mostly laboring at the white-collar dimensions of the trade—in services such as engineering, logistics, and information technology—and have anodyne names that tell you little about what they do. Take Advanced Systems Development I or, as it now prefers, ASD, which tells you even less. It has ridden the Pentagon's intensified focus on cybersecurity into contracts with multiple divisions of the Army, the Missile Defense Agency, the million-acre White Sands Missile Range in New Mexico, and the Joint Staff. For many of these companies, the work product consists mostly of interfacing with the Pentagon on behalf of their manufacturing facilities located far away.

Contrary to what we might expect, the area's military contractors are not most-heavily concentrated in an area next to the Pentagon called Pentagon City—that is dominated by apartments and megamalls. Instead, they have been clustered in a corridor behind Reagan National Airport, called Crystal City. Many of its residential and commercial buildings are connected by underground tunnels, meaning that it's quite possible to live there without ever going outside.

Here, for example, is Subsystem Technologies, which has done "weapons systems advance engineering analysis" for projects including the most expensive system of all time, the F-35 fighter jet, as well as offering, in its own words, "support in various areas, such as risk analysis, integrated product integrity analysis, vulnerability assessments, penetration testing, security mitigation planning, and security computer-based training; joint capabilities integration," and the list goes on.

One of Crystal City's high-rises, at 1235 Clark St., assembles a multitude of contractors, from small branches of Big Five prime contractors General Dynamics and Raytheon, to lesser knowns such as Syncadd Systems (Army, Navy, and Air Force contracts) and Concurrent Technologies (which we'll meet again in Pennsylvania), to the Air Force Deputy General Counsel.

Such assemblages, and indeed most of their fellow contractors across town, are invisible to the casual observer driving by. The exception to Pentagon contractor obscurity is the view from the waterfront, where Washington's warfare economy declares itself, literally, from the rooftops. Gazing across the river from, say, the terrace of the Kennedy Center, it's hard to miss the neon sign for Raytheon (which, following a merger with United Technologies, is now the second largest military contractor in the world) across the street from BAE Systems, currently number eight (it will much concern us in Chapter 8). Down the river a sign for the perennial number one, Lockheed Martin (coming up over and over in these pages), looms over Reagan National Airport. In between are hundreds of other non-behemoths.

This vista is about to acquire a new focal point: the dramatic "Helix" structure announcing Amazon's new second headquarters. (There will be no sign. Not that one will be needed.) It will push some military contractors toward other parts of the city, while providing amenities like restaurants and trees for the ones that stay. (One architecture critic described the trees running up the sides of the building as "expos[ing] Amazon workers to a cultivated facsimile of what they might find outdoors if they had time to be outdoors."[1]) Amazon is itself striving mightily to expand its own role as a contractor to its new neighbor. After a protracted challenge to Microsoft's $10 billion "JEDI" contract to put Pentagon information systems into the cloud, Amazon succeeded in derailing the contract. The procurement process started all over again.[2] And in August of 2021 the National Security Administration announced another contract award to Amazon for cloud services, costing *another* $10 billion.[3]

Out beyond the Beltway, in every state of the union, and in nearly every congressional district, is the rest of the military's domestic reach: the missile silos, in places like North Dakota and Missouri, the weapons arsenals in Nevada and Pennsylvania, for example, the vast network of military bases that reaches into every state. And the contractors: In fiscal year 2020 the DoD awarded them more than 3.6 million contracts.[4]

"National Security"

All of these are contributing parts of the National Security mission. The term had no real currency until the Cold War replaced preparation for a specific war with a military establishment permanently on call to pursue U.S. interests by force anywhere in the world. Congress codified this new mission in 1947 in the National Security Act, with amendments passed in 1949 reorganizing the War Department into the Department of Defense. The main centralizing features of the Act were: creating a new Air Force branch; creating a civilian Secretary of Defense invested with authority over all the military branches; establishing a National Security Council and a National Security Advisor to coordinate national security policy in the executive branch; creating the CIA; and, in 1952, before handing his job over to Eisenhower, Truman created the NSA. Analysts began referring to the result as the infrastructure of the National Security State.

But what the Act didn't do was define National Security. And what we mean by the term remains amorphous nearly 75 years later, while carrying almost talismanic power. These may be the two most powerful words in the language of U.S. policy.

Building the apparatus of this National Security State coincided with the debut of The Nuclear Age. In the 1950s, the threat to America became the threat of wholesale extinction, and it turned global. An internal poster at the NSA read "Plant security consciousness in your own mind," and "Cultivate security consciousness in the minds of others."[5] Such admonitions had plenty of success, as many Americans came to believe that protecting your family entailed stockpiling food in the basement and building a bomb shelter in the backyard.

Almost nobody does that anymore. But almost everybody is tempted to define the cause they care about as a national security threat. President Eisenhower got traction, which turned into money, for his interstate highway system by branding it the National Security Highway System. And science education in America got a huge funding boost after Americans started watching Sputnik make its way across the night sky. These days international competition over trade is frequently draped in "national security" clothing. The Trump Administration even tried to label imported steel from Canada as a national security threat.[6]

In the name of National Security, the reach of the NSA and other intelligence agencies has come to include the clandestine surveillance of millions, including U.S. citizens. The 9/11 attacks became a pretext for the Bush Administration to override, secretly, the legal constraints on such domestic surveillance. Reestablishing these constraints is still contested territory. And massive amounts of information are whisked away from public view, justifiably and otherwise, when marked "Classified."

Another consequence of living in a National Security State is this: If what constitutes national security has never been defined, and how to achieve it remains contested, how can we know how much money is enough to devote to it? When "security" is at stake, the case for erring on the side of *more* always starts out ahead. The Department of Defense's official National Security Strategy (NSS) perennially cites a set of national security needs that can't be paid for with the current budget, and then uses this disconnect to argue for more money. The alternative, of course, is to prioritize the missions and pare the budget to fit them.

What has been uncontested from the beginning is that providing the tools of military force involves the cooperation—the entanglement—of the public and the private sectors. While the government does some military production—in so-called Government-Owned Government Operated facilities (GOGOs)—since General Motors was enlisted to build tanks in World War II, most production has been outsourced to private contractors.

Yet the main architects of the National Security State—President Truman followed by President Eisenhower—definitely had their moments of skepticism about this permanent marriage of public and private sector military interests. Truman's came before his presidency began. As a congressman he made a national name for himself by convening the Commission on Wartime Contracting to uncover waste and fraud in the system.

Eisenhower's doubts came, or were most forcefully expressed, at the end of his presidency. In his famous Farewell Address he raised the alarm about

> this conjunction of an immense military establishment and a large arms industry [which] is new in the American experience. The total influence—economic, political, even spiritual—is felt in every city, every Statehouse, every office of the Federal government. We recognize the imperative need for this development. Yet, we must not fail to comprehend its grave implications. Our toil, resources, and livelihood are all involved. So is the very structure of our society. In the councils of government, we must guard against the acquisition of unwarranted influence, whether sought or unsought, by the military-industrial complex.

Early drafts of the speech called it the "military industrial congressional complex," a more complete descriptor.[7]

Eisenhower raised this alarm and was largely ignored. The "imperative need for this development" came under radical questioning three decades later, when its rationale—the Cold War against the Soviet Union—fell apart. But the "need" revamped and reasserted itself, and the complex came back as strong as ever. It is now poised to command more money, adjusted for inflation, than it had at any time during the Cold War. The term has acquired such potency that it has been applied over the years to all manner of imputed institutional power conspiracies, from the "prison industrial complex" to the "medical industrial complex" to even Minority Leader Mitch McConnell's 2021 descriptor for resistance to voter-suppression laws as the "outrage industrial complex."

This book will explore this military-industrial, public-private complex, and how it plays out beyond the Beltway. The economy created by military spending is deeply embedded in communities across America. We will visit a few of them to see how they came to be that way. In trips to six locations around the country, plus our militarized border and the apparatus of the hyper-weapons of the future, the book will connect this complex's big picture to its ground level. It will tell the story of how and why these pieces of it came to be where they are, who works in them, and how these pieces fit into the whole.

The tour will be far from a comprehensive survey of our vast and vastly complex military enterprise. It will, though, incorporate major manufacturing centers and out-of-the-way sites, and communities woven into the warfare economy by military bases, nuclear weapons labs, and the production of military aircraft, surveillance technologies, armored combat vehicles, artillery and missile launching systems, and ventures into exotic technological frontiers.

It will fill in some of the details about how the military economy works—its organization, and its means of perpetuating itself. The book will trace the lines of connection between these tour stops and our country's foreign policy, industrial policy, and budget priorities. It will, in other words, connect the microeconomics of these local defense-dependent communities to the macroeconomics that put them there.

The stops on the tour have been chosen with one other criterion in mind. Each place has, in some way and at some time, tried to become less dependent on the Pentagon, to find other useful things to do. We will look at these openings at the local level—in communities as well as individual companies—to a less-militarized economy. The book will make the case for what needs to happen for these efforts to succeed on a national scale.

What are the prospects that, all these years later, the "undue influence" of military industrial arrangements can be dislodged? In his first budget, President Biden could have begun the process by cutting the near-historically large military budget inherited from his predecessor. He didn't. And Russia's invasion of Ukraine sent United States military spending even higher.

But the Biden administration has taken a few steps in the direction of redefining national security and the means to achieve it. It declared up front that diplomats, not the military, would take the lead on shaping U.S. foreign policy. And in one of its most important steps toward redefinition, it committed to "Put the Climate Crisis at the Center of United States Foreign Policy and National Security."[8]

During his presidential campaign Joe Biden told the story of an early visit to the Pentagon as vice president for a briefing on the greatest danger facing our security: "Know what they told us it was?… Climate change. Climate change is the single greatest concern for war and disruption in the world, short of a nuclear exchange."[9] In this new decade two unprecedented national security challenges have converged on us: a global pandemic, perhaps the first of many, and climate changes threatening to become irreversible, leaving us without a habitable planet. No military forces on Earth can stop them. But the country's resources, too many of them currently commandeered by its military forces, have to be mobilized against them. And to prevent catastrophic climate change, the country's manufacturing capacity, too much of it devoted to supplying those military forces, must be redeployed toward creating a zero-emission economy.

Some parts of the new administration's early budgets, legislative proposals and administrative actions are trying to make that commitment real. Also real, though, are the powerful interests massed to prevent this: those who profit from a rising tide of federal money parked in the Pentagon budget, as well as the many profiting from climate denial. It will be the fight of our lives.

Notes

1 Philip Kennicott, "The helix is a distraction," *Washington Post*, February 21, 2021, www.washingtonpost.com/entertainment/museums/amazon-new-headquarters-the-helix/2021/02/17/.
2 Aaron Gregg, "Pentagon cancels $10 billion JEDI contract challenged by Amazon, ending long-contested cloud procurement deal," *Washington Post*, July 6, 2021, www.washingtonpost.com/business/2021/07/06/pentagon-cancels-10-billion-jedi-contract-challenged-by-amazon-ending-long-contested-cloud-procurement-deal/.
3 Aaron Gregg, "NSA quietly awards $10 billion contract to Amazon, drawing protest from Microsoft," *Washington Post*, August 11, 2021, www.washingtonpost.com/business/2021/08/11/amazon-nsa-contract/.
4 According to the federal government's main repository of data on its expenditures, usaspending.gov.
5 Dexter Fergie, "The Strange Career of 'National Security,'" *The Atlantic*, September 29, 2019, www.theatlantic.com/ideas/archive/2019/09/the-strange-career-of-national-security/598048/.
6 Aaron Gregg and Christian Davenport, "Trump says steel imports are a threat to national security. The defense industry disagrees," *Washington Post*, March 5, 2018, www.washingtonpost.com/news/business/wp/2018/03/05/trump-says-steel-imports-are-a-threat-to-national-security-the-defense-industry-disagrees/.
7 Bill Greenwalt, "Ike was wrong: The military-industrial-congressional complex turns 60," breakingdefense.com. https://breakingdefense.com/2021/01/ike-was-wrong-the-military-industrial-congressional-complex-turns-60/.
8 The White House, "Executive Order on Tackling the Climate Crisis at Home and Abroad," January 27, 2021, www.whitehouse.gov/briefing-room/presidential-actions/2021/01/27/executive-order-on-tackling-the-climate-crisis-at-home-and-abroad/.
9 Luke Darby, "How the Military Churns Out More Greenhouse Gas Emissions than Entire Countries," *GQ*, September 13, 2019, www.gq.com/story/military-climate-change-cycle.

1

OVERVIEW IN BRIEF

What should a country spend on its national security? How about this? As much as is necessary to protect its citizens, and not a penny more. As to the second part of the equation, nobody has really improved on Eisenhower's famous rationale crafted in his 1953 "Cross of Iron" speech—an early-term bookend to his Farewell Address—for "not a penny more."

> Every gun that is made, every warship launched, every rocket fired signifies, in the final sense, a theft from those who hunger and are not fed, those who are cold and are not clothed. This world in arms is not spending money alone. It is spending the sweat of its laborers, the genius of its scientists, the hopes of its children. The cost of one modern heavy bomber is this: a modern brick school in more than 30 cities. It is two electric power plants, each serving a town of 60,000 population. It is two fine, fully equipped hospitals.… We pay for a single destroyer with new homes that could have housed more than 8,000 people.[1]

As to the first part—how much is enough—that is the hard part.

What Does Our Military Budget Buy? A Few Basic Facts

The category "National Defense" occupies the first spot in our annual federal budget's 20 categories of federal spending. This category funds not just the Department of Defense (DoD), but also about two-thirds of the Energy Department (DoE), since most of DoE's money actually funds not energy policy but the country's nuclear weapons complex.

DOI: 10.4324/9781003293705-2

Following World War II the Pentagon tried to fix the dysfunction of service branches competing rather than cooperating by organizing them into Unified Combatant Commands: first solidifying the two theaters of World War II—Europe (and North Africa) and the Pacific—into permanent combat commands, followed in the sixties by a third command to "cover" South America, followed in the eighties by a command for the Middle East, and in the 2000s, another for North America and, finally, another for Africa. These commands are assigned jointly to two or more of the services but led by a single commander.[2]

These commands oversee a vast network of 750 military bases in at least 85 countries. Some of them are mere radar stations, while others are as large as mid-size cities, like Camp Humphreys in South Korea and the Baumholder Army base in Germany. To date, no other country has even tried to compete with this: Britain, France, and Russia combined to operate between 10 and 20 each. China has only one military base outside the South China Sea, though the U.S. global base saturation may be inspiring China's own expansionary plans.[3]

To these, six geographic commands have been added, four functional ones, covering transportation, nuclear forces, special operations forces, and cyber warfare. At the end of 2019 President Trump added another: the Space Force.

This is the superstructure in place to achieve global military dominance, which current U.S. military doctrine asserts we must have to protect ourselves. Our controlling National Security Strategy commits the military to prepare to win a war over Russia or China while holding off a second adversary, fight a global war on terrorism, maintain a large presence in the Middle East and Asia, and modernize our entire nuclear weapons arsenal. (There are some signs that the next official strategy will dial back a bit on some of these requirements).

What Forces Has the Pentagon Amassed to Serve this Goal (a Partial List)?

First are the people, including an active-duty force of nearly 1.4 million, most highly concentrated in the Army, followed by nearly equal numbers in the Navy and Air Force, and much smaller numbers in the Marines and Coast Guard. About 180,000 military personnel are operating beyond U.S. borders. The reserves add an additional 850,000, plus a civilian work force of 758,000.

A total of 63,000 enlisted personnel and 6,500 civilians are assigned to the Special Operations Command (SOCOM), which operates separately and more secretively in, SOCOM says, 70 percent of the world's countries.[4] Each of the four main service branches has its own special forces and dedicated arsenal. In addition, a classified number of intelligence service employees work secretively overseas in military operations beyond intelligence gathering.

As the military budget has grown, the Pentagon bureaucracy has grown with it. Paul Light, who studies the size of government at the Brookings Institution, counts 33 layers of bureaucracy at the top of DoD. Between 1998 and 2020 the numbers in the top-five tiers climbed from 193 to 629.[5]

The Strategic Command focuses on the equipment of nuclear war, including 3,750 nuclear warheads, 400 intercontinental ballistic missiles (ICBMs), 280 submarine-launched ballistic missiles, 66 strategic bombers, and 14 nuclear-powered ballistic missile submarines, plus the assorted systems attempting to give early warning of a nuclear attack and create a missile shield to protect against one.[6]

As of 2020 the Army's tools of conventional warfare include tanks and armored fighting vehicles, engineering and maintenance vehicles, amphibious landing vehicles, antitank weapons, artillery, and missile-launching platforms, including aircraft, helicopters, and drones. The Navy's arsenal included 53 tactical submarines, 11 aircraft carriers, 24 cruisers, 67 destroyers, 84 patrol and coastal combatant ships, 19 frigates, and 32 principal amphibious ships, for a total of roughly 300 ships, plus nearly 1,000 of its own combat-capable aircraft. In addition to its laser- and GPS-guided bombs, its air- and surface-launched missiles, its transport planes and missile-firing drones, the Air Force had 1,522 combat-capable aircraft, 46 of them nuclear-capable.[7]

The military budget funding these operations is divided into five major areas, providing funding for: Military Personnel (on average about 24% of the total, though with all expenditures including health care included, the percentage is substantially higher); Military Construction (2%); Operations and Maintenance (41%); Research, Development and Testing of new weapons (12%), and the Procurement of the weapons themselves (19%), for each of the four service branches (The Coast Guard is mostly funded through the Department of Homeland Security).[8] Each branch operates its own network of bases around the country, plus about a dozen that are shared by more than one service branch.[9]

Who Does What

> Procurement: contractors, including those that run Government-Owned Contractor-Operated facilities (GOCOs);
> Personnel: uniformed and civilian;
> R&D: the system of national laboratories, contractors, including universities, and think tanks such as the Rand and Mitre Corporations;
> Operations and Maintenance: military personnel and contractors;
> Military construction: military personnel and contractors.

A foundational element of the nation-state is the relationship between its public and private sectors. In the late twentieth century the Pentagon's piece of this relationship began to shift significantly, kicked off when Defense Secretary Dick Cheney asked contractor Haliburton (subsequently his employer) to study military outsourcing. (Halliburton thought it was a great idea.) Then the post-9/11 wars gave the drive to outsource Pentagon functions to the private sector, its great leap forward—one that Halliburton may have profited from the most. According to the Congressional Budget Office, by 2008 the proportion of private contractors to military personnel in the Iraq theater had reached 1:1.[10]

As it came into office, the Obama administration ordered DoD to examine whether more jobs could be brought in house to save money. According to Paul Light at Brookings, defense contractor lobbying soon shut this examination down.[11] And by 2021, the Center for Strategic and International Studies found that in the CENTCOM (Middle East) region, contractors outnumbered military personnel by a factor of 2.8 to 1.[12]

A 2020 study from the Costs of War project at Brown University found that the previous year more than half of the total defense budget went to private contractors, which was 164 percent higher than the spending on contractors in 2001. Though privatization is frequently touted as a way to lower costs through competition, the study found that 45 percent of these contracts—a higher percentage than with any other federal agency—were not competitively bid. And many of the rest of them were designated "cost-plus," that is, a guarantee up front to cover the contractor's costs plus an agreed profit. Some contracts also weaken competitive cost mechanisms by locking in lifetime service agreements and sole-supplier contracts.[13]

In a 2008 study the Director of National Intelligence's Office also called into question the idea that privatization saves money, with a finding that private contractors made up 29 percent of the U.S. intelligence's community's workforce while accounting for 49 percent of the community's personnel budget.[14]

As to how many people work for the Pentagon in private companies, no one really knows. The prime contractors aren't required to share information with the Pentagon about who their subcontractors are, let alone how many people work for them, and the subcontractors don't necessarily tell the primes that information about *their* subcontractors and suppliers.

The website governmentcontractswon.com listed 3.6 million individual Pentagon contracts in 2020, spread among more than 300,000 contractors. The top contractors are in the process of further consolidating their power, however, thereby reducing cost-controlling competition. According to a 2021 Bloomberg study, since 2011 the number of prime contractors has shrunk by 36 percent, even as the average revenue per company has grown by 83 percent.[15] While most private companies around the world have struggled to overcome the effects of the pandemic, military contractors mostly have not: their taxpayer-funded revenues have increased for five straight years.[16]

For decades, five companies—all of them U.S.-based—have held on to the top spots on the list of global military contractors: Lockheed Martin, Raytheon, Boeing, Northrop Grumman, and General Dynamics. They have jockeyed for position a bit among themselves during that time—Raytheon's 2020 acquisition of United Technologies allowed it to jump into the number two spot ahead of Boeing—but no other companies have really challenged their dominance. The acquisition also enabled Raytheon to reduce its dependency on the military market to 65 percent. Boeing's hold on the commercial aircraft market keeps its military-to-non-military focus at about 50-50. Northrop and General Dynamics are about 80 percent defense-dependent. While during its history Lockheed Martin has from time to time dabbled at making things other than weapons, this perennial head-and-shoulders leader now does almost nothing but military contracting (95%).[17]

How the Military Gets Its Money

Many stages have been inserted to form the gauntlet of the budget process, providing ample opportunity for our national security priorities to take some strange turns.[18] First the president submits his (or someday her) budget proposal, based on the requests of the individual departments, after which the House and Senate Budget Committees get to submit, and reconcile, their own budget blueprints, after which (according to plans that don't always get followed) the various Authorization Committees in both houses get to set the overall spending levels, and weigh in on defense policy and the spending specifics, and then meet in conference committees to reconcile their competing proposals. But it is the House and Senate appropriators, working with what 12 individual appropriations subcommittees send them, who hold the power to agree (or try to) on a final set of line items for the president to sign.

Not much about the budget process has actually worked the way it's supposed to for years, however. As political polarization has ratcheted up, agreement on a budget—Congress' central responsibility—has proven repeatedly elusive. So, in many years the "budget" becomes nothing but a Continuing Resolution, which freezes spending across departments at the previous year's levels (usually before raising them months later). Occasionally even this "agreement" doesn't happen until after the government runs out of money, and most of it shuts down.

There are actually two budgets: One covering the spending that Congress votes on every year ("discretionary spending"), and one covering the spending on the programs like Social Security and Medicare, whose levels are set by how much people use them ("mandatory spending"). Through all the upheavals and uncertainties of the process, there is one predictable result: The Defense Department, plus the Energy Department's nuclear weapons complex, will wind up with at least as much money as all the rest of the budget that Congress votes on every year put together. Add in the mandatory accounts, devoted to so-called "entitlements," and the military budget comes in at number two, after Social Security.

How Did We Get Here? The Military-Industrial Complex Origin Story in Brief

This enduring alliance took off in 1942 when the newly constituted War Production Board asked General Motors and hundreds of other manufacturers to convert their operations into suppliers for the war effort. GM stopped making cars and retooled its production lines to make jeeps and tanks. General Electric began making engines for fighter jets. Companies producing silk ribbons converted themselves to become parachute makers, typewriter manufacturers began making machine guns, and a roller coaster builder turned to producing bomber repair platforms.

During the Great Depression years big business interests had resisted Roosevelt's New Deal, fearing the encroachments of centralized government planning onto the turf of private enterprise. As this planning turned toward war, so did the recalcitrance of business to get involved.[19]

The urgency of changing their minds persuaded Roosevelt to offer several inducements. First, he gave big tax breaks to the major companies that were willing to build new war-production plants. Second, the government contracts for war work were structured as "cost-plus."

And, third, the industrialists turning to war work were given substantial control over the planning itself. In 1941 the president of General Motors, William Knudsen, was actually put in charge of the War Production Board's precursor, called the Office of Production Management. Each of these—tax breaks, cost-plus contracts and major roles in military industrial planning—would become features of military contracting that remain with us today.

By the end of the war, U.S. factories had converted their operations to produce almost 300,000 planes, 86,000 tanks, 64,000 landing craft and 6,000 naval vessels.[20]

It didn't take long for the potential conflicts of interest to surface between the patriotism of war production and the profit motive. The journalist I. F. Stone observed that "The arsenal of democracy is still being operated with one eye on the war and the other on the convenience of big business."[21] Harry Truman, as an obscure senator in the years before the war, had observed the padded contracts for shoddy materials that were a feature of military base construction in his home state of Missouri. As noted, he proceeded to project himself to national prominence by saving the country billions during the war, investigating waste, fraud, and war profiteering among military contractors.

By 1943, Roosevelt's confidence had grown that the war would end, and the Allies would win it. So, he added "and Reconversion" to the mandate of the Office of War Mobilization. The fear was that when the war ended, taking the massive economic stimulus of military spending with it, the U.S. would fall back into Depression. His administration knew they needed to avoid this by planning a transition to a peacetime economy.

As with the original war mobilization, Roosevelt had to contend with the pushback from military contractors against any plan that constrained their freedom to manage their own transition to civilian production in their own ways. So, he conceded most of the authority to write the rules for terminating military contracts and disposing of war-production plants to business and the military, helping to cement these interests into a permanent alliance.

Organized labor was worried that, in these hands, disposing of war production plants would entail disposing of their workers onto the street. Henry Ford II confirmed their fears on May 4, 1945, at the Ypsilanti, Michigan Willow Run Ford plant that at its wartime peak had been turning out a bomber an hour. He gave the workers an award for excellence and then told them the plant was now "expendable" and they were no longer needed. The leader of the United Auto Workers, Walter Reuther, responded that instead of just discarding the government's massive investment in the plant, why not turn these facilities toward producing the home-front infrastructure that had been sacrificed to the war effort? In consultation with his workers, Reuther drew up a detailed proposal, titled "Are War Plants Expendable?" to convert government-owned war plants to produce modern railroad equipment and low-cost housing for returning GIs.[22]

Two main factors conspired to ensure that his plan never made it past the drawing board. First was the contractors' allergy to any industrial planning beyond the military kind. And, second, the country's focus on converting wartime enterprises to serve key civilian priorities was disrupted by a whole new set of national security fears.

Once in office, President Truman expressed his roots as a New Deal Democrat in initiatives to create national health insurance, minority rights in employment, and new public power projects, among other efforts at federal industrial planning. But his efforts on behalf of these goals were quickly overshadowed by his focus on protecting the United States against its former World War II ally, the Soviet Union.

To deal with the consequences of his decision to introduce the world to the Nuclear Age, Truman began steering the federal budget toward the needs of a National Security State. The plans of 1943 for Reconversion were subordinated to the demands of Cold War Mobilization.

Funding for those needs is visible in the chart on the next page.

What the U.S. Military Costs

The *mountain range* on the following page tells this tale, from the onset of the Cold War to the present, factoring out inflation:[23]

Demobilizing from World War II triggered a precipitous decline in military spending—though it never went lower than its *highest point* during World War I. Thus began the postwar pattern of rolling hills of surge and decline in spending that, in the aggregate, nevertheless ratchet upwards toward the mountain peaks we see today.

The Korean and Vietnam wars' demobilizations left the military budget higher than it had been before these wars began. Following the Reagan-era military buildup of the 1980s, the miraculously bloodless end to the Cold War brought the steepest decline in Pentagon spending since World War II. But though the Cold War rationale for that buildup had disintegrated with the Soviet Union, post-Cold War spending never fell below where it was during most of the Cold War. And soon after, it began to climb again, well before the post-9/11 wars sent it back up close to the levels of World War II. Following the "surge" in spending during

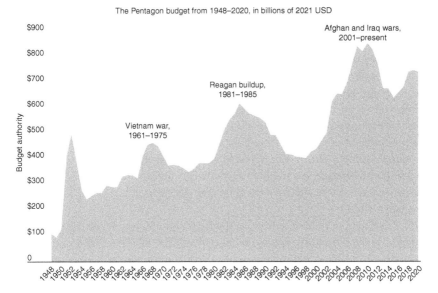

The Pentagon budget from 1948–2020, in billions of 2021 USD

FIGURE 1.1 The Pentagon budget 1948–2020, in billions of 2021 USD

Source: William Hartung and Ben Freeman, Center for International Policy Issue Brief: "Sustainable Defense: A Pentagon Spending Plan for 2021 and Beyond," December 2020.

his first two years in office, President Obama's efforts to end the wars in Iraq and Afghanistan created a modest decline. Then the Trump administration sent it climbing again. Between fiscal years 2016 and 2020, the Pentagon added $140.6 billion to its yearly total.[24]

As for the Biden administration, though it declared that diplomacy would take over the lead role in foreign policy from the military, its first budget left military spending essentially where Trump left it, close to its historically high levels.

What these Levels Include, and What They Don't

To fund the Afghan and Iraq wars, Congress added on top of the "base" National Defense budget a separate Overseas Contingency Operations (OCO) account. As the wars wound down toward the end of the decade, this account became more of a slush fund paying for DoD priorities having little or nothing to do with these wars. The 2020 budget request openly acknowledged this, saying that $98 billion of the OCO money was funding "base requirements," not wars.

OCO became a device for evading the spending limits imposed by the Budget Control Act (BCA), a ten-year deficit-reduction effort passed in 2011 setting roughly equal limits on defense and non-defense spending. That's because the law exempted the OCO account from these limits. Now that this deficit-controlling effort is over, and these wars appear for the most part to be ending, the separate

OCO account is disappearing. But its funds are simply being folded into an enlarged "base" defense budget. And following the OCO playbook, various parts of the military are hatching new efforts to carve out special funds beyond the regular budget, such as the Pacific Deterrence Fund to counter China.

There is also roughly $85 billion in the "black" (classified) budget covering the 17 major agencies of the U.S. intelligence community; most of this budget is believed to be included in the Pentagon budget, but since it's classified, we don't really know how much. We do know that it is making up an increasingly large proportion of the big prime contractors' business. In 2020 both Northrop Grumman and Raytheon reported double-digit growth over the previous year in classified (therefore less publicly accountable) defense business. According to Raytheon's CEO, classified contracting now accounts for about a fifth of his company's sales.[25]

Not included in these numbers are the federal programs outside the "National Defense" budget category, such as the more than $200 billion a year going to veterans, the $123 billion in interest paid to cover the portion of the national debt coming from decades of high military spending, and the Homeland Security costs of border security. While debate is ongoing about what pieces of federal spending belong under the category of "National Defense," it is pretty clear the real price tag exceeds $1 trillion a year.[26]

While adding to the Trump administration's enlargements to the Pentagon budget, the Biden administration's first budget did elevate the importance of non-military tools in securing the country, with real money. It increased the budget for diplomacy and foreign aid expenditures on such priorities as global health security, international climate programs and UN peacekeeping, by 12 percent, to $58 billion. In context, though, its allocation for military tools is still 13 times larger.[27] And the foreign aid budget includes billions to help other countries, including many in conflict zones, to buy U.S.-made weapons.

Is the U.S. Military Budget Enough? Too Much?

Answering this question must begin with what we are asking it to accomplish.

No other country has committed itself to maintaining a military presence on every continent and the ability to project force rapidly anywhere in the world. And while most military officials don't like the term "world's policeman" to describe the U.S. role in the world, no other country casts itself as upholder of the international order and its own interests across the globe. Defense analysts have laid out a strong case that this role acts more as provocation for resistance among the "occupied," armed and otherwise, than as guarantor of U.S. security.[28] The presence of U.S. bases in Saudi Arabia, for example, was the primary incitement for the 9/11 attacks. As this book's conclusion will outline, there are strong alternatives to this role, from which different force structures and far lower budgets could flow.

Can We Afford It?

Proponents of higher military budgets point to the relatively small percentage of national wealth—GDP—now allocated to the military, about 3.7 percent. But it's hard to fathom the logic of deciding that the military needs more money because the overall size of the private and public economy has grown.

It makes more sense to consider military spending as a portion of federal public investment—again, within the annual budget process, now accounting for as much as all other public priorities put together. And here we need to consider the costs of this concentration of resources to all other public purposes.

A major portion of our ballooning national debt comes from decades of deficit military spending. Many economists argue that deficit spending can be useful and necessary—as long as it improves the productivity of the economy as a whole. Such spending includes infrastructure repair and investments to create a healthy and educated workforce. Increasing our stockpile of fighter jets does not qualify.[29]

In the speech excerpt that began this chapter, Eisenhower laid down the basic idea of trade-offs for uncontrolled military spending. We now know that by identifying national security with military force we are ignoring, among other things, the national security threat of climate change that Eisenhower knew little if anything about. Part of the story told in these pages will be the tentative and limited steps some of the communities on this tour are making toward replacing defense dependency with contributions to this non-military fight of our lives.

Overkill?

Is it enough for the United States to spend more on our military forces than any other country in the world? Since the end of the Cold War, no other country has come anywhere close. In fact, the two most respected sources estimating national military expenditures, the Stockholm International Peace Research Institute (SIPRI) and the International Institute for Security Studies (IISS), peg U.S. spending at more than the next 11 countries *put together*. And the gap is widening: Back in 2016, that figure was closer to the next eight countries, and though the list includes China and Russia, most of the countries on it are U.S. allies. The alarms now sounding about the rise of China need this context: both sources estimate U.S. spending at least three times China's.[30] China's non-military spending on its Belt and Road Initiative, on the other hand, is building global influence beyond anything the U.S. military can accomplish.

We're Spending too Much if We're Wasting It

Pentagon waste has been with us since Truman began exposing it while the Pentagon itself was still under construction. New versions of the $600 toilet seat surface periodically, as do efforts to reform procurement systems to bring waste under control.[31] The astronomical amounts shoveled out in a hurry to fund the Iraq and Afghan wars generated an uncharacteristically serious, meticulous and sustained effort by dedicated inspectors general to document where that money had gone. Their accountings estimated waste in the Iraq War at $60 billion, and $100 billion in Afghanistan. And finally:

The Military Industrial Congressional Complex is Highly Organized to Inflate Military Spending

A mid-level congressional staffer reportedly attended a meeting with top generals discussing the 2018 troop surge in Afghanistan. They agreed unanimously that the action would make absolutely no difference to the war, but, they also agreed cheerfully, "It will do us good at budget time." And a former Air Force fighter pilot, Col. John Boyd, reportedly said years before that "People say the Pentagon does not have a strategy.… They are wrong. The Pentagon does have a strategy. It is: 'Don't interrupt the money flow, add to it.'"[32]

There is new momentum, in some parts of Congress and civil society, to the cause of putting the mountain range on a downward slope. (We'll look more closely at such initiatives in the concluding chapter.) A legislative proposal at the end of 2020 mandated a 10 percent cut in the military budget, with the money to be redirected to fighting the pandemic. This stirred the National Defense Industrial Association (the leading industry lobbying group) to commission a report from two Washington think tanks examining two scenarios: "an annual real 3 percent increase in defense spending and an immediate 10 percent cut." (Note that they left out the option of having the military live within its current means.) The report satisfied its funders by finding that "the 10 percent cut scenario would have devastating consequences for defense strategy and capabilities."[33]

Such reports are among an extensive portfolio of strategies the Military-Industrial Complex (MIC) employs to make sure this scenario is never tested. They include the steady stream of campaign contributions defense contractors make to members of Congress, especially the chairs of key committees with jurisdiction over military spending. And they include the advertising budgets from both the military and industrial arms of the MIC dedicated to associating weapons systems with cultural touchstones like the Super Bowl, which in 2021 hosted flyovers by all three of our deployed heavy bombers—the B-52, B-1 and B-2.

Here are a few more such strategies. We'll encounter others on the tour.

- **Keeping unauditable accounts.**
  To know whether you are buying only what you need, and not spending a penny more, you need to know what you are buying, how much it all costs, and where all the money is going. In part, because of the free rein business negotiated as the price of building weapons for World War II, when it comes

to the Pentagon budget, no one actually knows these things. Until recently it was the only federal agency that couldn't pass an audit. (The Homeland Security department, created by the 9/11 wars, now shares that distinction.[34])

DoD has been resisting this requirement since 1990. After years of promising they would get to it, in 2018 they finally made their first attempt. And each of the years since they have failed. In 2020, they paid public accounting firms $203 million to audit 24 separate Pentagon agencies. Seven of them passed—the same number as the previous year. Unfortunately, neither the Army, Navy, Air Force nor Marines were among them. The acting Defense Comptroller, Thomas Harker, said he expected they'd all succeed by 2027.[35]

Since 1995 DoD has been on the Government Accountability Office's High-Risk list designating agencies vulnerable to fraud, waste, abuse, and mismanagement.[36] Without a real accounting, all these practices are much easier.

- **Influence: The proverbial revolving door**

High-ranking contracting officials at DoD routinely set up lucrative second careers in the defense industry by going easy on the private companies sitting on the other side of the negotiating table. In a 2021 report, the Government Accountability Office found that between 2014 and 2019, 1,700 retired generals and admirals and former senior procurement officials went to work for the top 14 Pentagon contractors.[37] Taking up these jobs, they then begin earning their ample salaries by securing priority contracts from their former employer (DoD), for their new employers (private contractors). A 2018 study by the Project on Government Oversight found that 380 of these officials had been hired *that year* by defense contractors as lobbyists, board members, executives or consultants. One in four of them had been snapped up by the Big Five prime contractors alone.[38] Members of Congress and congressional staffers, especially those high up on the committees with defense budget jurisdiction, also frequently seize a piece of this action.

The practice gets more scrutiny when the door spins the other way, allowing military contracting executives to take top jobs at the Pentagon. True to its signature practice of doing out in the open what other administrations have tried to keep quiet, the Trump administration embraced the revolving door with enthusiasm. Following Gen. Jim Mattis as his first Defense Secretary, who had received somewhere between $600,000 and $1.25 million on the board of General Dynamics,[39] came two officials whose routes from defense firms through the revolving door were even more direct: Patrick Shanahan, a vice president at Boeing, and Mark Esper, Raytheon's top lobbyist. Both promised to recuse themselves from decisions relating to their former employers. But as defense analyst William Hartung observed, "If Shanahan were to step back from deliberations related to all [Boeing's products, including aircraft, bombs, drones, missile-defense systems, ballistic missiles, military satellites] he would, at best, be a part-time steward of the Pentagon."[40] Former Raytheon lobbyist Esper presided over the Pentagon while it permitted the merger of Raytheon and United Technologies, creating the second-largest defense contractor in the world.

The Biden administration has pledged to curb the worst abuses of the revolving door. Its Defense Secretary, former Gen. Lloyd Austin, received $2 million-plus on the boards of both Raytheon and United Technologies. Though the Biden rules lengthen the time government officials have to wait after leaving office before heading through the revolving door, Austin pledged at his confirmation hearing not to go through it at all. It's clear, though, that for many the door will keep spinning, although, in some cases, a bit slower.

- **Contract dispersion**

This book is about the seeding of the military economy across the American landscape. Though World War II planted most of these fields, the post-Cold War drop in the military budget propelled the major contractors to step up their own strategy for sprinkling those seeds wider and deeper, creating stronger political protection against future defense cuts.

By systematically spreading their contracts and sub-contracts they sacrificed the norms of industrial efficiency for an open campaign to make their production lines seem to be supporting local jobs everywhere.

The F–35 Joint Strike Fighter—again, the largest and most expensive weapons program ever devised—has an all-things-to-all-missions portfolio, including combat airstrikes, electronic warfare, and surveillance, with custom variants for each service branch. Plus, now it is being fitted for nuclear weapons. The all-things mandate has kept the project in development for three decades, working out an apparently endless succession of bugs. By 2013 its lead contractor, Lockheed Martin, was advertising that it had put pieces of the program in 45 states. By 2020 they had filled in three more. For 18 of these states the program does have a significant economic impact from multiple locations and more than $100 million to dole out. But the impression of having an impact in 48 states is exaggerated.[41] In Wyoming, for example, the F–35 has a presence in just one place employing ten people.[42]

But the spread continues to accomplish its political purpose. Among the scores of congressional caucuses—the Border Security Caucus, the Labor and Working Families Caucus and so on—the highly bipartisan Congressional Joint Strike Fighter Caucus attracted 130 members in 2020—27 more than the previous year—to propose funding 24 extra F–35s, at $77 million apiece, beyond what the Pentagon itself had requested.[43]

Here is one example of contract dispersal in action: In July of 2021 the Defense Department awarded Lockheed Martin an additional $231 million on top of an existing contract to supply equipment for the DDG 51-class destroyer and the FFG 62-class frigate. DoD was the main customer (80%), but some of these parts are going to Australia and Spain as part of the Foreign Military Sales program. According to the contract announcement, the company decided that the work needed to be performed in Baltimore,

Indianapolis, Fort Walton Beach, Florida, Farmingdale, New York, Saginaw, Michigan, Waverly, Iowa, Thomaston, Connecticut, and St. Peters, Missouri.[44]

Conclusion

Members of Congress routinely frame their support for higher military budgets as support for the troops and the "readiness" funds these troops need for their current operations, which are perennially described as "in crisis." But their actual budgetary decisions frequently seem to tilt toward their contractor-contributors instead. In 2019, for example, while agreeing with the Pentagon on a total budget, and decrying the "readiness crisis," Congress shifted money from the Operations and Maintenance account to R&D, that is, spending to set up future weapons purchases.[45]

In the following chapters, after a glimpse of its operations inside Congress, we will be looking mostly at how this system functions in communities across America. The wide-angle view of Congress's budget debate routinely features Republicans pushing for more defense spending against Democrats pushing domestic spending. As we'll see in the next chapter, observing the contract dispersal process observed up close tells a somewhat different story.

Notes

1 The "Cross of Iron" speech, April 16, 1953. www.eisenhowerlibrary.gov/eisenhowers/speeches. The National Priorities Project, nationalpriorities.org, updates these sorts of trade-offs, and breaks them down to the state and local levels.

2 Dana Priest, *The Mission: Waging War and Keeping Peace with America's Military* (New York: W. W. Norton Co., 2003).

3 See David Vine, *Base Nation: How U.S. Military Bases Abroad Harm America and the World* (New York: Metropolitan Books, 2015); www.theguardian.com/world/2019/may/03/china-will-build-string-of-military-bases-around-world-says-pentagon.

4 Nick Turse, "American Special Operations Forces Are Deployed to 70 Percent of the World's Countries," *The Nation*, January 5, 2017. www.thenation.com/article/archive/american-special-forces-are-deployed-to-70-percent-of-the-worlds-countries/.August.

5 *The Military Balance Volume 120, Issue 1* (London: International Institute for Strategic Studies, Taylor & Francis, 2020); www.iiss.org/publications/the-military-balance/military-balance-2020-book; Office of the Comptroller, Department of Defense, *National Defense Budget Estimates for FY 2020* (Green Book). https://comptroller.defense.gov/Portals/45/Documents/defbudget/fy2021/FY21_Green_Book.pdf.

6 Hans M. Kristensen and Matt Korda, "United States nuclear weapons, 2021," *Bulletin of the Atomic Scientists*, 77:1, pp. 43–63, https://doi.org/10.1080/00963402.2020.1859865.

7 *The Military Balance Volume 120, Issue 1* (London: International Institute for Strategic Studies, Taylor & Francis, 2020); www.iiss.org/publications/the-military-balance/military-balance-2020-book; Office of the Comptroller, Department of Defense, *National Defense Budget Estimates for FY 2020* (Green Book), https://comptroller.defense.gov/Portals/45/Documents/defbudget/fy2021/FY21_Green_Book.pdf.

8   Christopher T. Mann, "Defense Primer: The National Defense Budget Function (050)," Congressional Research Service, 7-5700, Washington, DC: March 17, 2017. https://crs reports.congress.gov/product/details?prodcode=IF10618.

9   John Harrington, "America's Largest Military Bases," wallstreet.com, September 6, 2018. https://247wallst.com/special-report/2018/09/06/americas-largest-military-bases/11/.

10 2 Congressional Budget Office (CBO), "Contractors' Support of U.S. Operations in Iraq," Washington, DC, Pub No. 3053, August 2008. www.cbo.gov/sites/default/files/110th-congress-2007-2008/reports/08-12-iraqcontractors.pdf.

11 "The true size of government is nearing a record high," Brookings, October 7, 2020, www.brookings.edu/blog/fixgov/2020/10/07/the-true-size-of-government-is-nearing-a-record-high/.

12 Mark Cancian, "U.S. Military Forces in FY 2021: Space, SOF, Civilians, and Contractors," Center for Strategic and International Studies, Washington, DC, January 8, 2021, www.csis.org/analysis/us-military-forces-fy-2021-space-sof-civilians-and-ontractors.

13 Heidi Peltier, "The Growth of the 'Camo Economy' and the Commercialization of the Post-9/11 Wars," (Providence, RI: Costs of War Project, Brown University, 2020). https://watson.brown.edu/costsofwar/files/cow/imce/papers/2020/.

14 Dana Priest, *Top Secret America: The Rise of the New American Security State*, (New York: Little, Brown, 2011) p. 320.

15 Travis J. Tritten and Paul Murphy, "Fewer Defense Companies in Military Spending Boom Raise Alarms," Bgov.com, March 8, 2021, https://about.bgov.com/news/fewer-defense-companies-in-military-spending-boom-raise-alarms/.

16 Joe Gould, "Riding the wave: Defense revenues rise despite a dark 2020," *Defense News*, July 12, 2021.

17 "Top 100 Defense Contractors in 2021," *Defense News*. https://people.defensenews.com/top-100/.

18 The National Priorities Project at the Institute for Policy Studies has an online exercise allowing citizens to compare their preferred federal budget allocations with the real ones; the gap between them is usually startling to those who try it.

19 Michael Heale, *Franklin D. Roosevelt: The New Deal and War*, (New York: Routledge, 1999).

20 "World War II Mobilization 1939–1943," encyclopedia.com, www.encyclopedia.com/education/news-and-education-magazines/world-war-ii-mobilization-1939-1943.

21 Alan Brinkley, "The New Deal and the Idea of the State," in Fraser and Gerstle, *The Rise and Fall of the New Deal* (Princeton, NJ: Princeton University Press, 1989) p. 103.

22 Ypsilanti, MI: Willow Run Local 50, UAW-CIO, 1945. www.wlym.com/archive/detroit/Walter%20Reuther/AreWarPlantsExpendable.pdf.

23 William D. Hartung and Ben Freeman, "Issue Brief: Sustainable Defense: A Pentagon Spending Plan for 2021 and Beyond," (Washington, DC: Center for International Policy, 2020).

24 "The top 10 defense contractors," *Bloomberg Government*, June 10, 2021, https://about.bgov.com/top-defense-contractors/.

25 Aaron Gregg, "Defense firms cash in on an 'unprecedented' wave of classified spending," *Washington Post*, January 31, 2020, www.washingtonpost.com/business/2020/01/31/classified-defense-spending/.

26 Mandy Smithberger, "Creating a National Insecurity State," TomDispatch.com, March 1, 2020, https://tomdispatch.com/mandy-smithberger-letting-the-pentagon-loose-with-your-tax-dollars/.

27 Author calculation.

28 See especially Chalmers Johnson, *Blowback: The Costs and Consequences of American Empire*, 2nd ed, (New York: Macmillan, 2004).

29 "Davis-Monthan Air Force Boneyard in Tucson: Layout, Operations, Tours, and Maps," AirplaneBoneyard.com. www.airplaneboneyards.com/davis-monthan-afb-amarg-airplane-boneyard.htm.

30 Nan Tian, Aude Fleurant, Alexandra Kuimova, Pieter Wezeman, Siemon Wezeman, "Trends in World Military Expenditure, 2020", (Stockholm: Stockholm International Peace Research Institute, April 2021) https://sipri.org/sites/default/files/2021-04/fs_2104_milex_0.pdf; "The Military Balance 2021," (London: International Institute for Strategic Studies, Routledge, February 25, 2021) www.iiss.org/publications/the-military-balance.

31 In my one trip to the Rose Garden, I got a front-row seat for the signing of the Weapons Systems Acquisition Reform Act of 2009 (WSARA). The fact that the bill passed both the House and Senate unanimously should have been a tip-off that its loopholes were big enough, as they say, to drive a truck through.

32 Andrew Cockburn, "How the US military got rich from Afghanistan," *The Spectator*, July 19, 2021, https://spectatorworld.com/topic/pentagon-rich-afghanistan-military-budget/.

33 Thomas G. Mahnken, Jack Bianchi, Regan Copple, Madison Creery, Jan van Tol, and Josh Chang, "America's strategic choices: Defense spending in a post-Covid 19 world," (Washington, DC: Center on Strategic and Budgetary Assessments, January 14, 2021). https://csbaonline.org/research/publications/americas-strategic-choices-defense-spending-in-a-post-covid-19-world.

34 "Independent Auditors' Report on DHS' FY2020 Financial Statements and Internal Control over Financial Reporting," (Washington, DC: Office of the Inspector General, Department of Homeland Security, November 13, 2020), www.oig.dhs.gov/sites/default/files/assets/2020-11/OIG-21-08-Nov20.pdf.

35 Marcus Weisgerber, "Pentagon Expects to Fail Another Audit, But Says Progress Made," Defense One, November 16, 2020.

36 Moshe Schwartz and Ray Gnanarajah, "Defense Primer: FY 2018 Department of Defense Audit Results," (Washington, DC: Congressional Research Service, Updated January 9, 2019). https://fas.org/sgp/crs/natsec/IF10913.pdf.

37 GAO, "Post-Government Employment Restrictions," September 2021, www.gao.gov/assets/gao-21-104311.pdf.

38 "Brass Parachutes: Defense Contractors' Capture of Pentagon Officials Through the Revolving Door," (Washington, DC: Project on Government Oversight, November 5, 2018). pogo.org/report/2018/POGO_Brass_Parachutes_DoD_Revolving_Door_Report_2018-11-05.pdf.

39 Jeremy Herb and Connor O'Brien, "Pentagon pick Mattis discloses defense industry work," *Politico*, January 8, 2017, www.politico.com/blogs/donald-trump-administration/2017/01/james-mattis-defense-disclosures-233331.

40 William Hartung, "Our Man from Boeing," (New York: TomDispatch, January 29, 2019). https://tomdispatch.com/smithberger-and-hartung-the-pentagon-s-revolving-door-spins-faster/.

41 Jeremy Bender, Armin Rosen and Skye Gould, "This Map Shows Why the F-35 Has Turned into a Trillion-Dollar Fiasco," businessinsider.com, August 20, 2014, 014, 9:14 AM, www.businessinsider.com/this-map-explains-the-f-35-fiasco-2014-8.

42 Lockheed Martin, "F-35 Lightning: Powering Job Creation for America and Its Allies," lockheedmartin.com, retrieved 7/21/21, www.f35.com/about/economic-impact.

43 Office of Congressman John Larson, "Joint Strike Fighter Caucus Announces Record Support for F-35," news release, Marc 17, 2020, https://larson.house.gov/media-center/press-releases/joint-strike-fighter-caucus-announces-record-support-f-35.

44 U.S. Department of Defense, "Contracts for July 20, 2021," news release. www.defense.gov/Newsroom/Contracts/Contract/Article/2701323/source/GovDelivery/.

45 Mark Cancian, "Congress Traded Operations & Maintenance for Modernization in 19 Appropriations," *Breaking Defense*, October 11, 2018, https://breakingdefense.com/2018/10/congress-traded-om-for-rdte-in-19-approps-bill/.

2

CONNECTICUT

A Choice Visible on Two Sides of a River

A Slice of Life at HASC

Unlike most congressional hearing rooms, the one assigned to the House Armed Services Committee (HASC), in the Rayburn House Office Building, has three full tiers of seats, arrayed in a graceful carved mahogany curve above the hearing table, and behind it a few cramped rows for the audience. Membership on this committee is, year after year, one of the most sought-after assignments in Congress.

On the morning of May 9, 2018, most of the commodious, black, soft, leather armchairs on those tiers are filled. Large oil portraits of previous chairmen, posed before flags or an aircraft carrier or other landscapes of military hardware, look down from the sidelines.

This morning's hearing takes a brisk walk through the provisions of the House's version of the National Defense Authorization Act (NDAA), which will be voted on that night. Passing this bill is the highlight and centerpiece of HASC's year.

HASC the only House committee routinely and widely recognized by its acronym has more members than any other. The next largest House committee is Appropriations; its subcommittee with jurisdiction over the military budget has more members than any other subcommittee. It is not hard to see why. As noted, between them HASC and the Defense Appropriations subcommittee control more than half of the money Congress votes on every year, money spent in congressional districts across the country. The legislators sitting in those chairs are there mostly to steer it toward their own.[1]

In other sessions the committee hears testimony about broad issues of defense policy and even debates them. While parochialism is sometimes visible in these sessions, it tends to be more subtle than it is today. Here, there are no witnesses and precious little debate. The speeches often come with perfunctory references to

DOI: 10.4324/9781003293705-3

how vital this or that expenditure is to national security, but these don't last long. Parochialism hardly bothers to hide during this exercise in mutual back-scratching.

The main story of American politics over the last decade is our descent into paralyzing partisan division. You'd never know it from what's taking place in this room. Except that by custom Democrats sit on one side and Republicans on the other, you can hardly tell the difference.

As they proceed expeditiously through the subcommittee reports, votes of the full committee affirming these decisions are mostly unanimous. A little skirmish— over one congressman's attempt to relax restrictions on yacht owners flying the U.S. flag—is quickly smothered when a colleague starts burying the idea in sarcasm. The prevailing mood of comity and courtly deference then resumes.

Eventually they reach the affairs of the Subcommittee on Seapower and Projection Forces. Its chair, Rob Wittman (R-VA) and ranking member Joe Courtney (D-CT), fall over themselves in praise of each other. Courtney notes that there's "scarcely anything we disagree on, and where there's differences you couldn't slip a loose-leaf piece of paper between those differences."

While they in fact disagree on gun control and cutting taxes for the rich and government spending in general and most other things, no piece of paper comes between their commitment to give the Pentagon more ships than the Pentagon thinks it needs.

The crux of this beautiful friendship is as follows: Nuclear submarines in the United States are built primarily in only two places: General Dynamics' Electric Boat shipyard in Groton, Connecticut, and Huntington Ingalls Industries shipyard in Newport News, Virginia. The two heads of the House subcommittee in charge of funding submarines represent those two districts. While other companies got into the act for a while, since the early 1970s Electric Boat and Newport News— and currently the team of Courtney and Wittman—have had exclusive rights as prime contractors and contractor champions for this major piece of the defense industrial base. In other words, our system of funding the military has given jurisdiction over the shipbuilding budget to the two legislators who are using it this day to engineer, as Courtney calls it, "the largest Navy contract in U.S. history" primarily for their own districts. Here, Congress's "power of the purse" looks a lot like the two nuclear submarine builders' power over the purse for nuclear submarines.

Courtney has spent more than a dozen years working his way up the HASC Seapower Subcommittee ladder. In 2019, when the Democrats took control of the House, he and his friend Wittman traded chairs. Back in his first reelection campaign Courtney had to run against the former commanding officer of Groton's Naval Submarine Base, upriver from Electric Boat. Courtney won. He knows that promoting submarines is the key to his political life.

Courtney has delivered. In his first term he got the nickname, "Two-Sub Joe," for his intense focus on making sure Electric Boat got to increase production of *Virginia*-class attack submarines from one to two a year.[2]

Then in 2016 he got the company locked into building the replacement for the current fleet of ballistic-missile nuclear submarines, called the *Columbia*-class. His subcommittee chair will have a piece of this one too. According to plan, the first boat will be built over the next decade, not going into service until 2031. All 12 of these boats are supposed to be built by 2042, and roaming the planet until 2085, at a total cost of $109.8 billion just to build them, and untold billions more to operate them for half a century.[3]

In this session of the 2019 NDAA, his objective is to up the ante: Call him "Three Sub Joe." The bill he and the chair get passed this day would add $1 billion *more than the President requested* for the Virginia-class subs—but only if the Navy commits to increasing production from two to three subs a year.

Bringing home his district's bacon thus has two dimensions: First, locking in lucrative projects for multiple-year funding, and second, getting legislators to agree to speed them up.

HASC this day goes along with the acceleration plan. But its Senate counterpart will not, despite the efforts of Connecticut's two senators, Richard Blumenthal, a Senate Armed Services Committee member, and Chris Murphy. Both are known as progressives, Murphy as perhaps the leading Senate advocate for a progressive foreign policy. And they occasionally vote against MIC interests. In 2020 both Murphy and Blumenthal voted for an amendment redirecting 10 percent of the Pentagon budget to human needs. At the same time, their advocacy for programs like the *Virginia*-class sub is steadfast. When Trump's fiscal-year 2021 budget request included only one *Virginia*-class sub, Courtney pulled out all the stops, with the senators' support, to make sure the final bill had two. Here was Blumenthal in celebration: "This bill's critical investment in strategic defense tools—submarines, helicopters and aircraft built in Connecticut—will keep our country secure, our troops supported, and our state's economy strong."[4]

The *Virginia*-class program has to compete with many other priorities in the Navy shipbuilding agenda, not to mention the priorities of the other services. Two-Sub Joe has so far failed to speed up the *Virginia*-class sub. But then there's the *Columbia*-class. In 2020 Electric Boat got a $10.4 billion contract to start work on the first two. This contract, Courtney said in a statement, "was years in the making."[5] *Columbia*'s bill, he notes, "is just gonna be huge," projected in fact to absorb upwards of 30 percent of the Navy's total shipbuilding budget between 2026 and 2030.[6] Though their focus, and power source, is shipbuilding, both Courtney and Wittman are also members in good standing of the Joint Strike Fighter Caucus, whose members unite to protect the F-35 fighter jet. Connecticut makes the engines for that one.

Connecticut's Military Triangle

Joe Courtney's state is not the most defense-dependent in the country, but it is right up there. As the third-smallest state in the country, it is 6th on the list of recipients of Pentagon dollars, a share that is more than three times greater than its share of the U.S. population.[7] Only three states—Virginia, Alabama, and Hawaii—derive more of their state GDP from the Pentagon than Connecticut does.

The state bases its military economy overwhelmingly on private contracting rather than on troops. In 2019 DoD spent $19 billion on private contracts in Connecticut—the 5th highest amount in any state—and only $700 million on military personnel (38th nationally). (States like Hawaii are the mirror image: Hawaii ranks 33rd in contract spending and 9th in spending on personnel.)

The strongholds of Connecticut's military economy form a triangle across the length of the state's coastline and up through its central core, nearly to the Massachusetts border. Courtney's district occupies one corner, where the Thames River empties into the ocean near the Rhode Island border. Head northwest to Hartford and you reach the second corner, where Pratt & Whitney has exclusive rights to make the engines for the F-35. The third corner of the triangle is in Stratford, down between New Haven and the border with New York, where the Merritt Parkway crosses the Housatonic River on the Igor I. Sikorsky Memorial Bridge. This is where Sikorsky's company now makes an array of military helicopter models, including the Black Hawk, which can be loaded up with forward-firing guns, rockets and air-to-ground missiles. Scattered around the triangle are hundreds of machine shops providing these major operations with parts. Alpha Q, for example, situated about halfway between Hartford and New London, supplies components to Sikorsky and Pratt & Whitney, among others.[8] The string of them along the 1-91 corridor from Hartford to the Massachusetts border has given that stretch of road the nickname Aerospace Alley.[9]

BOX 2.1 ARMS EXPORTS

In 2020 India sealed a $900 million deal with Sikorsky to buy 24 helicopters. India is loading up its military arsenal in response to its growing tensions with China, including a series of small border skirmishes that year. Russia has been its main supplier, but U.S. military contractors are gaining traction in the lucrative Indian market. In the global arms trade, U.S. contractors maintain a dominant position.[10]

While competing for the $740 billion U.S. military budget is the main event, exporting provides them a significant secondary market. For 2020 the Defense Department reported it had authorized $175 billion in arms exports, up from $170 billion the previous year.[11] All but $11 billion of these sales were divvied up by the Big Five defense contractors.[12] U.S. contractors spread their wares around nearly a hundred countries, the largest share going to the already-militarized Middle East.

Advocates for this dimension of U.S. foreign policy argue that these sales help build our alliances by making our weapons systems interoperable. They talk about building security capacity rather than funding wars. According to Andrew Miller, a former State Department official now with the Project on Middle East Democracy, "There was a belief that these countries wouldn't end up using this equipment, and we were just selling them expensive paperweights." And over the years the United States has tried various ways of controlling what its customers do with the weapons it provides. These assurances foundered when Saudi Arabia began dropping three billion dollars worth of Raytheon-made bombs onto Yemen, in its war on the Houthi rebels.[13] The war has dragged on for five years and killed by UN estimate more than a quarter of a million people, most of them civilians.

This devastating toll seemed to be too much for Joe Biden, who declared two weeks after he took office an end to "all American support for offensive operations in the war in Yemen, including relevant arms sales." He also froze $23 billion in pending arms sales to Saudi Arabia and the UAE, including a deal for 50 F-35 fighter jets his predecessor had signed just hours before leaving office.[14] During his first month in office, however, his State Department approved an $85 million sale of Raytheon missiles to Chile and $60 million in Lockheed Martin F-16s to Jordan. And three months into his administration, the deal with Saudi Arabia and UAE went through.

As long as the United States keeps exporting its weaponry, it will be paving the way for increased military spending: protecting American military superiority has always been connected to staying ahead of what the rest of the world has.

And beyond the questionable ethics of seeding the world with ever more lethal Made in America weapons, are the questionable economics.

First, the value of these sales to Americans, including job creation, is less than meets the eye. For decades the contractors have secured these trade agreements by promising to "offset" the cost for the buyer by moving production onto its turf. When the Saudis bought 150 Sikorsky Black Hawk helicopters for about $6 billion in 2017, parent Lockheed Martin predicted this would "support" 900 jobs. But half of them would be in Saudi Arabia.[15] And two years later, to beat out Swedish, Italian and U.S. competitors for a $15 billion contract with India for F-16 fighter jets, Lockheed offered to relocate its entire F-16 production line to Indian soil.[16]

Secondly, American taxpayers are funding significant portions of the contractors' arms trade profits. Of the $42 billion the contractors pulled in from this trade in 2017, nearly $10 billion was paid for by the government's Foreign Military Financing (FMF) program and other DoD authorities.[17]

The top three U.S. military contractors divide control of the triangle. General Dynamics owns Electric Boat. Lockheed Martin owns Sikorsky. The newly formed amalgam of Raytheon and United Technologies owns Pratt & Whitney. In 2013 number five, Northrop Grumman, pulled its operations in Norwalk, on I-95 down past Stratford, out of the state, though it retains a small division up in East Hartford.

Connecticut planted its manufacturing roots in the military-industrial complex long before most of the rest of the country. In 1798, when Eli Whitney's cotton gin operations were faltering and the U.S. was beginning to rearm, he became the War Department's first contractor, promising to supply the army with 10,000 muskets. (He got the contract despite never having made a gun.) Whitney's success was the beginning of Connecticut's gun-manufacturing industrial base, including startups, Colt, Remington, and Winchester. By the beginning of the Civil War, however, Whitney's operations had become Pratt & Whitney, and had moved on toward an expanded menu of military machining, eventually to be focused on aircraft engines.

Ukrainian immigrant Igor Sikorsky joined the early pioneers of American aviation in the 1920s. By the late 1930s he had turned to helicopters, inventing the first single-rotor model that could reliably maintain a stable course. By 1943, Sikorsky was building military helicopters for the U.S. in World War II and has remained one of the anchors of Connecticut's military economy ever since. The world's largest military contractor, Lockheed Martin, will turn up in most of the stops on this tour. Until 2015, though, it was a missing piece of Connecticut's warfare economy. That was the year United Technologies, which had acquired Sikorsky in 2004, sold it to Lockheed for $9 billion.

And finally, in the third leg of the Connecticut triangle are the state's submarines. The first submarine appeared in U.S. waters during the Civil War: The Confederacy built a steam-powered model that finally sank a Union ship in 1864, after many Confederate sailors had died trying. The Electric Boat Company designed the first sub officially commissioned by the U.S. Navy in 1900, subcontracting out

FIGURE 2.1 A *Virginia*-class submarine heading down the river past New London

Source: United States Navy via wikimedia commons

construction to other shipyards until 1931. That year they brought the work in-house by building the enormous manufacturing plant downriver from the Naval Shipyard in Groton. In 1954 they added a nuclear-powered model to the diesel electric fleet. And, when in 1959 they were first equipped with nuclear weapons to be delivered anywhere in the world by ballistic missiles, submarines were also standing up the third leg of the nuclear triad.[18]

The two biggest ticket items in DoD's procurement budget anchor Connecticut's military economy. The F-35 Joint Strike Fighter is the biggest. The last Trump defense request proposed giving the program $11.4 billion, and ultimately Congress gave it more money—$12.9 billion—to make more of these planes than the Pentagon wanted. In the early 2000s DoD had funded GE to build a second engine for the F-35, to be made in Ohio. Congressman John Larson (D-Pratt & Whitney) lobbied furiously, and successfully, to nip this in the bud: Pratt now has the exclusive rights to supply the plane's engines. In September of 2020 the Navy awarded Pratt a $500 million contract for F-35 engine spare parts, 93 percent of which were to be made in East Hartford.[19]

The *Virginia*-class submarine currently underway comes in second on the price list. The 2021 budget provided $7.2 billion to cover the cost of two boats. But factor in the costs of the new *Columbia*-class, and Connecticut's submarine franchise surges into the lead. And, between financial years 2020 and 2021, delays in developing the new boat pushed its annual price more than half a billion higher.[20] (Electric Boat does have another facility doing some of the work up the coast in Quonset Point, Rhode Island, shipping segments of these boats back to Groton to be incorporated into the finished product. A non-incidental fact: The chair of the Senate Armed Services Committee is now Rhode Island's senior senator, Jack Reed.)

While Connecticut's congressional districts concentrate on different segments of its military economy, the state's congressional delegation, as noted, presents a united front in protecting all of them. Pull back to look at the bigger budgetary picture, though, and this economy's two anchor programs are on something of a collision course.

As troubles and costs of the F-35 program have continued to mount, so have the voices of alarm, pointing out that fully funding this program would crowd out funding for much of the rest of the rest of the procurement wish list.

Meanwhile, the Navy budget supporting the subs of Electric Boat threatens to do the same. For years the Navy's stated goal, if questionable, has been to have 355 ships, up from the current total under 300. Getting there, according to January 2021 testimony from Navy officials, would require increasing the Navy's budget by a total of $120 to $130 billon over ten years. In addition, military planners are beginning to grapple with the conventional wisdom that their aircraft carriers, whose models range from $3 billion to $13 billion apiece, are sitting ducks.[21] So the Navy has begun to focus on building a lot more small ships. To do all this, according to the Chief of Naval Operations, would mean reapportioning the DoD budget to give the Navy a larger share.

In short order after taking office, the Biden administration ordered a review of Pentagon programs they might want to adjust. It was a short list, and shipbuilding and the F–35 were on it. Its first budget request shaved the F–35 program from 96 to 85 planes (Congress added some of them back); it prescribed building the same two *Virginia*-class subs, but at a slightly lower cost (from $7.2 to $6.9 billion). [22]

Both federal budget watchdog agencies—the Congressional Budget Office and the Government Accountability Office—have also raised concerns that cost overruns will make the gap between what these ships ultimately cost and what is budgeted for them even worse. The number one target of their concern: the *Columbia*-class ballistic missile submarine, the centerpiece of Electric Boat's long-term plans.[23]

Can the Navy close this gap? Documents the *Navy Times* uncovered early in 2021 provide new reasons to doubt it. They reveal one of the Navy's favored ideas for making more room in the budget for shipbuilding: eliminate "unnecessary" expenditures on oversight. The idea was to cut personnel in the Naval Audit Service—its internal watchdog on the lookout for waste, fraud, and abuse. The budget covers 290 personnel whose job is to investigate problems with hundreds of thousands of Navy contracts at a time. The proposal would cut this force by more than two-thirds.[24]

Jobs

In making its case for more Pentagon spending, the military-industrial complex relies least as much on the jobs all this spending creates, as on national security needs.

Manufacturing jobs in the United States overall have been losing ground to the service sector for decades, a decline usually attributed to jobs shipped overseas, and automation replacing humans. Connecticut's manufacturing jobs base has declined from a peak of about 300,000 in the 1980s to about 160,000 now, but it remains a larger proportion of the state's workforce than in most states.[25] And the core of this base is military contracting.

These facts are related. As we've seen, the federal government has invested in its military industrial base far more than any other country on earth, and more of its research dollars than in any other sector of its economy.[26] And Connecticut has put most of its manufacturing eggs in this basket. Electric Boat is 100 percent defense dependent. Sikorsky is mostly defense-dependent. Pratt & Whitney, with a new "turbofan" jet engine that is popular with its commercial customers, has a military-commercial split that hovers around 50-50.[27]

The Trump administration's (and, for now, the Biden administration's) military spending increases have at least temporarily boosted the state's manufacturing jobs. Electric Boat is building a new facility for a longer version of the *Virginia*-class sub, and another one for the new *Columbia*-class. Electric Boat has already hired 15,000 new workers and expects to hire another 15,000 more.[28] And the F–35, as currently planned, will keep Aerospace Alley going for quite a while.

But beyond the coming budget battles over those programs are other pressures on those jobs. In addition to being militarized, manufacturing is more unionized than most other economic sectors. Connecticut is no exception. The Teamsters represents Sikorsky workers, the International Association of Machinists and Aerospace Workers (IAMAW) represents the Pratt workers and those of another Raytheon subsidiary in East Hartford, Hamilton Sundstrand. An old-fashioned labor arrangement at Electric Boat has representation divided up among the Metal Trades Council, the Boilermakers (now associated with nuclear reactors), the IAMAW, and the Sheetmetal Workers. Most of the small shops supplying these mega operations are not unionized.

The major manufacturers have a potent tool, beyond international outsourcing and automation, to use against their unions: move the work to non-union "right to work" states, or extract concessions by threatening to do so. While most of Electric Boat's operations remain in Connecticut, there's another reason, beyond the chair of SASC, that some have been moved to Rhode Island: this operation is a non-union shop. And Pratt & Whitney has built a highly automated plant in (non-union) North Carolina to produce some of its F-35 engines.

Pratt has assured the union that this is not a threat to Connecticut jobs: the F-35 orders, plus the commercial "turbofan" engines will keep them employed long into the future. The union is not so sure. Current contract language does make it difficult to shift work to North Carolina, but there are several closed Pratt plants in the area where the work already headed to North Carolina could have gone, and didn't.

Two Labor Visionaries

In the middle of Connecticut's battles over its military jobs for the last three decades were John Harrity and Bruce Olsson. After finishing college in the mid-seventies, they and their girlfriends tooled around Europe, the Middle East and North Africa for a couple of years in a rented camper before taking jobs at small machine shops back in the Hartford area.

The union movement attracted both of them to this line of work. Harrity says his dad worked a production line at GE, and "I always felt [he] wasn't treated fairly … and I wanted to see what I could do about it…. Figured the labor movement was a place you could really make some changes." Before training as a machinist, Olsson got the "union bug" working at a state facility for severely disabled women, where he organized his fellow workers to block the state's attempt to increase work hours with no increase in pay. The small machine shops where they both landed to learn the trade weren't unionized: The action was at Pratt & Whitney. So that is where they both went, working their way up in the machinists' union, as shop stewards, then taking turns as the union's labor representative to the company, negotiating grievances and contracts, plus political work.[29]

While the union's fights with the company were punctuated by some successes, the long slow slide of unionized manufacturing jobs—at Pratt & Whitney, in Connecticut, and in America at large—was well underway. The Reagan military buildup of the 1980s was accompanied by a sustained effort at union busting, so military budget gains "didn't necessarily translate" to job gains, Olsson says. At Pratt "it became a pattern—every four months or so 1000 people would go out the door."

During most of its 20th and 21st century history, organized labor has largely stood behind high levels of Pentagon spending.[30] With a manufacturing base disproportionately focused on military production, this is where the jobs are. Studies have repeatedly demonstrated, though, that the same amount of spending would produce far *more* jobs if directed elsewhere. Researcher Heidi Peltier, now at Brown University, found that $1 billion spent on the military would generate 11,200 jobs, as compared to 26,700 spent on education, 16,800 on clean energy, and 17,200 on health care. Even spreading the money around through tax cuts generated more jobs than targeting it to the military.[31]

As Harrity points out, though, machinists are highly trained and skilled as manufacturing workers. "Most of them are not going to become teachers." If the military budget is to be cut, they need a "just transition" to new kinds of useful manufacturing.

Labor and Economic Conversion

What do defense workers do when defense spending takes a dive? Beginning with Walter Reuther's detailed proposal for redirecting World War II defense plants toward housing and rail transport (see p. 14 in Chapter 1), they have periodically made the case for keeping their jobs while shifting to making things the country needs more than ever-higher numbers of ever-fancier weapons.

During most of its history, Harrity and Olsson's machinists union has been one of the largest defense-dependent, and therefore defense-promoting, unions in the country. But in the decade leading up to the end of the Cold War, the disjunction of Reagan-era military budgets from the fortunes of the IAMAW workforce had led its president, William Winpisinger, to begin touting economic conversion, that is, redirecting the U.S. budget, its economy and its manufacturing base toward civilian production and using labor–management cooperation to get there. He joined the board of the National Commission for Economic Conversion and Disarmament, a group of economists, public officials, and labor and business leaders dedicated to this goal.[32]

Conversion advocates had a few models to build on. Back in the mid-seventies, layoffs, or "redundancies" were mounting at the UK's Lucas Aerospace, about 50 percent defense-dependent, and the largest manufacturer of aircraft systems and equipment in Europe. In response the unionized workforce pioneered a search for new products that would save jobs. This search began with a questionnaire for shop stewards, inventorying the equipment at the factory, the skills of the work-force, and ideas for what else they could make there. It revealed a breadth of both technical expertise and technology with wide potential new applications, from the proximate—their recirculating ballscrew for aircraft flight controls could be used in industrial machine-tool control systems—to the visionary—their aerodynamics and aerofoil design knowledge, added to their electrical and mechanical expertise, could be applied to the then-emerging field of wind power.

In addition to the inventory, their resulting plan, developed with help from several engineering and technical colleges, included: an assessment of the social utility of the company's products—existing and proposed—and detailed proposals about the products, the production process, and the workforce development program that would be needed to meet them.

For a time, some factions of the British government supported using this project as a model for broader industrial planning involving organized labor; these ideas were swept away by the wave of conservative control under Margaret Thatcher. Well before this, Lucas Aerospace had rejected the project at its own company as a violation of its managerial prerogatives—the ones that identify managers as the people who plan, decide, and manage, and workers as the ones who work.[33]

But the idea of labor–management cooperation to develop alternative work at flagging defense plants sparked interest in the United States. In the mid-eighties a group of International Brotherhood of Electrical Workers (IBEW) workers making circuit boards for the *Seawolf* submarine at a Unisys plant in Minnesota traveled to England to meet with the Lucas workers. A finding of contracting fraud against the American company had been shrinking the workforce. So, they tried a version of the Lucas experiment: a small state grant allowed them to hire a consultant to survey the workforce on skills and technology and to develop a list of products that were both socially useful and technically feasible. The company rejected the proposal, closed down the plant, and developed one of the products at (non-union) plants in Utah.[34]

National legislation appeared on the horizon to buttress isolated efforts like these. In 1989 House Speaker Jim Wright gave the Defense Economic Adjustment Bill (H.R. 101) the honor of first place on the congressional calendar. This bill mandated the creation of a Defense Economic Adjustment Council, co-chaired by the secretaries of Commerce and Labor, to "encourage the preparation of plans for non-defense-related public projects" that could help pick up the slack from reduced defense spending. Other titles in the bill funded community-planning grants and assistance to workers in the event of major defense contract cancellations. And there was Title III, which would mandate the creation of Alternative Use Committees to develop detailed, regularly updated plans for non-military production as a condition of major defense contracts. The bill died in committee, and its official summary recorded in August as "Unfavorable Executive Comment Received from DoD."[35]

In Connecticut, 1991 was the year Harrity's and Olsson's union scored a big win for organizing protections at Pratt. But it was also the year the end of the Cold War was beginning to hit the Pentagon budget, which shrank by a third overall from its Cold War peak and two-thirds in weapons procurement.[36] Between 1985 and 1995 Connecticut's share of defense procurement dropped by 64 percent (in fixed 1992 dollars), from $7.1 billion to $2.5 billion.[37] Right after the union's organizing victory, Pratt closed two plants and laid off everyone who worked there.

Labor Tackles the End of the Cold War

While Winpisinger had been well ahead of the post–Cold War curve on conversion planning, it took the curve itself to get the AFL-CIO on board. At its February 1992 annual meeting in Bal Harbour, Florida, the AFL-CIO's Executive Council released a "Statement on Economic Conversion."

> The decline in direct military threats to U.S. national security and the reduction in military spending require an economic conversion program for the transfer of economics resources and workers from military to civilian production. Such a program would ensure that those who built the nation's defenses need not suffer in times of peace.

After criticizing the meager amounts provided so far to cushion the blow of military budget cuts, the statement outlined its policy prescriptions.

- A national commission in which labor, industry and government together plan and coordinate conversion-related activities.
- Community committees in defense-dependent areas, where labor, management and local leaders can work together to develop conversion plans.
- In-plant Alternative Use Committees to engage labor and management in joint exploration of civilian market possibilities, with sufficient advance notice of defense procurement cutbacks to allow time to develop such plans.
- Incentives to help firms convert existing facilities from military to civilian use.
- Programs for defense worker retraining and other transition support.

It ended with this: "We urge Congress to allocate a significant share of federal budget savings from defense cutbacks for use in economic conversion planning and assistance."

In August of that year the School for Workers at the University of Wisconsin Madison convened a conference called Defense Industry Conversion: Strategies for Job Redevelopment, co-sponsored by the state and national offices of the AFL-CIO, as well as the most defense-dependent individual unions: the Machinists, Boilermakers, Electrical Workers and United Auto Workers. Participants came representing workers from one end of the country (Pratt & Whitney, Electric Boat) to the other (General Dynamics in San Diego.) They looked at defense budget scenarios and their projected impact on jobs, at existing federal and state programs to deal with these effects, and at the need for a civilian industrial policy, including finance for alternative product development, to drive the transition and more involvement from workers in the process.

A handbook distilled from the conference offered a roadmap to the conversion process and linkages to available resources at the state and federal levels that could be tapped to facilitate conversion at the plant level. Attendees came away from the conference split between those who thought they'd been equipped with specific tools to approach the problem of finding civilian alternatives and saving jobs, and those who remained convinced that their companies had few realistic prospects beyond defense contracting.[38]

Harrity and Olsson were in the first group. "We came back from the conference thinking about what we could do," Olsson says. "We had a rally at UTC headquarters [United Technologies Corporation, now absorbed into Raytheon Technologies]. We went to the [Connecticut] congressional delegation, the AFL-CIO legislative director, the White House Public Engagement Office." And they joined forces with other New England unions, including the UAW and the Teamsters at Sikorsky and formed a coalition called "A Call to Action." It fleshed out a proposal that, he says, "in a lot of ways resembled the Green New Deal," focused on converting defense industries to produce the infrastructure of clean transport and clean energy.

Two months after the conference, Bill Clinton's victory speech declared the election,

> a clarion call for our country to face the challenges of the end of the cold war and … [t]o face problems too long ignored—from AIDS to the environment to the conversion of our economy from a defense to a domestic economic giant.[39]

During the campaign Clinton promised a dollar-for-dollar reinvestment of defense funds into the civilian economy.

This didn't happen. Between 1993 and 1997 federal funding for the conversion of the military economy amounted to about $16.5 billion—a tiny fraction of the defense dollars cut during the post–Cold War period. It included retraining funds for displaced defense workers and community-adjustment planning, plus a couple of tiny demonstration projects that were actually funded efforts by defense companies to move into civilian production. About $220 million went into building up the commercial shipbuilding industry. But 85 percent of the cumulative defense savings during the post–Cold War period, amounting to about $116 billion, went into deficit reduction.[40] This result diluted the investment value of the "Peace Dividend," preventing it from becoming the foundation for the kinds of civilian industries envisioned by, among others, the "A Call to Action" coalition. The prospects for what economists call "demand-pull," picking up the slack in the economy and attracting military contractors to major new markets, took another hit after control of Congress shifted to Republican hands in 1994.

And calls to reverse the post–Cold War cuts to Pentagon spending grew louder. While Colin Powell, Chair of the Joint Chiefs of Staff, began pointing to the demise of the Soviet Union to observe that, "We are running out of enemies," defense hawks began arguing for new military budget increases by invoking the fallback enemy: "It's a dangerous world out there." Others leaned on the idea that we might someday have one: We needed to "prevent the emergence of a peer adversary." On 9/11, they found their enemy, and instead of a police action to find and capture terrorists, they launched two wars, framed as a Global War on Terror (GWOT). Its price tag is estimated at $6.4 trillion, and counting.[41] So much for a Peace Dividend.

Connecticut's contributions to the War on Terror were limited. It is hard to use nuclear-armed submarines and cutting-edge fighter jets to kill terrorists. However, in the money-no-object post-9/11 world, budgeteers left expenditures on such systems intact and simply added equipment for the wars we were actually fighting on top. Harrity and Olsson went back to defending and promoting strengthened protections for union workers. Harrity worked his way up to become head of Connecticut's Machinists Union, and Olsson became head of legislative affairs at IAMAW headquarters outside Washington, DC.

Harrity remembers one "great day" in 2001 when the trucks in the act of moving Pratt equipment to Texas had to turn around. According to their labor agreement, the company had to make "every reasonable effort" to keep work in Connecticut. But they had the company's representative on record calling the move "a no-brainer, given the cost structures," meaning, primarily, lower labor costs in non-union Texas. That didn't sound like they'd given a lot of thought to alternatives. So, when the trucks were already on the road, the union secured an injunction blocking the move. "It was like a great scene from a movie," Harrity says, "when the trucks came back to East Hartford and backed into the well, everybody left their work stations and went down there chanting, 'Union! Union!'" The work never did move to Texas. The North Carolina plant, though, is still hanging over them, he says, as part of the company's "long game."

Harrity's other Conversion Experience

In 2012, the year Harrity took over as president of Connecticut's Machinists Union, he picked up an article in *Rolling Stone* titled "Global Warming's Terrifying New Math," by Bill McKibben, the relentless climate change visionary, organizer and proselytizer. Harrity called the article "a revelation." He began educating labor groups on climate change as "the most critical issue for the rest of our lives." It

FIGURE 2.2 John Harrity with his "personal hero," John L. Lewis, at the 2004 Machinists Convention in Cincinnati

Source: Photo by John Harrity, used with permission

became his life's work to defeat the faulty math that equated reducing greenhouse gas emissions with job killing.

Harrity wound up chairing the Connecticut Roundtable on Climate and Jobs, a coalition of 31 affiliated groups connecting state labor unions and religious and environmental groups to this goal, and joined the national Labor Network for Sustainability. He also worked his way into several decision-making rooms, winning seats on various state agencies with pieces of a green agenda. One was the Manufacturing Innovation Fund. Another was the Connecticut Green Bank, which leverages private investment in green projects with pennies from residents' electric bills. When the state tried to defund the Bank "in the dead of night" during "a rough year for state finance," Harrity, as its only labor representative, had to maneuver hard for its survival.

In 2014 he also represented organized labor on the "Commission on Connecticut's Future." Deficit reduction measures in the 2011 congressional Budget Control Act were taking a bite out of the military budget, and federal money from the Pentagon's Office of Economic Adjustment was coming to defense-dependent states so they could figure out how to help their economies adjust. Advocacy by civil-society groups like the New Haven Peace Council ensured that the state legislation creating the commission would specify membership to include not only relevant state officials and big and small business, but also labor representatives and one member each from a peace organization and an environmental organization.

The bill charged the commission with outlining a plan for Connecticut's economic renewal, emphasizing a turnaround for its manufacturing job base and "the retention and expansion of the state's economic base industries" [read: defense]. But the commission was also supposed to plan for "the diversification or conversion of defense-related industries with an emphasis on encouraging environmentally-sustainable and civilian product manufacturing."[42]

Harrity and the environmental and peace advocates proposed a collection of working groups to dig into such topics as: ways the state could capitalize on promising technology areas like fuel cell corridors and offshore wind development; strengthening the focus of existing state agencies on economic diversification; setting up finance mechanisms for diversification, such as revolving loan funds; a state Office of Diversification, or assign at least one staff person dedicated to this task.

"Our argument" for diversification, Harrity said, "aside from the abhorrence of war, which not everybody feels, is that it's precarious to put all your eggs in one basket. Dependence on the military over time had led the state economy to gyrate wildly depending on how much military spending there was."

But instead of being allowed to vote on the final recommendations, the commissioners were only allowed to advise, and some advice (pace Orwell) was more equal than others. The final report reflected the conflicted message of Connecticut's approach to its heavily militarized economy: In principle a more diversified economy would be good, but not if it diluted attention to the main imperative. The recommendations included some language on fuel-cell development and on creating tax incentives for green technology development and added the goal of reducing defense dependency to the scope of the Manufacturing Innovation Fund. But retaining and expanding "the state's economic base industries" was front and center. The main charge to the governor and legislators was that they press for guaranteed full funding of defense contracts. And no office or staff person focused on diversification, the report said, was necessary.[43]

Since then ...

... all six years notching the highest global temperatures ever recorded have occurred. The battle to do something about this is way behind schedule, and perilously close to being too late. But there are signs of hope for the economic transition that will be necessary. The United States has a president who is putting policy behind the idea that fighting climate change is a top national security priority, requiring an "all of government" approach. And, like Harrity, he is centering that fight on creating American jobs.

One *New York Times* writer cited a UAW paper, arguing for building up U.S.-made electric car battery production as influencing the Biden campaign to build an economic policy around this linkage. The head of the Alliance for American Manufacturing—a coalition of unions and a few large manufacturers—called the Biden administration's green job development plan, "the closest thing we've had to a broad industrial policy for generations, really."[44] And, before he died, the president of the union of unions, the AFL-CIO's Rich Trumka, called the Biden plan for a big, bold infrastructure bill "the most important climate bill of all time."[45]

Where Are the Machinists?

In 2020 the Connecticut's two senators joined 31 of their Senate colleagues in co-sponsoring "The Clean Economy Act," a similar proposal purporting to, as Murphy puts it, "put us on a path to net-zero emissions by 2050, boosting the economy in the process.... We don't have another moment to waste."[46] Murphy's press release is signed by a long list of environmental and public-health organizations, headed by four unions. The Machinists Union was not there.

Harrity is still focused on changing that. In 2016, 1,100 local union delegates met in Chicago for the IAMAW's quadrennial national convention. Harrity introduced a resolution committing the union to make climate change a priority, and to work for the just transition of its workers to jobs focused on solving it. The resolution was "based on the threat to our members and to working people and humanity in general." Going into the convention Harrity had spent weeks working behind the scenes on building support for the resolution.

> The resolution comes up and then the president goes to the microphone and asks who wants to speak on the resolution, come forward and do so. Five people speak against it. The president says: Anyone here wants to speak in favor? I was of course the only one.

Harrity acknowledged to the assembled delegates that it would be hard for them to vote against their leadership. But his years of studying the issue made clear the "unimaginable effects that are coming if we don't do something about it." He told them,

> [t]here've been times in the union where we hesitated. Like on secondhand smoke because we represented tobacco workers.... Like on the civil rights movement because we were afraid of alienating at that time our mostly white membership. Finally, we moved, and now we shake our heads at what took us so long. Climate change is the most critical issue that's going to affect all of us for the rest of our lives. This is a moment when we can be in the lead on this.

Harrity showed the assembled delegates a picture of his grandson, who he said was counting on him to make sure the world is livable in the boy's lifetime, and asked them to think of their own grandchildren before they voted.

> [After their voice vote the president] said the Chair was in doubt [about which way the vote had gone]. Which was a real gift. I'd talked to him a lot beforehand. The resolution was opposed by the executive council. Also by resolutions committee. But it got the only standing [individual] vote we had at the convention. It won 605 to 500. Remarkable.

It was, Harrity says, probably the highlight of his union career.

It didn't, however, produce the visible results in IAMAW policy that he'd hoped for. For the most part the leadership remained, and remains, focused on securing defense appropriations to keep their workers working. And back at the state level, Connecticut's military economy has been riding fairly high on Trump-and-Biden administrations' Pentagon contracts.

How do the workers feel in general about their work? At Pratt and the other Raytheon Technologies companies, Harrity says,

> there's not a whole lot of 'We're building the things that protect our country.' Not any particular patriotic zeal about the products. The company would try to whip that up—they'd bring in for example Air Force pilots to big assemblies, and they would thank the workers [for] building these jet engines to help them defend democracy. But there's not a whole lot of zeal. If people came in one day and were told they were making turbines to generate power, everybody would have been fine with that.
>
> There's always been more of a pro-military pride coming out of Electric Boat. Some of that is because they put a premium on hiring vets. They had to pass a security clearance to work there and they wanted people who were enthusiastic about the product.
>
> If you worked at Pratt it would be possible to not really think about were you supporting the military and what did it mean. At Electric Boat all you're doing is making a gigantic weapon. So there's no escaping it.
>
> [Those subs are] probably the most technologically complex product that is made[,] … a modern marvel. Unfortunately every one of [them] carries enough weaponry on it to kill all life on the planet. That's the downside.

As for the congressional delegation, Harrity says his conversations with all of them make clear that

> [d]espite their support for defense contracts they're really a progressive bunch. They talk about being the arsenal of America and all that. I think their attitude comes down to: If the country is going to make this stuff we want as much of that here as we can get. But [Congresswoman, and new chair of the House Appropriations Committee, Rosa] DeLauro would be thrilled if more of the defense budget could be spent on domestic or international needs. It's impossible for even progressive politicians to not have a lot of verbiage about patriotism which in our country is synonymous with supporting the military.

Harrity is trying again to move his union to put climate change at the center of its concerns. Though the victory of his 2016 resolution didn't produce noticeable change at the top, "I began to get calls from locals around the country that were interested in how do we deal with climate change." So he helped develop a questionnaire that enabled workers to raise the issue and its impacts with their locals: How has it affected your job? Your life outside your job? What do your kids think of climate change? Do you think your union should be involved in this issue or not?

Covid moved the 2020 IAMAW quadrennial convention to Sept of 2021. Harrity introduced another resolution mandating that the union do a nation-wide survey to determine how many jobs are dependent on fossil fuels, where they're located, and what union members want to do about it. He was working the phones to gin up support, up until the enduring pandemic postposed the convention, again, to 2022.

Conclusion

Openings to a New Future

Connecticut unions have won the first project labor agreement in the country for a Greentech project. The state requires that the jobs that building and maintaining the first wind farm off its coast will be union jobs. Unionized American workers will not be building the towers and the turbines—those will be European made—but will be installing generators and cables and maintaining the operation.

And in March of 2021 the Biden administration announced a multi-agency effort to build wind power installations up and down the East Coast, creating "thousands of good-paying union jobs."[47] The previous month the City of New London signed an agreement with Danish wind power manufacturer Orstad, and the relevant utility to turn an expanded State Pier in New London—across

FIGURE 2.3 Artist Jennifer Gottlieb's rendering of the new pier with offshore wind components on their way out to sea

Source: "State Pier Infrastructure Improvements Project;" photo courtesy of Connecticut Port Authority www.ctportauthority.com/

the river from Groton—into the hub for launching these offshore wind projects. Harrity reports that a 2018 visit to Denmark by the Connecticut Building Trades union helped get this ball rolling. "This makes Connecticut's role as a leader in the offshore wind industry official," Governor Neal Lamont said, "with New London now poised to become the premier commercial east coast hub for this sector and our state set to become a leader in the transition to renewable energy and the fight against climate change."[48]

The Thames River has been dominated by the stalwarts of Connecticut's military economy, Electric Boat, and the submarine base. Now they will look across the river at the makings of a non-military future. With this new kind of employment, Harrity says, "The Southeast Connecticut economy can begin to diversify."[49]

To reiterate: Union workers will be launching and maintaining the towers, but so far, they won't be building them. Too many eggs in the basket of military manufacturing mean that America lags far behind Europe in building a wind energy manufacturing base.

Connecticut has plenty of assets it could apply to changing that.

Notes

1 Markup of H.R. 5515 NDAA, full committee hearing, for FY 2019 (ID:108275), www.youtube.com/watch?v=uXjlP5ytgGI&t=5415s.
2 www.courant.com/opinion/editorials/hc-ed-courtney-endorsed-for-congress-again-20161025-story.html.
3 "Navy *Columbia* (SSBN-826) Class Ballistic Missile Submarine Program: Background and Issues for Congress," Congressional Research Service, updated February 19, 2021. https://crsreports.congress.gov/product/pdf/R/R41129/179.
4 www.theday.com/military-news/20201203/submarine-funding-restored-in-final-version-of-defense-bill
5 www.defensenews.com/naval/2020/06/22/us-navy-announces-intent-to-ink-10-billion-in-contracts-for-first-2-columbia-subs/.
6 Paul McLeary, "Esper Echoes Reagan Buildup, Calls for Billions More for Ships," *Breaking Defense*, September 16, 2020. https://breakingdefense.com/2020/09/esper-echoes-reagan-buildup-calls-for-billions-more-for-ships/.
7 www.defense.gov/Newsroom/Releases/Release/Article/2470586/dod-releases-report-on-defense-spending-by-state-in-fiscal-year-2019/source/GovDelivery/; state population 3.7 million/U.S. population 330 million; CT share of defense economy, 3.6%.
8 https://alphaqinc.com/about.
9 John Harrity's remarks come from phone interviews conducted on February 15, 2021, and February 21, 2021.
10 Paul McLeary, "India Inks $900M Deal For Sikorsky Sub-Hunting Helos As Tensions With China Spike," *Defense News*, May 14, 2020, https://breakingdefense.com/2020/05/india-inks-900m-deal-for-sub-hunting-helos-as-tensions-with-china-spike/; www.sipri.org/yearbook/2020.
11 "FY 2020 Security Cooperation Numbers," Department of Defense Security Cooperation Agency, December 4, 2020. www.dsca.mil/news-media/news-archive/fy2020-security-cooperation-numbers.

12 Dan Auble, "Capitalizing on conflict: How defense contractors and foreign nations lobby for arms sales," OpenSecrets.org, *Center for Responsive Politics*, February 25, 2021, www.opensecrets.org/news/reports/capitalizing-on-conflict.

13 Michael LaForgia and Walt Bogdanich, "Why Bombs Made in America Have been Killing Civilians in Yemen," *New York Times*, May 16, 2020, www.nytimes.com/2020/05/16/us/arms-deals-raytheon-yemen.html.

14 Valerie Insinna, "Just hours before Biden's inauguration, the UAE and US come to a deal on F-35 sales," *Defense News*, January 20, 2021, www.defensenews.com/global/mideast-africa/2021/01/20/just-hours-before-bidens-inauguration-the-uae-and-us-come-to-a-deal-on-f-35-sales/.

15 Jonathan Caverley, "America's Arms Sales Policy: Security Abroad, Not Jobs at Home," *War on the Rocks*, April 6, 2018, https://warontherocks.com/2018/04/americas-arms-sales-policy-security-abroad-not-jobs-at-home/.

16 "Lockheed says it sees demand for 200 F-16 fighter jets, and it wants to move a US plant to India to build them," *Reuters*, January 22, 2019, www.businessinsider.com/r-lockheed-sees-potential-exports-of-200-f-16-jets-from-proposed-indian-plant-2019-1.

17 Aaron Mehta, "America sold nearly $42B in weapons to foreign countries in 2017," *Defense News*, November 29, 2017, www.defensenews.com/pentagon/2017/11/29/america-sold-nearly-42b-in-weapons-to-foreign-countries-in-2017/.

18 Roger Franklin, *The Defender: The Story of General Dynamics* (New York: Harper and Row, 1986).

19 U.S. Department of Defense, "Contracts for September 4, 2020. www.defense.gov/Newsroom/Contracts/Contract/Article/2337845/source/GovDelivery/.

20 news.usni.org/2021/06/07/cost-estimates-for-lead-boat-in-columbia-class-program-grow-by-637m.

21 Fox Van Allen, "Meet the U.S. Navy's new $13 billion aircraft carrier," cnet.com, www.cnet.com/pictures/meet-the-navys-new-13-billion-aircraft-carrier/9/.

22 "Center for Arms Control and Non-Proliferation Fiscal Year 2022 Defense Budget Request Briefing Book."

23 "Navy Force Structure and Shipbuilding Plans: Background and Issues for Congress," *Congressional Research Service*, January 26, 2021. https://fas.org/sgp/crs/weapons/RL32665.pdf.

24 www.navytimes.com/news/your-navy/2021/02/23/navy-looking-to-slash-the-budget-of-its-internal-oversight-office/.

25 www.nam.org/state-manufacturing-data/.

26 For years the American Academy for the Advancement of Science has published data showing that federal defense R&D spending exceeds all non-defense R&D spending put together. In 2018 they stopped counting late-stage DoD development funding, and so R&D defense spending fell slightly behind. Yet it remains by far the largest U.S. R&D expenditure. www.aaas.org/programs/r-d-budget-and-policy/historical-trends-federal-rd.

27 Phone interview with John Harrity, February 22, 2021.

28 Ana Radelat, "Connecticut bets on manufacturing renaissance, but hurdles remain," *Connecticut Mirror*, December 24, 2019.

29 Phone interview with John Harrity, February 10, 2021, and with Bruce Olsson, February 28, 2021.

30 Lance Compa, "Labor and the Military," in eds. Suzanne Gordon and Dave McFadden, *Economic Conversion: Revitalizing America's Economy* (Cambridge, MA: Ballinger Publishing Company, 1984).

31 https://watson.brown.edu/costsofwar/costs/economic/economy/employment.

32 I worked there during the post–Cold War period.

33 Hilary Wainwright and Dave Elliott, *The Lucas Plan: A New Trade Unionism in the Making?* (London: Allison and Busby, 1982).

34 Fred Rose, "Coalitions in Practice," in *Coalitions Across the Class Divide: Lessons from the Labor, Peace and Environmental Movements* (Ithaca and London: Cornell University Press, 2000); Miriam Pemberton, "Remembering Claudette Munson" August 17, 2011, https://ips-dc.org/remembering_claudette_manson/.

35 www.congress.gov/bill/101st-congress/house-bill/101.

36 Greg Bischak, "US Conversion after the Cold War, 1990–1997," Bonn International Center for Conversion, July 1997.

37 "Connecticut's Defense-Related Industry: Spending, Employment and Dependency," *The Connecticut Economic Digest*, Connecticut Departments of Labor and Economic and Community Development, September, 2011.

38 Miriam Pemberton, "'How Will This Help Me Save My Plant?' ECD Convenes Labor Conference on Conversion," *The New Economy*, National Commission for Economic Conversion and Disarmament, Summer 1992.

39 www.nytimes.com/1992/11/04/us/1992-elections-celebration-excerpts-victory-speech-president-elect-clinton.html.

40 Bischak.

41 www.brown.edu/news/2019-11-13/costsofwar.

42 www.cga.ct.gov/2013/act/pa/2013PA-00019-R00SB-00619-PA.htm.

43 Personal knowledge, based on contemporaneous notes, of the author, who testified before the Commission and worked with the labor-peace-environment coalition.

44 Noam Scheiber, "The Biden Team Wants to Transform the Economy. Really." *The New York Times Magazine*, February 11, 2021. www.nytimes.com/2021/02/11/magazine/biden-economy.html.

45 www.nytimes.com/2021/03/01/business/infrastructure-biden-stimulus.html.

46 www.murphy.senate.gov/newsroom/press-releases/murphy-blumenthal-join-31-senators-in-introducing-legislation-to-achieve-net-zero-greenhouse-gas-emissions-in-the-us-by-no-later-than-2050.

47 www.washingtonpost.com/climate-environment/2021/03/29/biden-wind-power/.

48 Greg Smith, "New London secures host agreement with offshore wind partners," *The Day*, February 26, 2021. www.theday.com/article/20210226/NWS01/210229506.

49 Phone interview, September 21, 2021.

3

JOHNSTOWN, PA

From Coal to the King of Pork

We travel now about 400 miles west, from a Mecca of Pentagon contracting to one of its backwaters. Connecticut's roots in the military economy dig deep into the state's history. Pennsylvania's Johnstown built its military economy in the 1980s out of chutzpah and whole cloth.

What forces draw military contractors into the spots they occupy on the American landscape?

Geography, for one. Shipyards have to be on the coasts of course. The massive flat open spaces near Fort Worth, Texas, nicely accommodate America's largest manufacturing facility for military planes—it's more than a mile long—and their adjacent airfield.

Also, history. While this military footprint is always evolving, World War II drew many of its basic outlines: a vastly expanded network of military bases in every state and the contractors clustering on and around them; a few key concentrations of the "aerospace" industry (southern California and Texas) and the tank plants (Michigan, Ohio, and Indiana) and so on.[1]

And, as we've seen so far, contractors are also where they are because of politics.

In the case of Johnstown, it was politics. Johnstown became a military economy town late in the game, primarily through the efforts of one complicated, proverbially larger-than-life man.

A Legacy of Coal and Steel

Water channeling riverbeds into the Appalachians formed Johnstown's geography. Two of them, joining forces about 65 miles east of Pittsburgh to make the

DOI: 10.4324/9781003293705-4

Conemaugh River, carved out the narrow, deeply and beautifully gorged valley where Johnstown sits.

The coal in these mountains became the region's competitive advantage, absorbing waves of immigrants—early on Germans, Irish and Italians mostly—to get the coal out. Freight cars of the Pennsylvania railroad began rolling through town in 1850 and, by the Civil War, Johnstown's coal-fired industry was the biggest producer of iron in the country. Two experimenters then came to town to work the bugs out of the steelmaking process, briefly turning Johnstown into the largest steel producer in the country. This preeminence lasted five years, until Andrew Carnegie out of Pittsburgh started raiding some of Johnstown's workforce for his operations, and pushed Johnstown into second place. Second place still meant new waves of immigrants, now largely from eastern Europe, disembarking at the train depot and heading to jobs in the blast furnaces. One of Andrew Carnegie's proteges, Charlie Schwab, who ran Bethlehem Steel for 35 years, described his child's- eye view of the steelworks from 20 miles away:

> Along toward dusk tongues of flame would shoot up in the pall around Johnstown. When some furnace door was opened the evening turned red.... And the murk always present, the smell of the foundry. It got into your hair, your clothes, even your blood.[2]

During the 1880s the demand for steel in the United States tripled, first horizontally, to double the country's rail lines, and then vertically, to provide the backbone for its skyscrapers.

Carnegie and his cadre of Pittsburgh steel magnates also acquired a reservoir perched on the lip of a gorge 14 miles upstream from Johnstown, where they built a summer getaway resort for their families and called it the South Fork Hunting and Fishing Club. Many suspect that their subordination of safety engineering to accommodations for the fish, and spacious carriage trails across the dam, contributed to the collapse of the dam on May 31, 1889. Ten minutes after the wall of water reached Johnstown, most of the town was destroyed, and more than two thousand of its inhabitants were dead. Following a harrowing emotional and physical reconstruction, the "Great Flood" eventually became not only Johnstown's tragedy but its claim to fame. (Music lovers from far-flung states still turn up in June for Johnstown's "Flood City Music Festival.")

Johnstown clung tenaciously to its good thing. A month after the deluge, extraordinary measures dragged the first of the steel mills back up and running, and they remained the community mainstay for another century.

Johnstown's identity as a steel town reached its peak in the 1940s and 1950s, putting around 13,000 people to work supplying infrastructure to the post-World War II economic boom. Then, over the next decades, the U.S. steel industry slowly imploded, a casualty, among other things, of increased

FIGURE 3.1 Johnstown, Pennsylvania

Source: Wirestock Creators/ shutterstock

domestic and foreign competition and of the regulations finally controlling the depredations of a century of coal and steel pollution: During his boyhood, a reporter for the local *Tribune-Democrat* newspaper recalls the Conemaugh River running orange.[3]

Bethlehem Steel began closing its plants in the Johnstown area during the late 1970s. Unemployment soared and, in 1992, the company left town for good. So did a lot of its workers—by then, the population had plunged from the steel-infused amplitude of 70,000 to under 30,000, with more decline to come.

How to Build a Military Economy—From Scratch

Johnstown needed a salvage plan, and its new congressman came up with one. John Murtha, an elfin-faced man with a bearlike body, was running the Johnstown Minute Car Wash in 1974 when, as Bethlehem Steel began pulling out, he won a congressional seat by 122 votes. His devotion to Johnstown ran deep—there are six Murthas on the list of victims of the Great Flood. Unlike the legions of his congressional colleagues morphing into creatures of Washington, Murtha's loyalty to his hometown never wavered.[4]

The graph on p. 15 depicts the boom-and-bust cycles of U.S. military spending. Murtha came to Washington during the post-Vietnam valley, on the way to the mountain of Reagan-era buildup. Murtha found he had both the appetite and aptitude for the arts of congressional power-broking and horse-trading. These skills soon secured him the plum prize of a seat on the House Committee on Appropriations, where, as Willie Sutton would say, the money is.

As we've seen, the 12 Appropriations Subcommittees hash out the individual line items in the budgets for each federal agency, which (if all goes well) then are amalgamated in a final Appropriations bill. The lion's share of the money goes through the House Subcommittee on Defense. So, Congressman Murtha's task became undertaking the maneuvering necessary to get appointed to that subcommittee. And this became his strategy to steer its money to his district.

It should be said that Murtha's affinity for this subcommittee was not a matter of business alone. While the devotion of members of Congress to "the troops" can often sound more like trope than conviction, Murtha's was close to the bone. More than a decade after enlisting in the Marines to fight in Korea, he had decided to leave his assignment in the National Guard to go back to combat in Vietnam. As the first Vietnam vet elected to congress, he became one of the staunch "defense hawks" of the Democratic Party, seeing no daylight between support for the troops and fatter budgets for the Pentagon.

That lasted for decades, until in 2005 he turned around and jeopardized his standing in Congress, and with his own constituents, by becoming a leading critic of the Iraq War. It was, he said, "a badly flawed policy wrapped in illusion." Talking to National Public Radio that year from his district office in Johnstown, he invoked President Lyndon Johnson's assurances about the Vietnam War: Johnson "said over and over again how well it was going.… We're hearing the same thing now. Just because they say it does not make it so."[5] Murtha wanted the troops to risk their lives only in wars that, by his lights, made sense.

Earmarks

What didn't seem to change was his support for ever-increasing funding for the Pentagon. "All politics is local," House Speaker Tip O'Neill began preaching during Murtha's first decade in Congress, and no one took this to heart more than his confidante, Murtha.

The economic foundations of his home base had all but collapsed. Its local assets—its mountains of coal, its mills, its confluence of rivers—were of limited use. Politics as an economic development strategy would have to take over.

You can steer Pentagon money into your district in a variety of ways. You can do it the way Joe Courtney and Rob Wittman do it, by leading the subcommittee controlling spending on a class of weapons that your districts are virtually alone in being able to build. Or you can become a reliable vote for a massive program that is built all over the country (n.b. the F-35 Joint Strike Fighter) and make sure your district gets its piece.

Or you can ensure that one line item in the budget specifically and explicitly assigns—earmarks—money to a military project in your district, circumventing the competitive bidding process, so that by law, the money can't go anywhere else. By 1989, Murtha had worked his deal-making arts up the chain to become chair of the Defense Appropriations subcommittee. He held on to this post, or, when Republicans were in control, to the position of its ranking member, until his death in 2010. He began inserting earmarks into his defense bills ensuring that new defense contracting businesses would begin sprouting in Johnstown.

Congress created its first earmark back in 1789. It contained the classic element: a quid pro quo. In exchange for its support for federal funding to construct lighthouses in states along the Atlantic coast, the Pennsylvania delegation had inserted the money to build a pier in Philadelphia.[6] But earmarks' heyday came much later, and Murtha made it happen. In 1970, four years before Murtha went to Washington, the defense appropriations bill included about a dozen earmarks. By 2006, it held 2,879.[7]

And a remarkable number of them went to Johnstown: between 1992 and 2008, about $2 billion worth.[8] Some years, Johnstown, Pennsylvania, population under 30,000, was the beneficiary of more earmarks than any other city in America.[9]

Although the desks on the House floor are mostly unassigned, one of them at the back on the right came to be known as "Murtha Corner." Members of Congress could often be seen congregating there securing appropriations for military contractors in their districts and hammering out the quid pro quos. They knew that an offer from one of those contractors to set up a branch facility in Johnstown, or to send one of its subcontracts Johnstown's way, would help a lot.

Ray Wrabley chairs the political science department at the University of Pittsburgh at Johnstown. He used to invite Murtha frequently to talk to his classes. Murtha defended his parochial deal-making, Wrabley says, by calling himself "a full-throated defender of spending money—all kinds." It was mostly military money because that's the committee he sat on. He believed appropriating increasing sums to the Pentagon would enhance national security, but also, "if it's going to be spent he'd rather it be spent in his district rather than somebody else's."[10] He also argued that doing defense contracting in Johnstown saved the taxpayers money over doing the same work in high-priced Washington.

FIGURE 3.2 Congressman Murtha testifying before the Senate Foreign Relations Committee on the Iraq War

Source: Office of Congressman John Murtha via Wikimedia Commons

Ways and Means

What kind of military economy do you try to create in a struggling mountain town that has almost none?

Back in 1987, just before taking control of the subcommittee, Murtha secured an earmark giving a five-year $27 million Navy contract to a local nonprofit startup that called itself Metalworking Technology. This was Murtha's attempt to base Johnstown's new industry on its established manufacturing expertise in metal bending, machining, welding, and so on.

> "The idea," says Mike Hruska, now the chief customer success officer of a local IT and business consulting business, was to create a centerpiece of a defense economy…. When you have nonprofit applied research in the middle, they can solve problems for those other companies, or as they get work, [their research] could be spun off to others for production…. That never *really* happened, but it was the intent.[11]

Rather than manufacturing experience, the Metalworking Technology CEO, Ed Sheehan, brought knowhow on maneuvering for defense contracts from his previous job back in Northern Virginia. When Murtha assumed the subcommittee chairmanship a few years later, he began providing the company with around $60 million in earmarks annually.[12]

The military economy Murtha wound up building in Johnstown, though, looks less like an outgrowth of metalworking expertise than a grab bag of goods and services pulled from all over the defense budget: Along with pieces of weapons systems, there were, and are, companies providing supplies and training for personnel, and services for military installations across the service branches. Metalworking Technologies was renamed "Concurrent Technologies," an elastic name worthy of Crystal City, Arlington, Virginia, that could cover whatever projects Murtha could bring to it. Hruska goes on:

> The principle of selection for Murtha's earmarks tended to be: What could a start-up business get up to speed quickly to do, and who in the Johnstown region did he know who, with enough federal money, could do it. Or as Hruska puts it, One might say he took whatever seeds he had in his hand and threw them in a field…. Or he planted a variety of things to see what might grow together…. Someone else might say the seeds he had in his hand [were] who he had the most power over, and [to whom he] could say: "You need to put something in my town."

What do you make for the Pentagon if you are a start-up without much experience making anything? One attractive option is to offer your services to manage others who do. A case in point was a company called Mountaintop

Technologies. Its CEO, David Fyock, met Murtha in the 1980s when working as a lobbyist for the local electric company. Soon after Murtha became chair of the House Appropriations Subcommittee on Defense, Fyock decided to try his hand at the defense contracting business. Hiring lobbyists of his own became part of the business plan—specifically, Murtha's brother Kit and three former Murtha aides, who after 1999 collectively earned $725,000 representing the company. Mountaintop had an office a floor below Murtha's district office.

In 2002, Murtha proudly announced that he had added earmarks in that year's defense bill, awarding three contracts worth $13 million to Mountaintop. The largest had them overseeing others to find military uses for the Bombardier CL-415, a plane that could pour water on fires. (None were found.) As Fyock told it, "We were the ones who found the experts and took their knowledge and made it available." Taxpayer watchdog groups wondered why this middleman role was really necessary, and why for military ventures as disparate as robotics, battle-field anesthesiology and emergency communications, Mountaintop was the best candidate to undertake them. Fyock had the answer: "We get the work because Congressman Murtha and his staff are well aware of our capabilities."[13]

Beyond creating new companies in Johnstown from scratch, the strategy featured inducing major prime contractors to set up shop in Johnstown. Two of them did: Lockheed Martin and Northrop Grumman. That same year of 1987, while Murtha was solidifying his power base on the subcommittee, Lockheed Martin created a Johnstown subsidiary, Lockheed Martin Aeroparts. The company supplies new and repair parts for a variety of aircraft, including the F-16 fighter jet and the C-130 transport plane. But the gravitational force pulling in more and more of the military procurement budget has absorbed much of this facility's operations as well: the F-35.

Also pulled into its forcefield is Martin-Baker, a British company which, in 1986, launched its U.S. subsidiary in Northern Virginia. In 2000, Murtha convinced it to move to Johnstown. Starting out as an airplane manufacturer, the company had redirected its mission after pilot/co-owner Valentine Baker was killed in 1942 during an emergency landing. The company devoted itself to developing and manufacturing the first ejection seats allowing fighter pilots to escape a crashing plane. From their now-influential spot in Johnstown, they secured the contract to build these seats into the F-35.[14] As we'll see, ejection seats have joined the list of this plane's many troubled features.

The fruits of Murtha's power weren't confined to military projects. He cut deals with other appropriators that funded an array of projects in Johnstown, most of which bear his, or his wife's name: the John. P. Murtha Regional Cancer Center. The John P. Murtha Technology Center. The Joyce Murtha Breast Care Center. The John P. Murtha Center for Public Service and Competitiveness.

Most notorious was the National Drug Intelligence Center, which he got funded the same year he took control of his subcommittee and put into the shell of Johnstown's extinct department store. Throughout its life, this Center had to contend with one question: Why do we need a National Drug Intelligence Center in the Pennsylvania mountains when we already have one in Washington, DC.? Someone asked him at the ribbon cutting: Why put this here? His answer: "Because this is where I wanted it."[15] Until Murtha died, a total of $500 million in earmarks kept it alive.[16]

Corrupt? Illegal?

The other key component of the feedback loop between Murtha's powerbase and local defense contracts was contributing to John Murtha's election campaigns. Mountaintop Technologies executives, for example, gave $40,200 to the cause of his reelection.[17]

In keeping with its contract dispersal strategy, Lockheed operates its political influence game on a national scale. Murtha's power brokering dovetailed nicely. During the representative year of 2008 the company spread $2.5 million in campaign contributions to 53 Senators and 100 Members of Congress, equally split between Democrats and Republicans. Their targets were, of course, concentrated among the members of the committees with control over the Pentagon budget.

They gave Murtha $34,900 that year. The ranking Republican on his committee, Kay Granger, beat him out by raking in $59,700. The explanation: She was the congresswoman from Fort Worth, Texas, where most of Lockheed's F-35s get their final assembly. Only three others were ahead of these two on Lockheed's list: that year's two presidential contestants and one Chris Myers ($132,420), who never made it to Congress at all.[18] This anomaly is easily explained: He launched his unsuccessful congressional campaign from a platform as one of Lockheed Martin's vice presidents.[19]

When people think about corruption, it is usually the kind of pay-to-play system that benefits the lifestyles of the corrupted. Occasionally, not often, its perpetrators do time in prison. The most notorious might be Randy "Duke" Cunningham (R–CA), a colleague of Murtha's on the Subcommittee on Defense, who went to jail for steering more than $200 million to two defense contractors in exchange for $2.4 million in contributions. (Trump included Cunningham in his flurry of last-minute pardons.) Unlike Murtha, representing one of the poorest cities in Appalachia with no defense industry to speak of at the start, Cunningham represented a wealthy San Diego district concentrating more defense assets than anywhere else in the country, including half of the Navy's Pacific Fleet.[20] The contractors maneuvering for a piece of that action helped him get his own yacht and Rolls Royce. His trial featured his bribe menu, where he specified the amount of the bribe that would secure the earmark desired. A starting bid was $140,000, plus that yacht, which would be required to win a $16 million Pentagon contract.[21]

In contrast to many, perhaps most, of his colleagues, personal enrichment appears not to have figured much in Murtha's agenda. No Rolls Royce showed up in his driveway. His motivators, it seems, were amassing power and using it to benefit his friends—including his brother—and his district. (And, presumably, the ego boost of having his name on all those buildings in town.)

In 2008 Murtha arranged $48.2 million in earmarks and received a total of $493,950 in contributions. That's a lot of deals to negotiate and money to keep track of. Enter the lobbyists to streamline this operation. Many were his former employees. A former staffer and friend on the defense appropriations subcommittee, Paul Magliocchetti, formed the lobbying firm PMA Group and became Murtha's most important facilitator of deals. He represented seven of Johnstown's defense contractors that year, including Concurrent Technologies and Mountaintop Technologies. Murtha provided Magliocchetti's clients with $30 million in earmarks and they provided him a total of $301,850 in donations to his campaign.[22]

Was this (illegal) bribery? Such arrangements had been heading down that slippery slope for years, certainly. More and more members of Congress were joining the slide, fearful of missing out on a system that allowed them to secure, and tout, special benefits for their constituents. A 2009 study by the Center for Public Integrity found that three-quarters of Murtha's subcommittee members had worked out similar arrangements, in which "former staffers became lobbyists for defense contractors; the contractors received earmarks from the representatives, and the representatives received campaign contributions from the lobbyists or the contractors."[23] The study was called the "Murtha Method." His leadership as an innovator and promoter of the system earned him the title "King of Pork."[24]

Melanie Sloan, director of the watchdog group Citizens for Responsibility and Ethics in Washington (CREW) said in 2009, "What Murtha is doing everybody else is doing. It's just to such a higher degree that it becomes shocking."[25]

Where is the legal, as distinct from the ethical, line? It is crossed when arrangements become explicit quid pro quos between favors and money. Murtha flirted with the line for years. In the late seventies his methods attracted the attention of the FBI, who named him as an unindicted co-conspirator in the "Abscam" public corruption investigation that convicted one senator and six representatives. A surveillance tape caught Murtha initially putting off, while appearing to entertain, a $50,000 bribe to arrange a visa for an "Arab sheik" in exchange for investments in Johnstown. "After we've done some business, I might change my mind," he said. "I think with a tie to the district, there's no problem getting [the visa] taken care of…. I do business like this all the time to get companies into the area."[26]

In 2006 CREW began publishing an annual reckoning of the "Most Corrupt Members of Congress." Murtha was flagged that first year as a "Member to Watch." By 2008 he was on the list. Cited first as rationale was his relationship with the PMA Group, whose defense contractor clients had received at least 60 of his earmarks, totaling $95 million, and donated more than $274,000 to his campaign. Next was Concurrent Technologies Corporation, which had paid PMA $302,000 to lobby for them. Also cited was Murtha's threatened retaliation toward another congressman for trying to get rid of the $23 million earmark for his National Drug Intelligence Center. "I hope you don't have any earmarks in the defense appropriations bills because they are gone," Murtha is quoted as saying, "and you will not get any earmarks now and forever."

In November of 2008, federal agents raided the offices of PMA and the home of its CEO Paul Magliocchetti. PMA closed down and Magliocchetti went to jail, for reimbursing friends, family members and business associates for the hundreds of thousands of dollars in campaign contributions to Murtha and other congressmembers.[27]

Murtha never backed down from defending his methods. "If I'm corrupt," he declared in a 2009 interview, "it's because I take care of my district."[28]

When students in Ray Wrabley's political science class asked him about the Most Corrupt Members list Murtha would reply that he was lining the pockets of his neighbors, not his own. On the mountain of campaign contributions from defense contractors, he would say, "They're not buying me, they're paying me because I'm already doing what they want."

But in 2011 it was revealed that the FBI had opened a criminal investigation into Murtha and some of the lobbyists in his circle.[29] The walls appeared to be closing in. The investigation was short-circuited in 2010 when, suffering from complications to gall bladder surgery, Murtha died.

Whither Earmarks?

Potential corruption and illegality aside, this is the major knock-on earmarks: It is the president's and the Congress's job to think about the national security interest as a whole, and to decide where to spend money in service to that common interest. Horse-trading among parochial power brokers takes those deliberations in a different direction.

It is not a settled question. Former Senate Majority Leader Harry Reid defended them in 2014, saying "[I]t is wrong to have bureaucrats downtown make decisions in Nevada that I can make better than they can make."[30] This was after the Republican majority decided to eliminate them. (Some argue this never entirely happened—that some of them just got hidden in the budget more creatively.[31]) The argument for bringing them back is that when this vehicle for dealmaking went away, the impulse to reach bipartisan agreement on anything took a hit, making the divisive trend in our politics worse.

In Johnstown today, Murtha is widely revered and his practices defended. Everybody was doing earmarks they say. The work is going to be done some-where. Why not Johnstown, a place that *really* needs it?

Mike Hruska, the local computer executive, has a somewhat different take. Growing up in Johnstown, he left what looked like its economic death spiral, until Murtha's machinations gave the town a pulse. He started his own company,

Problem Solutions, in computer software development and consulting. In the early years the business was 90 percent dependent on Pentagon contracts.

Unlike most of his fellow contractors, Hruska had his misgivings.

> There was general reliance on the economic spin that was put on by the defense industry here. The value of earmarks. Don't worry, they'd say, the congressman has us. People take care of him, and he takes care of us. I said wow, that's great, but what are we going to do ten years from now? What are we doing to create a sustainable and resilient economy of the future?[32]

One local, who didn't want to be public about his skepticism toward the Murtha defense contracting plan for economic development, called it "Murthadone."

The Military Market Contracts, 2011–2015

The hit from the sudden death of the King of Pork was only one of a confluence of factors bearing down on Johnstown's military economy.

Congress took notice of the expanding budget deficit, ignored during a decade of votes for tax cuts and surging military spending. The year Murtha died they passed the Budget Control Act (BCA), a ten-year framework putting roughly equivalent caps on spending for defense and domestic needs. Almost immediately Congress turned around and began passing two-year "relaxations" of the budget constraints they made a show of imposing on themselves. But the law did set the Pentagon budget on a path toward cuts of nearly 10 percent.

And a few months after Murtha died, Congress put a moratorium on earmarks.

The loss of its one-man gravitational force pulling military dollars into Johnstown meant that when the national market contracted, this spot on the Pentagon economy's landscape took a harder hit than almost any other. In 2014 the Pentagon hired an economic consulting firm to assess the effects of the budget cuts. Its report identified the land that Murtha built as the second most-deeply impacted area in the nation, after Oshkosh, Wisconsin.[33] The report estimated that, between 2010 and 2012, $782 million in Pentagon contracts and resulting economic activity had leaked out of Johnstown, equivalent to $5,400 per resident.[34]

For a brief time, Murtha's chief of staff, Mark Critz, succeeded him. Hruska, the software entrepreneur, remembers "Everyone said, 'Oh great, Mark will take care of us.' People failed to realize the power that someone like Congressman Murtha had accumulated over the years [that Critz didn't have.] And things kind of started to move away."[35] The world Murtha built out of Pentagon dollars began to shrink as contractors he'd lured in began to leave, and some of the ones he'd created locally shut their doors.

Northrop Grumman, for example, is currently the world's fifth-largest military contractor, formed by the merger of two defense giants during the post–Cold War defense industry consolidation. It makes both the B-2 bomber, at $2 billion a copy, and its successor the B-21, as well as intercontinental ballistic missiles, satellites, drones, and array of other weapons systems, including parts of the F-35. We'll visit one of its strongholds in the next chapter. Back in 2005, to stay on Murtha's good side, Northrop also established a beachhead operation in Johnstown.

One highly lucrative piece of the Pentagon pie has been around since 1983, when President Reagan hatched his dream of a system that could shield the U.S. from nuclear attack.[36] This benign-sounding idea has actually been the catalyst for a new arms race, as more and more countries fear an attack from a potentially invulnerable enemy and so feel the need to buy their own missile defenses. From 1985 to 2019, the United States has spent $200 billion devising, making, tinkering and testing (and manipulating the tests for) an array of systems, from the ground-based to the space-based, from missiles to lasers, trying to fulfill this dream. After a few successes and failure after failure, none have remotely achieved the invulnerability of a "shield." Yet allied with their contractors, Congress remains bullish on the dream of missile defense, providing its assemblage of programs more than $20 billion in fiscal year 2021. More on this in Chapter 7.

Northrop's product line in Johnstown featured a piece of the Kinetic Interceptor Program, a land-based system that was supposed to hit nuclear missiles soon after they were launched. In addition to its repeated test failures, it had another problem: to knock out a just-launched missile, the system would have to be installed near the launch site, an impossibility for most of the likely U.S. targets such as Russia, China, and Iran.

The Obama administration's first military budget killed the $4 billion program, which Northrop had been counting on to keep its Johnstown workforce busy. Reverses like this, on top of Murtha's powerful finger no longer on the scales, and the general budget shrinkage driven by the Budget Control Act, led Northrop to fold its tents in Johnstown.[37]

Many of the contractors homegrown in the fertilizer of Murtha earmarks didn't last long after he died. The month that Murtha died, for example, Mountaintop Technologies started furloughing workers.[38] By 2012, it had closed its doors.

The military economy has not entirely evaporated in Johnstown, as Murtha warned it might when he was "long gone." He called his annual celebration of this economy the Showcase for Commerce. It really only showcases one kind of commerce. Every year during his reign over defense appropriations, more than a hundred contractors from as far away as Europe and California would come to display their newest military gadgets in Johnstown's hockey arena and talk up how essential they are to America's national security. Workshops on how to get defense business would fill up every year. Generals and ex-generals would attend. Announcements of Johnstown's haul of defense contracts that year would be announced. Tanks and artillery pieces would line up outside.[39]

Shutting down for Covid in 2020, the Showcase reemerged in 2021, with Deputy Defense Secretary Kathleen Hicks joining its "John P. Murtha Breakfast" on screen.[40] Hruska, the computer guy, sees this as a legacy event that may need some reinvention, to "attract a broader group of people" by reaching beyond the military economy toward "what the future economy is going to be—internet of things, sensors, 3D printing, AI learning, lots of other things."[41]

What Now?

On a sunny day in early March 2019, Frank Janakovic, mayor of Johnstown, sits in a chair upholstered in Pittsburgh Steelers logos, with Steelers, Pirates and Penguins memorabilia occupying most inches of wall space around him. Janakovic is an even-tempered man with a walrus mustache and big problems. His annual State of the City address, delivered the night before, forthrightly laid out the city's problems, including, on top of its poverty rate and opioid crisis, $25 million in unfunded pension liabilities that a shrinking and aging population was not going to be able to cover. The 850–1000 abandoned houses that should come down if the $7,000 per tear-down cost could be found. And the wages of 20–30 years of neglect to the sewer system: a $140 million state-mandated project to eliminate stormwater run-off and replace everybody's sewer lines. "It needs to happen," he says that morning, "but tell that to the homeowners that have to foot the bill."

Over the lip of Johnstown's mountain ridges, new suburbs, and the industrial parks housing most of the defense contractors, have grown. In the valley and its lower mountain sides the visible remains of those who left town—their vacant and deteriorating houses--blight street after street. The 2010 census recorded a poverty level in Johnstown of 34 percent, one of the highest in Pennsylvania.[42] And the city's opioid crisis rages.

Johnstown has been operating for more than 20 years under a special state designation for "Distressed Cities," giving them special taxing privileges and

FIGURE 3.3 Gautier Works steel mill, now mostly vacant

Source: Historic American Buildings Survey/Historic American Engineering Record/ Historic American Landscape Survey Collection; Library of Congress

other mechanisms designed to bring their budgets into balance. They are trying to move on from this special "status." The problem, Janakovic says, is the stigma. "If I'm a business looking to relocate, why would I want to go into a "distressed community"?[43]

A month after his speech, the news came from new Census figures that Johnstown's population had dropped another one percent during the previous year.[44] The 2020 census showed Cambria County's population contracting by 7.1 percent over the previous decade.[45] Amy Bradley, president of the local chamber of commerce, and Bill Polachek, CEO of local contractor JWF Industries, believe it is "around the corner from stabilizing."[46] Ray Wrabley, the University of Pittsburgh-Johnstown political science professor, thinks the town is "teetering."

A Plan for Defense Diversification

City leaders have launched a multitude of plans ("Vision 2025"; "Comprehensive Plan: Toward a Sustainable Future 2030"; "Destination Cambria") to reverse Johnstown's decline.

John Dubnansky, a compact man with outsize enthusiasm for Johnstown's potential, heads the Cambria County Department of Economic Development. He mentions the Pentagon study identifying Johnstown as one of two communities in the nation most affected by defense budget cuts, calling it an important wake-up call for contractors and subcontractors who haven't taken steps to diversify beyond the defense market. "It is a reality check," he said. "We need to develop a plan to diversify."

Johnstown got support for this planning effort from the Pentagon's Office of Economic Adjustment (OEA), which also funded Connecticut's Commission on its future. OEA, one of many Defense Department agencies sitting in high-rises along the Potomac, was created in 1961 to help defense-dependent communities adjust to base closures or major contract cancellations with technical assistance and funding for a community planning process. Knowing that its intent to end the wars in Iraq and Afghanistan would deliver a hit to many of these communities, the Obama administration beefed up OEA's funding to try to reduce both the economic impact itself and the backlash to it from those who would favor jacking up Pentagon budgets instead to keep the military economy humming. From its perch as the second-biggest casualty of the contracted military economy, Johnstown was one of OEA's prime beneficiaries. The task was to find the next phase of Johnstown's economic identity, following its historical trajectory from coal to steel to defense contracting to—what?

The idea, adapted from the base closure process (more on this in Chapter 5), is to assemble local stakeholders—business leaders, economic development experts, public officials, other community leaders, and defense workers—to do a "SWOT" analysis (identifying community Strength, Weakness, Opportunity and Threat). From this baseline the diversification strategy is supposed to emerge.

In Johnstown, John Dubnansky was in charge. The planning phase focused most intently on identifying regional industry clusters: the concentrations of industrial categories in the local economy. Then the idea is to network these components of the local industrial base with other nearby manufacturing centers and companies to create hubs of local economic strength. Industrial policy on a local scale, in other words.

Johnstown's OEA process identified metals manufacturing and information technology as having the strongest crossover potential from military to non-military production. These two, they noted, also shared strong potential to connect to the economic boom town of Pittsburgh. A third identified strength, tied to the area's extractive legacy, was energy, particularly the potential to partake of the natural gas boom opened up by the fracking of the Marcellus Shale—covering a huge gas field under Pennsylvania and six other states.

Their Cambria County Defense Transition Plan included an extensive directory and analysis of the state and local assets—educational, nonprofit, business and economic development and workforce organizations—that might be useful in the transition, noting that new entities focused on specific industry clusters might be necessary. It also drew lessons from case studies of previous efforts at defense industry transition.

The Metals Manufacturing group thought they needed outside help in evaluating the alternative market potential of defense products: those with experience in innovative product designs for metal products who could help them figure out whether and how their products could be retooled for other industries, what similar products could be fabricated using the firm's capabilities, and how to expand those capabilities. And they talked about linking themselves to the federally funded additive manufacturing (3-D printing) hub in Youngstown and Pittsburgh, as well as developing greater capabilities in digital manufacturing.[47]

The Information Technologies group explored ways to build a "Bridge to Pittsburgh"—tapping into the IT Mecca there by making the commute from Johnstown easy, or satisfying some of Pittsburgh's need for IT workers with remote work out of Johnstown, or luring Pittsburgh companies to open branch offices in Johnstown.[48]

Where Do Things Stand Now?

The Trump administration's campaign to boost defense spending blunted some of the momentum behind these plans. But Dubnansky says his town's defense sector is nowhere near its Murtha-era heyday, and he doesn't expect it to grow. "We want to keep the ones we have," he hastens to add, while realizing that the growth of that industry "follows congressional powers."

The city solved some of its financial problems in 2020 by privatizing its sewer system, generating the $25 million they needed to fix their pension issue and

begin capital improvements. They've extended their "distressed community" designation a little longer, for tax purposes.

And they seem poised to build on this strategy of making Johnstown's economic plight into an asset. First an Intuit (Turbo Tax, QuickBooks) partner named
Concentrix came to town with 250 new jobs—part of the Defense Transition
plan's focus on building a bridge to Pittsburgh's information hub. Following a
four-year lobbying effort, including a visit from Intuit's CEO, Johnstown has been
picked to join Intuit's Prosperity Hub Program. Since the company's original
CEO grew up in West Virginia, Dubnansky says, he focuses his corporate responsibility efforts on "depressed areas that need a helping hand," in seven towns in
Kentucky, Tennessee, Virginia, West Virginia, Pennsylvania, and Oklahoma. His
thinking is that "if he develops businesses here they can be customers."

In addition to creating local jobs with its partner companies, Intuit will open an
Economic Development hub in downtown Johnstown for local entrepreneurs and
existing businesses, and has made videos to lure them in.[49] "I can use their name,"
Dubnansky says, to grow other businesses. "Nobody wants to be the first one
in—it's risky. Intuit was happy to be the one." He credits the Defense Transition
process, along with Johnstown's several other "visioning" groups, for convincing Intuit that the city was not only "distressed" but had enough community
"momentum" to make this work.

Johnstown's Contractors: Three Different Paths

Defense-dependent economies diversify when they grow and attract civilian
business, as well as when their defense contractors start doing other things: either
staying with government contracting for civilian agencies (in the kind of market
they know) or developing goods and services for the commercial marketplace.

Some of Johnstown's contractors, as we've seen, have either closed down or
moved out of town. Those staying have fanned out in one of three directions.

Getting Out

Some have exited the defense market, predominantly or altogether. Mike Hruska's
Problem Solutions, for example, was 90 percent defense-dependent in 2010 and,
by 2019, had become 86 percent commercial. The following year, merging with
a Minnesotan virtual learning company, Allen Interactions, Hruska has kept all of
his people employed, and indeed has expanded his workforce.

Making the transition he "had to start talking to a whole different set of people,
marketing differently, changing the way we operated as a business." To do defense
contracting, you've got one customer, he observes, and marketing to that customer
means hanging out in DC and going to defense business conferences. To market
his company in the commercial world, "the best way to do it is to go press the
flesh, build relationships," which he's doing on trips all around the country.

He's happier with the pace of the commercial world. "Anything I've ever done in the defense industry takes like eight to twenty months to get there," he says. Further, "the RFP [request for proposals] cycle is extremely long … and the cost of bidding is inordinately complex." He finds it more satisfying doing "short-term nimble computer projects." And in the commercial sector "you don't have all the crazy acquisition regulations and procurement cycles."

To help build Johnstown's commercial capacity, Hruska runs an entrepreneurship meetup group that convenes monthly on zoom and has grown to 460 members. He envisions Johnstown as a place where small tech start-ups can flourish. "We've been a one-company town forever: mining, then steel, then large defense contractors." What he read somewhere around 2007 has stuck with him: "We don't need another 800-person company; we need 100 eight-person companies."

One of Hruska's proteges worked at Concurrent Technologies designing technology that could make water potable for soldiers in the field. In 2020 he left the company to turn this technology toward a homegrown problem: mine effluent polluting the area's groundwater. He formed INNOH2O, which manufactures water treatment equipment for the northern Appalachian coal region.

Staying In

Murtha's empire has contracted but not imploded.

Heading the list of its primes are Lockheed Martin Aeroparts and Martin Baker, both companies firmly planted in the F-35. Each has both profited from, and been bedeviled by, this connection.

One of the enduring features of defense contracting, and a source of many of its bugs, is its practice of concurrency. Columbia University industrial engineering professor Seymour Melman began raising the alarm about this contracting procedure during the 1970s and 1980s. Standard practice in industrial design, he pointed out, begins with a research and development phase, followed by the preparation and testing of a prototype, followed by improvements to the design, followed by more testing. "This process repeats until a prototype has withstood operational tests that satisfy the management…. Not until then does the new model go into production."

According to the Pentagon's tradition of concurrency, he wrote, these steps are performed simultaneously, with defects discovered either in the factory or in the field, and corrected on already-produced and delivered equipment. He identified concurrency as one of the Pentagon's "cost maximizing" practices. It is "the most expensive way known to carry out revisions in industrial design."[50]

Pentagon whistleblower Ernest Fitzgerald, a friend of Melman's, succinctly captured why the Military Industrial Complex is so devoted to this practice. "There are only two phases of a [weapons] program," he said, with tongue only partially in cheek. "The first is, 'It's too early to tell.' The second is, 'It's too late to stop.'"[51] In other words, multi-billion-dollar weapons systems are rushed into production before we know whether they will work, and then the sunk costs are so great that, the argument becomes, they are too big to fail. It's a principle that proponents of the F-35 are living by.

In 2018, following a series of reports critical of the F-35, the Government Accountability Office (GAO), the federal government's principal watchdog agency, recommended that Congress consider withholding development funding for the program until a long list of defects have been fixed. The report pointed out that Lockheed began producing the planes with less than 1 percent of testing complete. It also noted that in 2008 the company took money from testing and put it into manufacturing, over GAO's objections.

Congress ignored this advice, and accelerated production. It is poised to do so once again.

The United States has required a "stealth" skin for only a few of its planes, in part because the process is so hard to pull off. The B-2 bomber became notorious in the late 1990s as the $2 billion plane "that couldn't go out in the rain": its outer coating was prone to deteriorate in conditions like rain and humidity.[52] The process has been improved, Lockheed assures us, with robots applying the coatings to the "extremely precise thickness tolerances" required.[53]

This is one of the assigned tasks of Lockheed Aeroparts' facility in Johnstown. According to the GAO, though, the stealth features are responsible for about half of the litany of defects that have dogged the program all the way along. And concurrency is the main culprit: As Lockheed acknowledged, "[T]he rework done to bring the plane up to requirements is driving up the amount of money and time spent producing an airplane."[54]

Nor has Martin Baker's work making F-35 ejection seats been a smooth ride. In 2011 the Pentagon's director of Operational Test and Evaluation recommended delaying the plane because its ejection seats had not been tested. Since the plane was already about five years behind schedule, his recommendation was rejected.[55] Then in 2016 the Air Force considered replacing Martin-Baker's seats out of concern that lighter pilots faced potentially fatal neck injuries from the current design. Before merging with Raytheon, United Technologies began working on an alternative. But Martin Baker's efforts to correct the defects were "too late to stop": Lockheed Martin's general manager of the F-35 program said "The details of the kind of testing, cost and schedule of integrating another seat would really be out of scope right now." So, Martin Baker got to keep its most important contract.[56]

Other defects in the program have proliferated since then, though, so the Johnstown F-35 production lines are in danger of slowing down.

Then there is Johnstown defense contracting's largest employer, Concurrent Technologies. CTC remains mainly in the defense market, active in software engineering for the U.S. Army Space and Missile Defense Command.[57] CTC had to begin laying off staff in 2016 after losing a contract in metalworking services for the Navy, which it had held for nearly three decades.[58] But CEO Ed Sheehan worked to ride the Trump administration's Pentagon spending increases toward new defense market growth.[59]

Some of CTC's defense work has civilian potential. The military is still the largest source of R&D funds for green technology. For example, CTC has developed a working prototype of a hydrogen fuel cell power unit for the Air Force, as well as a Wastewater Reuse System that, as noted, is being commercialized.

But CTC has also pursued a *different* kind of diversification strategy. Building on its origins as a creature of John Murtha's art of the deal, it began to diversify its stable of congressional champions. In 2007 Murtha was joined by four other congressmembers, two Republicans and two Democrats, in proposing $18 million more in earmarks for Concurrent (for a total of $226 million over four years). One of these congressmembers took over as chair of the defense appropriations subcommittee when Murtha died. Concurrent had already opened up branch offices, making campaign contributions, in each of their districts.[60]

Straddling: Johnstown Welding and Fabrication (JWF)

Bill Polacek's father John couldn't make his job at Bethlehem Steel support his nine children, so he put a welding machine on the back of his pickup and started Johnny's Welding. Bill was his only employee. After the company closed up shop in 1992, Bill eventually cobbled together the money to buy its 500,000 square foot Lower Works plant, then a graveyard of adjoining gray hulks sitting in town by the river. He grew a business there doing an assortment of commercial metal-bending work.

Then he followed Johnstown's move from steel to the defense market, as his friendship with Murtha turned into lucrative Pentagon contracting. In 2007 JWF Defense Systems was born. Its first contracts, applying extra armor to the Humvees bound for Iraq, turned into work fashioning armor for a wider variety of military vehicles. Its customers have included Lockheed, General Dynamics, and BAE Systems.

The modest defense downturn in 2011 contracted the workforce and led Polacek to look for new civilian markets. He's found them in a variety of metal work, such as a contract to make stairwell flex-gates for flood protection in the New York City subway.[61] And outside his main building are stacked the metal equivalent of jersey walls, which some engineers argue are the preferred—lighter and more flexible—alternative to the concrete kind.

Polachek's biggest move out of the defense market has been a return to Johnstown's roots in subterranean extraction, but with a new twist. Appalachia's recovery strategy from the implosion of coal mining has turned to hydraulic fracturing, or fracking, the technique of getting to natural gas reserves by pumping huge amounts of water underground to release the reserves. The Cambria County Defense Transition plan cites Johnstown's water resources as a competitive advantage in adding value to these massive projects. But using these resources for extraction has created a legacy of pollution that Johnstown is still struggling to remove. And fracking loads the water up with heavy metals and even radioactivity, which can contaminate the groundwater. So Polachek has turned his company's metal-bending capabilities to building storage containers—"frack tanks"—for waste water. There the water can be diluted for reuse, he claims, or treated.

In 2019, Polacek characterized his business as a well-diversified 50-50 mix of military and non-military work.[62] A year later, the story had changed. New military contracts fueled by Trump budgets had jacked JWF's defense dependency to 70 percent. And Polacek looked at the forecast for economic effects of Covid-19 and decided that defense was going to be "a good place to be."[63] At least temporarily, his reading of the tea leaves was correct: The defense industry prospered during the epidemic, while commercial industry did not. "Financially, it's great," one defense-industry analyst said. The major contractors are "swimming in excess cash." Federal aid pumped nearly $5 billion into the industry, mostly to increase progress payments, that is, to give them more money up front—a Pentagon-designed assist that commercial companies didn't have.[64]

Capitalizing on Change

Johnstown is doing its best to pull itself up. But here's the big picture: real diversification, in Johnstown and across the country, can't happen unless alternative public investment creates new economic engines to rival military spending. In a rebuttal to a *Politico* article denigrating Johnstown, Wrabley and the president of his university, Jem Spectar, argue for big "transformational infrastructure investments with special emphasis on communities like Johnstown, to create more well-paying jobs for our people, stimulate economic growth and create a more hopeful longer-term economic trajectory."[65]

Enter the Biden administration's framework for infrastructure spending. In addition to funding the kinds of jobs Johnstown's workforce needs, it could help connect the town to the prosperity beyond its ridges in places like Pittsburgh. The bill's provisions targeting help to rural America is especially timely to Johnstown, whose declining population threatens its federal funding as a Metropolitan Statistical Area by reclassifying it as rural.[66] And its climate-change provisions could open up the chance for Johnstown's manufacturers to join the great project of helping the country convert to run on clean energy and transportation.

While a few have dabbled around the edges of the green economy, as for example Concurrent's fuel cell project for the Navy, this is for most of them an opportunity waiting to be seized.

The town lost its biggest chance to date to move beyond fossil fuels when Gamesa moved away in 2014. The Spanish-based company is a world leader in wind power, with systems in 90 countries.[67] In 2005 it built a $25 million facility outside of Johnstown, with the help of $2 million in state grants, and began employing 250 people; 150-ft. wind-turbine blades began rolling out of

Cambria County, and large wind farms began sprouting on the ridges outside of town.[68] A year later, the company jettisoned its aerospace business to focus solely on renewable energy. But eight years later, it was gone.

Why? Professor Ray Wrabley points a finger at opposition to the plant from some environmentalists, whose concerns about such issues as interrupted bird flight paths blinded them to the benefits of good local manufacturing jobs tackling the climate crisis. The company cites another reason. In December of 2013 Congress allowed a Production Tax Credit for windpower to expire. Again. A few weeks after the credit vanished, Gamesa, staring at the absence of more stable supports such as a national renewable energy mandate or carbon pricing, announced it was closing its local plant. Sixty-year-old Joe Kline was one of the layoffs. In his previous job, he mined coal.[69]

The Biden administration's infrastructure plan is all about using fiscal and regulatory tools to give the Gamesas of the world (and their homegrown American competitors) a place to stand.

In September of 2021, Johnstown got an all-too-familiar reminder of their local stake in a zero-emissions economy. The rains that flooded Louisiana and New York brought the water levels at the former South Fork Hunting and Fishing Club, where the Great Flood of 1889 began, higher than one local geology professor said he'd ever seen them.[70] While the levees held, two thousand people were evacuated as a precaution. With Johnstown's geography and history, such events loom large over the town's psyche and make the climate-change-driven increases in flooding a future they must try to avoid.

That same month came another plot twist: the news that Johnstown's local leaders, including Mayor Jankovic, were reviving ideas of coming full circle—back to steel-making. Declaring that "climate change is the challenge of this generation," U.S. Steel has pledged allegiance to a net-zero GHG emissions goal by 2050. To get there it has acquired the first LEED certified steel mill in the United States and is building electric arc furnaces to run on renewable energy sources. Cities across the country are said to be competing to site the company's $3 billion project to put two of these furnaces within a "mini-mill." If Johnstown got the project, it could create 300 jobs in town—far from the thousands of Johnstown's steelmaking past, but also from its past of choking air and orange water.

The idea of steel mills coming back to Johnstown seems more nostalgic than realistic, though. Meeting with a company representative, one local legislator reported that "He didn't say no … but he didn't want to give us any false hope, either."[71] Non-union Arkansas and Alabama are the more likely destinations.[72]

Conclusion

Over the better part of two centuries, Johnstown has had an education in the perils of putting all your eggs into one economic basket: from coal, to steel, and now military contracting.

The earmarks plot also thickened in 2021, when the narrowly Democratic congressional leadership brought them back, sanitized as "Community-Focused Grants." The idea was, again, that a few deal-sweeteners targeted to key Republican districts might induce a little more "bipartisan" support for key legislation. (Some Republican beneficiaries, though, seemed fine with taking the earmark and voting against the legislation).

The leadership set some stipulations on the practice, to tamp down the worst of its abuses. Murtha's modus operandi would have passed muster with some of them: Members have to declare they have no personal financial interest in their earmark, and that local officials support the project. Murtha would have passed. But earmarks for private for-profit companies are disallowed: This one Murtha would have failed.[73] And as earmarks come and go, and are hidden and embraced, one constant is that they are supposed to be small, individual side deals at the periphery of the budget. The Murtha Method, of using his power to redirect his district's economy with legendary quantities of earmarks, would have failed that test, too.

But though Murtha opened doors for him in the defense business, local contractor Bill Polacek also reports getting two pieces of advice not quite in keeping with the image of the "King of Pork." First, Murtha said, "I don't want you to rely on earmarks too much. I'll help you get your foot in the door, but then I want you to earn the business. After I'm long gone, I don't want this town to evaporate."

And, perhaps most surprising of all, Polacek quotes Murtha, the mastermind of Johnstown's military economy, as follows: "Be careful how much defense you take on, because the country can't afford this budget."[74]

Notes

1 Ann Markusen, Peter Hall, Scott Campbell and Sabina Deitrick, *The Rise of the Gunbelt: The Military Remapping of Industrial America* (Oxford: Oxford University Press, 1991) p. 18.
2 David McCullough, *The Johnstown Flood* (New York: Simon and Schuster, 1968) p. 23.
3 Personal interview with David Sutor, March 5, 2019.
4 McCullough, p. 274.
5 "Murtha: Military Supports Call for Iraq Withdrawal," All Things Considered, NPR, Dec. 1, 2005. www.npr.org/templates/story/story.php?storyId=5035043.
6 Tim Ryan, "Harry Reid says Congress used earmarks for 200 years." *Politifact*, May 13, 2014, www.politifact.com/factchecks/2014/may/13/harry-reid-says-congress-used-earmarks-200-years/.
7 Steve Ellis, "Earmarks Don't Work," Taxpayers for Common Sense, Jan. 18, 2018.
8 "Meet Congress' 'King of Pork,'" CBSNews.com, April 4, 2008, www.cbsnews.com/news/meet-congress-king-of-pork/.
9 Taxpayers for Common Sense, "President Signs Earmark-Laden Spending Bill," www.taxpayer.net/budget-appropriations-tax/president-signs-earmark-laden-spending-bill/.

10 Personal interview, Ray Wrabley, (U-JT) March 7, 2019.
11 Mike Hruska, phone interview. April 1, 2019.
12 Jason Zengerle, "Murthaville: The city that pork built." *Real Clear Politics*, September 1, 2009, www.realclearpolitics.com/2009/09/01/murthaville_the_city_that_pork_built_220492.html.
13 Zengerle.
14 Martin-Baker, "About," http://martin-baker.com/about/.
15 Dennis B. Roddy, "Obituary: John P. Murtha/ Powerful Johnstown congressman," *Pittsburgh Post-Gazette*, February 9, 2010, www.post-gazette.com/news/nation/2010/02/09/Obituary-John-P-Murtha-Powerful-Johnstown-congressman/stories/201002090275.
16 CBSNews, "Meet Congress' 'King of Pork.'"
17 Carol Leonnig, "Justice Department Probes Pa. firm tied to Murtha," Inquirer.com, May 25, 2009, www.inquirer.com/philly/news/nation_world/20090526_Justice_Dept__probes_Pa__firm_tied_to_Murtha.html.
18 Open Secrets, "Lockheed Martin File: Recipients," opensecrets.org, www.opensecrets.org/orgs/recips.php?id=D000000104&chamber=&party=&cycle=2008&state=&sort=A.
19 www.esquire.com/news-politics/a5152/new-jersey-1108/.
20 James McCartney with Molly Sinclair McCartney, *America's War Machine* (New York: St. Martin's Press, 2015) p. 44.
21 Brian Ross, "From Cash to Yachts: A Congressman's Bribe Menu," abcnews.go.com, March 2, 2006, https://abcnews.go.com/Politics/story?id=1667009&page=1.
22 "The Murtha Method," The Center for Public Integrity, September 9, 2009, https://publicintegrity.org/politics/the-murtha-method/.
23 "Murtha Method."
24 CBSNews.com, April 4, 2008.
25 Zengerle, "Murthaville."
26 Zengerle, "Murthaville."
27 Paul Singer, "FBI Saw Dark Side of Rep. John Murtha," *Roll Call*, October 24, 2011, www.rollcall.com/2011/10/24/fbi-saw-dark-side-of-rep-john-murtha/.
28 Roddy, *Pittsburgh Post-Gazette*.
29 Singer, "FBI Saw Dark Side."
30 Tim Ryan, "Harry Reid says Congress used earmarks for 200 years," *Politifact*, May 13, 2014, www.politifact.com/factchecks/2014/may/13/harry-reid/harry-reid-says-congress-used-earmarks-200-years/.
31 Winslow T. Wheeler, "Those Porky Pentagon Earmarks Never Really Went Away," *American Conservative*, January 11, 2019, www.theamericanconservative.com/articles/those-porky-pentagon-earmarks-never-really-went-away/.
32 Phone interview, Mike Hruska, April 1, 2019.
33 "Final Report: Cambria County Defense Transition Study," November 17, 2015, https://bloximages.chicago2.vip.townnews.com/tribdem.com/content/tncms/assets/v3/editorial/6/e1/6e19fa98-f3c2-11e6-ae10-8ba92e3150bc/58a4c2df2e388.pdf.pdf.
34 "Cambria County Defense Transition Study, p. 6.
35 Hruska.
36 Frances Fitzgerald, *Way Out There in the Blue* (New York: Simon and Shuster, 2000).
37 Randy Griffith, "Weapons contract halted: Northrop Grumman dealt setback," *The Tribune-Democrat*, June 3, 2009.

38 Mike Faher, "MountainTop Technologies furloughs another 11 workers," *The Tribune-Democrat*, September 30, 2010, www.tribdem.com/news/local_news/mountaintop-technologies-furloughs-11-more-workers/article_05eceee2-1c41-5c70-a84a-e4819bdca80e.html.

39 Personal interview with Ray Wrabley, March 7, 2019.

40 Dave Sutor, "DoD's Hicks tells Showcase audience: Small businesses key to military innovation," *Tribune-Democrat*, September 2, 2021, www.tribdem.com/news/dods-hicks-tells-showcase-audience-small-businesses-key-to-military-innovation/article.

41 Phone interview with Mike Hruska, February 23, 2021.

42 United States Census Bureau, "QuickFacts: Johnstown City, Pennsylvania," July 1, 2019, www.census.gov/quickfacts/fact/table/johnstowncitypennsylvania/PST045219.

43 Personal interview with Frank Janakovic, March 7, 2019.

44 David Hurst, "Data: Region's population continues to shrink," *Tribune-Democrat*, April 29, 2019, www.tribdem.com/news/familiar-trend-data-show-region-s-population-continues-to-shrink-ahead-of-2020-census/article_207d4140-695f-11e9-aeef-f34cae7e0fbb.html.

45 Dave Sutor, "Census shows high population decline in Cambria," *Tribune-Democrat*, August 13, 2021, www.tribdem.com/news/cambria-county-loses-population-again-new-census-data-show/article_9d99204a-fbca-11eb-8be7-174ab94a328a.html.

46 Personal interview with Amy Bradley and Bill Polachek, March 5, 2019.

47 "Cambria County Defense Transition Study."

48 Personal interview with John Dubnansky, March 5, 2019.

49 For example, www.youtube.com/watch?v=JIT4kQcIDGM.

50 Seymour Melman, *Profits Without Production*, (Philadelphia: University of Pennsylvania Press, 1983) pp. 212–213.

51 Mark Thompson, "A Tribute to Pentagon Whistleblower Ernest Fitzgerald," Project on Government Oversight, February 5, 2019. www.pogo.org/analysis/2019/02/remembering-ernie-fitzgerald/.

52 Tim Weiner, "The $2 Billion Stealth Bomber Can't Go Out in the Rain," *New York Times*, August 23, 1997, www.nytimes.com/1997/08/23/world/the-2-billion-stealth-bomber-can-t-go-out-in-the-rain.html.

53 Neal Seegmiller, Jonathan Bailiff, and Ron Franks, "Precision Robotic Coating Application and Thickness Control Optimization for F-35 Final Finishes," *SAE International Journal of Aerospace*, Vol. 2, No. 1, March 2010, pp. 284–290, www.ri.cmu.edu/publications/precision-robotic-coating-application-and-thickness-control-optimization-for-f-35-final-finishes/.

54 Valerie Insinna, "Stealth features responsible for half of F-35 defects, Lockheed program head states," *Defense News*, March 5, 2018, www.defensenews.com/air/2018/03/06/stealth-features-responsible-for-half-of-f-35-defects-lockheed-program-head-states/.

55 David Axe, "Stealth Jet Could be Unsafe for Flight Training," *Wired Magazine*, November 1, 2011, www.wired.com/2011/11/joint-strike-fighter-unsafe/.

56 Valerie Insinna, "F-35 Ejection Seat Concerns Have Not Reached Lockheed Martin," *Defense News*, July 7, 2016, www.defensenews.com/digital-show-dailies/farnborough/2016/07/07/f-35-ejection-seat-concerns-have-not-reached-lockheed-martin/

57 Dave Sutor, "Showcase contracts mean hundreds of millions for local companies," *Tribune-Democrat*, May 30, 2014, www.tribdem.com/news/local_news/showcase-contracts-mean-hundreds-of-millions-for-local-companies/article_3a5fab89-faba-53ad-922e-19eff9dcc8f3.html.

58 Personal interview with Ray Wrabley, March 7, 2019.
59 Jocelyn Brumbaugh, "Defense companies taking slow, steady approach," *Tribune-Democrat*, February 26, 2017, www.tribdem.com/news/vision-2017-defense-companies-taking-slow-steady-approach/article_9919cafa-f9fa-11e6-875a-abbd531e0220.html.
60 Robert O'Harrow, "A Contractor, Charity and Magnet for Federal Earmarks," *Washington Post*, November 2, 2007, www.washingtonpost.com/wp-dyn/content/article/2007/11/01/AR2007110102691.html.
61 Dave Sutor, "Contracts awarded at Showcase bring millions to local companies," *Tribune-Democrat*, June 2, 2018.
62 Personal interview, March 5, 2019.
63 Russ O'Reilly, "Area manufacturers remain on job but watching supply chain changes," *Tribune-Democrat*, March 18, 2020, www.tribdem.com/corona_virus/area-manufacturers-producing-delivering-shipping-but-watching-supply-chain/article_19b350bc-68a4-11ea-81ac-4b00cfa8547c.html.
64 Aaron Mehta and Valerie Insinna, "Chaos, cash, and COVID-19: How the defense industry survived—and thrived—during the pandemic," *Defense News*, March 15, 2021, www.defensenews.com/industry/2021/03/15/chaos-cash-and-covid-19-how-the-defense-industry-survived-and-thrived-during-the-pandemic/.
65 "In Defense of Johnstown and a rebuttal of the Politico article," *Tribune-Democrat*, November 13, 2017, www.tribdem.com/news/jem-spectar-and-ray-wrabley-in-defense-of-johnstown-and-a-rebuttal-of-the-politico/article_8edd0102-c82a-11e7-93d0-13595b871b3e.html.
66 Russ O'Reilly, "Johnstown could lose metro status," *Tribune-Democrat*, March 24, 2021, www.tribdem.com/news/johnstown-could-lose-metropolitan-label-reclassification-would-deal-a-blow-to-funding-for-local-programs/article_3fb8413a-8c04-11eb-ad19-0f509e8c2e31.html.
67 Siemens Gamesa, "About Us," www.siemensgamesa.com/en-int/about-us.
68 Kathy Mellott, "Gamesa closing Cambria plant," *Tribune-Democrat*, January 28, 2014, www.tribdem.com/news/local_news/gamesa-closing-cambria-plant/article_9e2ca3fc-0880-5f20-af81-8194f45e7274.html.
69 Mellott, "Gamesa closing."
70 Joshua Byers, "'77 flood survivors: Day 'brings back memories,'" *Tribune-Democrat*, September 2, 2021, https://tribune-democrat-cnhi.newsmemory.com/.
71 Russ O'Reilly, "Johnstown leaders make plans to court U.S. Steel," *Tribune-Democrat*, September 26, 2021, https://tribune-democrat-cnhi.newsmemory.com/.
72 Patricia Sabatini, "U.S. Steel announces plans to build a mini-mill," Pittsburgh Post-Gazette, September 16, 2021, www.post-gazette.com/business/pittsburgh-company-news/2021/09/16/U-S-Steel-3-billion-mini-mill-Big-River-Steel-electric-arc-furnaces-carbon-neutral/stories.
73 Paul Kane, Marianna Sotomayor and Tony Romm, "Earmarks are back as lawmakers seek deals," *Washington Post*, March 22, 2021, www.washingtonpost.com/powerpost/earmarks-biden-infrastructure/2021/03/21/5a9d15ca-88c6-11eb-bfdf-4d36dab83a6d_story.html.
74 Personal interview, Bill Polacek, March 5, 2019.

4

SOUTHERN CALIFORNIA

Green Capital of the World or Aerospace Central?

In Connecticut we found a military contracting Mecca dominated by the top three primes—Lockheed, Raytheon, and General Dynamics. Southern California beats that, adding major Boeing and Northrop installations into the mix with Lockheed, plus General Dynamics-spinoff General Atomics, and a Raytheon foothold south of San Diego. For 70 years, California received more money from the Pentagon than any other state. While slipping behind Texas and Virginia in 2020, its haul for both private contracts and military personnel totals more than $60 billion per year, or one-twelfth of the U.S. total. But California's overall economy is huge—it's usually described as the world's fifth largest—and is far more diversified than, say, Connecticut's. So, the percentage of its GDP tied to its military economy ranks the state way down at 28th.[1] Nevertheless, during the Cold War, California claimed the title of "Aerospace Capital of the World."

The roots of this title reach back to American aviation's pioneering early days. During the 1920s the Lougheed brothers (as they then spelled it) set up shop in Burbank, while their collaborator/competitor Donald Douglas was getting started in Santa Monica and El Segundo. As their companies evolved, the competition eventually came to be between Lockheed Martin and Boeing. Another flying enthusiast, John Northrop, worked for both Donald Douglas and the Lougheed brothers before striking out on his own with the enterprise that grew into Northrop Grumman. Other aircraft startups moved in, including General Dynamics, down in San Diego, as did clusters of small machine shops and parts suppliers to service them. Located on what were then the fringes of Greater Los Angeles, they built mostly airframes for the civilian aviation market. The engines came from Connecticut's well-established engine manufacturing base.

Southern California's warm cloudless skies, permitting year-round outdoor construction and open spaces for testing, offered this industry's perfect conditions.

DOI: 10.4324/9781003293705-5

By 1937 California had accumulated a quarter of U.S. aircraft manufacturing, and nearly half of its workforce.

World War II quickly turned these aircraft builders into military contractors. Since most of them were already clustered in Southern California, the military consolidated most warplane contracts there. Also important was the War Department's desire to decentralize production away from the East Coast, and to position aircraft for the Pacific Fleet.

War mobilization transformed a cottage industry with the techniques of mass production. In 1940, North American Aviation (which later became North American Rockwell and is now a part of Boeing) operated one plant with 6,000 employees. By 1943 it had five plants with 92,000 employees, producing 42,000 planes in total for the war effort. Between 1939 and 1945 Lockheed grew from 2,500 workers to 60,000, building 19,000 planes. In 1943 40 percent of the Los Angeles workforce was building a total of 190,700 planes. Adding women to the workforce made this precipitous expansion possible, as did government subsidies covering the relocation expenses of workers from all over the country.[2]

Following the war, aircraft employment in Los Angeles dropped to 44,600—still three times its prewar levels—and then began to rise again with the temperature of Cold War tensions. And making warplanes became subsumed in a newly defined enterprise called "aerospace."

Lockheed began its transition to aerospace in 1943, with an Army contract to design and build a jet fighter. By 1945 Boeing-precursor Douglas was at work on surface-to-air missiles, and Hughes, precursor to Raytheon, on the air-to-air version.[3] In addition to trying (and failing) in this market, Northrop focused on developing bombers capable of carrying the entirely new megaton payloads. Hughes took the lead in developing the advanced electronics that began to account for a larger and larger share of the costs of military aircraft.

By 1953 California had surged ahead of New York and Michigan to become number one in total Pentagon contract awards, where it remained until fiscal year 2020, when as noted it fell to number three, behind Texas and Virginia. In 1990, Los Angeles County was getting twice as much from the Pentagon as any other county in America.

The Military Economy Crashes

But when the Cold War ended in the early 1990s, the rationale for ratcheting Pentagon spending to fund a perpetual arms race collapsed with it. Military budget cuts followed, engineered by one Dick Cheney, defense secretary for President George H. W. Bush. And Los Angeles watched its aerospace-heavy economy go south—further south than at any time since the Great Depression.

The defense industry is notorious for its boom-and-bust cycles. Military economies across the country generally understand the bargain they make: In exchange for high-paying Pentagon-funded jobs, they are susceptible to the cycles in which these jobs come and go, as the answer to the military budget question, "How much is enough?" varies according to foreign policy and economic politics. The boom times of the Reagan buildup had boosted national military spending by 60 percent. Now, as noted, the bust was cutting that spending by a third, and the procurement budget—the main event funding private contractors—by two-thirds.

This bust cycle slammed Los Angeles's aerospace Mecca harder than almost anywhere else. The 13 different military planes built there during the 1980s dwindled to two: the B-2 bomber and the C-17 transport. Between 1988 and 1994 the number of defense contracts awarded to Los Angeles County fell by nearly 40 percent. And the membership of the unions representing most LA defense workers— the United Auto Workers (UAW), International Association of Machinists (IAM), and the International Brotherhood of Electrical Workers (IBEW)—declined from 62,000 in the late 1980s to 18,300 in 1994.[4]

Because Los Angeles hosted a wide assortment of contractors—unlike one-company defense towns such as Seattle (Boeing) and St. Louis (McDonnell Douglas, now Boeing)—LA's defense workers were used to "job hopping" from one contractor to another as necessary. When Northrop began laying off workers, for example, Lockheed could pick them up, and vice versa. This system worked well to smooth out the disruptions caused by individual contract losses. Until it didn't. In the post–Cold War crash, the layoffs were happening city-wide. There was nowhere in the area for the workers to go.

Nakamoto

During this time, Don Nakamoto was waist-deep in the cascade of layoffs, trying to hold back the flood. He represented the LA branch of John Harrity's union, the International Association of Machinists and Aerospace Workers (IAMAW). Nakamoto's local was 90 percent defense-dependent, representing the workers from Lockheed, McDonnell Douglas, United Technologies, Hughes, and General Dynamics, in locations spread all over LA County.[5]

When Nakamoto first started with the union in 1987, there were between eight and nine thousand members at Lockheed alone. By the time he left eight years later, there were between 2000 and 2500. And he was up against the same long-term forces faced by the workers at Pratt & Whitney: Lockheed had begun began moving production jobs from LA to Marietta, Georgia, where they could cut costs in non-union facilities.[6]

Then, on May 8, 1990, "My boss [at the union] was driving into work," Nakamoto says, "when he heard on the radio that Lockheed was shutting down the entire operation based in Burbank, including the corporate headquarters." As many as 4,500 jobs were going away. It was, the company said, part of a complex effort to respond to the Pentagon budget cuts. Another IAM member, Frank Williams, said, "They didn't even have the courage to tell us that they were going to pull out." Nakamoto adds that,

FIGURE 4.1 Don Nakamoto

Source: Photo courtesy of the author, used with permission.

> [l]ess than six months before, we had met with top Lockheed management and they assured us that there was no plan to move any projects or people or conduct any more layoffs. We talked to them a month before [the shutdown notice]. And there was no mention of it. They totally deceived us.

Ken Varney had 20 years at Lockheed under his belt at that point. That day he envisioned his future: "After I've exhausted my job fairs and applications in other aircraft industry (companies), then I['ll] have to take a seventy percent cut in my wages to survive, probably flipping hamburgers." For much of his union's workforce, Nakamoto says, those grim predictions were accurate. "[These workers] had a skill set that was in high demand, and then all of a sudden there was absolutely no need for it anymore."[7] While they could sign up for brief outplacement services, only 1 or 2 percent were getting substantial retraining.[8] By 1995, the ranks of Southern California's laid-off aerospace workers had swelled to 210,000.[9]

At the Federal Level

The Clinton administration adopted two main strategies to deal with the contraction of the defense industry. First were the programs to help companies, workers, and communities adapt to new markets. In addition to those programs outlined in Chapter 2, the administration's flagship was the Technology Reinvestment Project (TRP). It funded teams of defense and commercial companies plus other partners such as academic and economic development institutions, labor unions and nonprofits, to commercialize defense technologies. We'll look at one notable TRP success in Chapter 8 and, in the present chapter, one failure of follow-through.

In keeping with President Clinton's characteristic have-your-cake-and-eat-it-too style, his conversion program also hedged its bets. The program's technology policy and incentives privileged "dual-use technology," that is, technology with both military and civilian applications, which steered contractors away from more decisive moves toward civilian markets.[10]

At a dinner in 1993, now dubbed "The Last Supper," new Deputy Defense Secretary William Perry told the major defense contractors that they needed to scale back their massive excess capacity to produce military hardware the country would no longer need. The administration would provide financial help for them to merge with each other.

At a rapid clip, they did. In 1994, Lockheed merged with Martin Marietta to create what remains today the largest military contractor in the world. It immediately set in motion plans to acquire General Dynamics's rocket division, followed by Rockwell defense and space operations. Also in 1994, Northrop acquired Grumman Aerospace Corporation based on Long Island, New York; Northrop Grumman then proceeded to absorb Westinghouse's defense unit. And so on. In 1997 the last of the major post–Cold War mergers fell into place when Boeing acquired McDonnell Douglas, and a month later the defense sector of Hughes Electronics Corporation, which the *Los Angeles Times* called "long a symbol of Southern California's dominance of the U.S. aerospace industry," was swallowed up by Raytheon.[11] That same year Lockheed Martin even made a bid to acquire Northrop Grumman. That fell through. But five years after "The Last Supper," an industry formerly of 12 major military aircraft manufacturers had shrunk to four.[12] Wall Street encouraged this predatory strategy—labeled "pure play" within the closed circle of military production.[13]

The Clinton administration's policy to encourage mergers among its faltering defense contractors made a certain kind of sense: there was not enough work to sustain all of them. But there were two unintended results. Classic monopsony theory would predict the first: As these companies devoured each other, the clout of the remaining behemoths grew. One *Washington Post* writer predicted that "President Clinton's most enduring legacy in national security will be his role in creating a handful of extraordinarily powerful defense contractors."[14] And with only one or two contractors left to compete for each major aerospace contract, they became too big to fail, and could use this new leverage to push prices, and profits, higher.

And, second, the scramble to acquire or be acquired and to manage the radical requirements of staying in business on fewer contracts, preoccupied the majority of the contractors. It diverted the energies and attention that might have been applied to the alternative: keeping their employees busy by working seriously on adapting their assets to civilian markets.[15]

Industrial Policy: Is there Only One?

For 40-plus years the United States had concentrated its talents and treasure around the mission of winning the Cold War. It organized the lion's share of the federal government's resources around this goal which, in turn, centered the country's industrial capacity on military production. This was our de facto industrial policy. The term itself was mostly taboo, equated with un-American Soviet-style five-year plans and with impeding the free market by giving government the license to "pick winners and losers." Only the Pentagon was allowed to do that.

The abrupt end of the Cold War mission allowed the country to pick up its head and contemplate a new one. The suitable replacement needed to be large, complex, and critical to the country's security and welfare. The accumulating evidence pointed in one direction. The U.S. environmental movement that had been gaining strength over 20 years now had a new focal point: curbing greenhouse gas emissions. Saving the planet was no longer a matter of projects like cleaning up polluted streams. It required revamping the energy and transportation infrastructure of the nation, its building materials, and its agricultural systems.

In its policymaking for the post–Cold War period, the Clinton administration took some modest steps in this direction. Its Technology Reinvestment Project identified five key priorities, one of which was: Redirecting the fruits of our 40-year investment in military supremacy to the challenge of climate change. In 1994 the nonprofit called the National Commission for Economic Conversion and Disarmament organized a Technology Conversion Conference in Washington, DC, which brought together government and labor officials—with experts in such fields as fuel cells, mass transit, and solar energy—to look at what role military manufacturers might be able to play in moving them forward.[16]

California in the Vanguard

But it was California, specifically its southern metropolis, that came closest to building a comprehensive industrial policy around that goal. Among the reasons was Los Angeles's "City of Dreams" spirit of technological innovation, reaching back to early aviation pioneers like Lougheed and Northrop, and accelerated by the Cold War arms race.

But the critical catalyst came from the state's ambient crisis conditions. Back in the summer of 1943, the Los Angeles climate collided with its teeming freeways to produce a smog attack that shrank visibility to three blocks and visited the people in its path with burning lungs and nausea. Two decades later the state established the first tailpipe emissions standards in the nation. In 1963 the federal Clean Air Act authorized California to set stricter standards than the nation as a whole, or any other state. Governor Ronald Reagan signed the law creating the California Air Resources Board and giving it the power to enforce these standards in the state. Then in 1990 the state legislature took the additional step of requiring manufacturers to produce an increasing number of zero-emission vehicles.

The California Air Resources Board became a pillar of a green industrial policy because it conceived its role not only as a regulator but as a collaborator with the public, the business sector, and local governments to solve the state's air quality problems.[17]

A month after Don Nakamoto heard the news that Lockheed Martin was shutting down its Burbank plant, the Los Angeles County Board of Supervisors commissioned an economics research outfit called the Los Angeles Economic Roundtable to come up with a strategy to deal with the city's aerospace industry's collapse. In March of 1992, with funding from the federal Economic Development Agency, the plan arrived.

The plan proposed basing the strategy on "an integrated statement of public goals for mass transportation, environmental quality, alternative energy vehicles, and job creation for high technology workers." It proposed connecting the challenge of defense diversification to the work of a Center for Clean Energy and Power Sources, a joint effort of Cal Tech, USC, and UCLA. These universities had set up five collaborative teams working on developing the technologies of hybrid vehicles, fuel cells, alternative fuels, solar power systems, and advanced batteries, and transferring them for use by commercial manufacturers.[18]

Major industrial transitions are difficult; most start-ups fail; most manufacturers would rather keep doing what they're doing than venture into the unknown. The strategy outlined key forms of assistance to get over these humps. They included seed funding targeting products and processes already proven but needing more R&D to get to market; such technical assistance as incubators, prototype testing, securing federal and state R&D awards, management restructuring and exporting; revamping the state job training system to better serve laid-off defense workers, and to retrain them for the new work.

The plan also discussed ways of "recycling" the abandoned defense plants littering the landscape, proposing that one be used as the center for development and manufacture of a new advanced surface transportation industry in Los Angeles County. And it examined the coordination among public and private actors that would turn piecemeal efforts into a true regional industrial policy.

One of these coordinating efforts was Project California, the brainchild of the California Council on Science and Technology, funded by contributions from several public authorities, utilities, and corporations. The group identified Los Angeles's competitive advantages growing out of the aerospace industry's know-how in systems integration, remote imaging and sensing, satellite communications, and composite materials, and connected them to the most promising emerging markets, including mass-transit command and control systems, advanced telecommunications, electric vehicles, alternative fuel vehicles such as fuel cells, and high-speed rail. Like the collaborators on the Economic Roundtable strategy report, they emphasized the public benefits of this industrial transition—in reduced pollution, more efficient transportation, and cleaner energy, as well as the need for intensive regional coordination among business, labor, and government to make it happen.

For each of the industries targeted they developed a concrete action plan, involving a combination of standard setting and regulation to propel new market demand, public procurement to underwrite these emerging markets, and public R&D funds to enable new and existing companies to enter them.[19]

The initiative that checked the most of these boxes was CALSTART, launched in June of 1992. Its mission connected three big dots: the state's ground-breaking emissions standards, an aerospace industry in need of new work, and Californians' famous love affair with their cars. Building an electric car industry would satisfy all three.

Congressman Howard Berman's district included Burbank, where Lockheed had just left town. He put one staffer to work full-time figuring out how to make the vaunted "peace dividend" into a springboard for clean technology development in Southern California.

Adapting Aerospace Technology: Lon Bell

Putting out feelers for who might be working on this, the staffer came up with one Lon Bell. During the Vietnam War, Cal Tech engineering students like Bell routinely walked into lucrative jobs in the aerospace industry. He had set his sights instead on taking military technologies and finding commercial uses for them. An engineer visiting campus from the Sandia (New Mexico) National Laboratory talked about a device used in arming nuclear missiles that could serve as a crash sensor. "It seemed to be a perfect candidate," Bell thought. "It required little capitalization and fit my skill set." His first company made sensors for private aircraft that could locate downed planes.[20]

Then in the early 1970s federal safety regulation mandated the invention of the airbag. Here was a massive new market that depended on technology that would sense crashes and trigger the airbag. Bell and his Cal Tech friends had one. Eventually they sold the company "at quite a profit" to TRW Automotive, and Bell went to work managing the airbag sensor division. With a worldwide customer base in the auto industry—Toyota, Nissan, Porsche, BMW and so on—the division employed 1,600 people. "We had a global technical product," he says, "highly proprietary, derived from nuclear missile technology, with highly positive social value."

After five years, Bell was ready for a new entrepreneurial project. His son, an engineering student, got involved in a competition to solve the technological challenge of building a solar-powered car. Looking to help, Bell asked himself, "Where do people push extremes, push against the limits of the possible?" The aerospace industry, was his answer. It had developed lighter, stronger materials, solar cells that were more efficient, electronic converters that were smaller. He became a mentor to his son's project, helping them solve technical problems.

"They competed in driving a long distance over multiple days," he says. "You couldn't take parts from a conventional car and put them in—tires, sets, engines, steering wheel, brakes. All had to change."

Coming off this project, Bell looked at the layoffs cascading through the aerospace industry, and also saw the long-term need for cleaner technologies; and he had years of "direct experience with practically every automaker in the world." His idea for a new project fell into place.

Bell's technical expertise matched up with the political and strategic know-how in Congressman Berman's shop to conceive CALSTART. "Berman saw the way the union was being massacred," said Don Nakamoto, the union rep for Lockheed's laid-off machinists.

> [He] became the conceptual catalyst for a pilot project that might be replicated across Southern California and beyond. Bell was the nuts and bolts guy who could make it happen. They began figur[ing] out who would be the stakeholders in the process. … And knocking on doors.

Working with Los Angeles Mayor Tom Bradley's chief of staff, they convened players, including the major aerospace contractors and commercial manufacturers, engineering and environmental research firms, public utilities, the Air Resources Board, labor leaders, and state and local officials—to get the kind of buy-in that the Project California and Economic Roundtable blueprints had said would be needed. In 1992 CALSTART was born with 40 institutional members, a number that quickly grew to 84.

Following a stint as an environmental reporter, Bill Van Amburg, now CALSTART's executive vice president, was working at So Cal Edison, one of its members, when he was asked to emcee the organization's kickoff event.

> Wow, I thought, we have the worst air in the nation, and yet we've got highly skilled engineers and technical people [in the defense industry] working on power control, electronics … all of which will be needed in this new emerging area.… I helped them package the description of themselves, and liked it so much I ended up joining the organization.[21]

They decided to focus first on three related areas: the infrastructure for electric vehicles—that is, charging stations—building a showcase electric vehicle; and electric buses.

Congressman Berman, a labor lawyer who had represented the United Auto Workers among other unions before running for Congress, reached out to Nakamoto. Casting about for jobs for his workers that would beat burger flipping, Nakamoto was definitely interested in the project. But, in addition to what Nakamoto calls his dedication to the union, Berman was also friends with the executives of Lockheed, his district's largest employer. The company's sudden move to close the Burbank plant without mentioning it to the union had stirred up a public relations maelstrom. So, Berman negotiated a deal: CALSTART would move its advanced transportation R&D and manufacturing operations into Lockheed's shuttered Burbank facilities, at the price of $1 a year.

"I had this very long list of all the parts of a car—the steering system, suspension system, brake system, cooling, windows, frame and so on," Bell says.

> We said, who might be able to contribute technology? We went to Hughes Aircraft, which later became Delco, and they provided the motor and the controller. Kaiser Aluminum, people who made plastic panels, and solar cell companies. So, we had this fabulous building that could house multiple companies as an incubator. About twenty companies started to design and develop these technologies.

Sen. Dianne Feinstein and other politicians began coming around.

A small cadre of Don Nakamoto's laid-off machinists began assembling the prototype of an electric car with an array of new technologies—carbon parts, aluminum, and solar. Nakamoto says it was "light years ahead of what was out there." It made its debut at the Los Angeles Auto Show, and soon was chosen as the pace car in the 1992 Monaco Grand Prix.

In these early days CALSTART also paid attention to the infrastructure that would be needed to make cool electric cars into viable transportation. Van Amburg says they installed between 300 and 500 charging stations around the city.

> Some technologies were directly transferred from defense, such as an inductive paddle Hughes developed for safe underwater power transfer. [And] we showed that there's an opportunity for public-private partnership with the state's environmental and social goals matching the commercial industry's capabilities.

But this nascent electric car industry, with the potential to replace all the lost aerospace jobs, create millions more, and drastically reduce greenhouse gas emissions across the globe, needed financing to realize those outcomes by going beyond prototype into full production.

Finance: The Pentagon versus Everybody Else

When a defense contractor wins a contract to make a new weapons system, the Pentagon usually covers the research and development costs, either directly by paying for an R&D contract or indirectly as part of overhead (so-called "independent R&D"). And, of course, the Pentagon pays the manufacturing costs, and for a nice pre-negotiated profit on top.

As noted above, an even sweeter deal has been part of U.S. defense contracting since its early days—the "cost-plus" contract.[22] This arrangement creates an incentive for contractors to bid low to win the contract (subject to the government's notoriously elastic "cost realism" measures), knowing that, at the end of the process, they'll get paid the true, inflated price. This is particularly the case for massive, multi-year contracts which, at a certain point, become (it is claimed) too big to fail, that is, uncancellable.

For example, Secretary of Defense Dick Cheney tried unsuccessfully to default the contractor over the massive cost overruns of the A-12 fighter jet. Twenty years of litigation ensued.

Periodically the public and their members of Congress look at the huge waste in this system and call for reform. The Pentagon negotiates more fixed-price contracts than it used to. But the contractor lobbyists make sure that the cost-plus maneuver, and its numerous variants (cost-plus-fixed-price, cost-plus-incentive fee; cost-plus-firm-fixed-fee, and so on) still live.

In civilian manufacturing this system was nowhere to be found. CALSTART cobbled together piecemeal start-up funds from the Federal Transit Administration, the California Energy Commission and its Department of Transportation, plus private dollars from its member companies, and a modest amount of money that Congressman Berman was able to insert into federal appropriations bills. It was nothing like the comprehensive financing routinely provided for a military contract.

Nor, crucially, did they have the guaranteed market the Pentagon provides to its contractors. "So many market forces were working against us," Nakamoto says. And "light years ahead" may have been "too far ahead." California residents weren't exactly clamoring to get out of their cars into electric cars whose limited range and scarce charging locations were not enticing. Nor were the automakers eager to build them. The Big Three—General Motors, Ford, and Chrysler-- were in fact actively and vehemently opposed.[23]

California Struggles to Birth a New Industrial Policy

As for the major defense contractors, they were mostly indifferent and dismissive. They put their representatives on the CALSTART board, but Nakamoto says they were mostly communications people rather than people with decision-making power.

> I don't think they sincerely wanted to be involved; they just put their name in there to avoid public criticism. In my meetings with them behind closed doors they said it was ridiculous for them to get involved in any of this stuff.

CALSTART's groupthink approach may also have hurt the project, Nakamoto believes. Instead of focusing on creating a basic vehicle with extended range, they may have gotten a little side-tracked into exotic stuff—heated seats for example, and proto-GPS navigators. (Bell's heated and cooled car seat company, developed with technology originally used to cool the warhead on a nuclear missile, did take off, selling to car companies all over the world—just not for electric cars.)

Bell says CALSTART filled a need, not for a plentiful source of manufacturing jobs, but for a "quasi-government non-commercial enterprise to synthesize and do early planning before it's commercially attractive." Nakamoto was in it for the jobs, though, and for a long time, there weren't many.

California implemented some other pieces of its industrial policy frameworks during this period. One was the California Manufacturing Technology Center, part of a federally funded network that was trying to provide the manufacturing equivalent of the Department of Agriculture's extension centers. The Center offered technical assistance in such fields as process/product development, technology transfer, systems integration, strategic planning and marketing—all relevant to the challenges of aerospace contractors trying to move into commercial manufacturing.[24]

And some individual companies were making the move. Most were small and medium-sized enterprises like Aura Systems, which turned its experience working on missile defense toward producing fuel-efficient generators and hi-tech sound systems.[25] In a business survey by the Los Angeles County Economic Development Corporation, 60 percent of the defense suppliers and 29 percent of the subcontractors reported pursuing commercial work; only 10 percent of the prime contractors said the same.

Among this latter group, Hughes Aircraft, having been acquired by GM, showed the most enthusiasm for the challenge. Their designers in Torrance, in southwest LA between El Segundo and Long Beach, turned from building power systems for fighter-jet radar to those charging stations for electric cars, which could resupply a car's batteries in 20 minutes. Their most famous conversion project: DirecTV.[26] Northrop Grumman took $8 million from the Southern California Transit District, plus a grant from the Clinton administration's Technology Reinvestment Project, to build a lightweight all-electric bus prototype, but then showed no interest in taking it into production.[27]

How to lift Southern California out of its post–Cold War trough? Two schools of thought contended over the right strategy. The first proposed a creative, multi-pronged industrial policy to take the lead in developing new industries wedded to solving the local problem of LA's smog and the planet's problem of climate change. The second said the state needed to become more "business-friendly" by lowering its taxes and lifting its onerous regulations, including its strict emissions standards.

Most of the primes were casting their eyes toward the national policy scene, looking for reasons to avoid thinking about turning their swords into plowshares. As noted in Chapter 2, they found at least four big ones.

First was the Clinton administration's failure to reinvest the defense savings in enough civilian manufacturing opportunities to take up the slack in the economy that those savings created. Much of the "peace dividend" was instead spread out and diluted by tax cuts and deficit reduction. The demand–pull of this modest civilian reinvestment was insufficient to dissuade most of the prime contractors from their inclinations to hunker down in the remaining realm of military contracts.

Second, the prime contractors looked at the post–Cold War fiscal shift away from defense spending and figured it would shift back. In the late 1990s, it did.

Third, they joined with an array of public officials, starting at the top, who were redefining the idea of conversion to include arms exports: offloading overseas what they couldn't sell to the U.S. government (See sidebar, Chapter 2). Lockheed Martin, for example, underwrote a major conference promoting the expansion of NATO into Eastern Europe, that is, into a potentially huge new export market for Lockheed's military hardware.[28]

And, finally, the contractors refined the techniques they use to this day to skew federal spending toward the defense side of the budget: more sophisticated targeting of campaign contributions for members of Congress with the most influence over the budget, and spreading subcontracts for maximum political advantage.

This is indisputable: 30 years ago, had the blueprints for turning California's aerospace calamity into a decarbonized industrial base been allowed to succeed, and to drive a national transition, we would have a better chance of averting climate catastrophe today.

California's Military Mecca Hangs On

Southern California has never quite recovered its Cold War status as the capital of aerospace manufacturing. In addition to moving production overseas, prime contractors have moved headquarters and many major manufacturing facilities to other states: going where the money is (Washington, DC) as well as to states whose right-to-work laws, lower taxes, and fewer regulations hold the promise of fattening their profits. Still, as noted, California continues to get more Pentagon dollars than all but two other states. As high tech looms larger in the Pentagon's plans, Silicon Valley now siphons off an increasing share. But the southern part of the state still concentrates most of the money.

Time now for an abbreviated tour. It will travel from south to north, touching down in the three main hubs of Southern California's military economy.

We'll start in the spot where the Pentagon's dollars are most concentrated. That would be San Diego. It ranks third in the country in total contract dollars, following Fairfax, Virginia, where most DC-area contractors are located, and Tarrant County, Texas, where Lockheed Martin moved most of its aerospace manufacturing, and where 1,500 other Pentagon contractors have also set up shop.[29]

San Diego

In addition to its convergence of contractors, San Diego leads the nation in military personnel. More than 100,000 of them are spread among Marine Corps bases at Miramar and Camp Pendleton, and naval bases at Point Loma, Coronado, and in San Diego itself. And large numbers—currently about 240,000—wind up staying after they leave active duty, attracted by the year-round welcoming weather and the company of other vets.[30]

The city's geography—particularly its sheltered deepwater harbor—created its destiny as a site for shipbuilding, repairing, and porting. World War II put this mission on steroids. San Diego's contractors were filling Navy orders 24 hours a day, including building 467 mass-produced cargo and troop-carrying freighters called "Liberty Ships."[31] War work more than doubled San Diego's population.

In the Nuclear Age that followed, as surface shipbuilding took on a diminished role, San Diego's military economy did its best to make the transition to Cold War purposes. Launched in 1955, General Atomics focused on building the tools of Cold War surveillance: radar, satellites, and the new world of "automated airborne surveillance," that is, drones. General Atomics is now California's fifth largest defense contractor, with 15,000 employees worldwide.

Today, while Navy contractors still pull in the majority of San Diego's Pentagon contract dollars, they are no longer front and center in the Navy's warship-building mission. None of the flagship programs—building submarines, aircraft carriers, destroyers, or the troubled Littoral Combat Ship—now operate on the West Coast. San Diego's principal shipbuilder, Nassco, short for National Steel and Shipbuilding Corporation, is a subsidiary of General Dynamics, mostly building auxiliary and support ships that supply naval operations with ammunition, dry cargo, and oil.

Diversification?

San Diego's Cold War industrial base has spawned some successful crossover civilian ventures. ViaSat, for example, once primarily a defense contractor, has reduced its defense dependence by diversifying into commercial product lines such as satellite broadband.[32] Cubic Corporation supplies command and control information systems to both the military and to civilian agencies running mass transit networks, though it bills itself mostly as a military contractor.[33]

Like Johnstown, and Connecticut, San Diego did receive grants from the Pentagon's Office of Economic Adjustment (OEA) that were supposed to help the city's military economy to diversify itself beyond defense. The first grant produced a 2018 report, entitled "Mapping San Diego's Defense Ecosystem," which showed scant interest in that goal, however. Its conception of how to "enhance the resilience of local defense contractors" features that old post–Cold War favorite, "diversifying" by pushing arms sales overseas. Citing the 23 percent of San Diego firms already involved in the arms export market, the report observes that "Further promoting and supporting out-of-region sales will allow defense contractor firms to diversify beyond the local defense economy."[34]

A brief mention of free or discounted services helping "local defense contractors who are interested in pursuing new avenues for commercialization" looks like an afterthought added to fit the OEA grant's requirements.

Los Angeles

Most of Los Angeles's military contractors are clustered on the outskirts of the city.

Up the coast from Long Beach in El Segundo, the Los Angeles Air Force Base is now part of the Trump administration's Space Command. Private contracting at the base includes parts of Boeing's satellite manufacture and Raytheon's work on Tomahawk missiles. In January of 2021 the Defense Department announced its intent to "capitalize on small launch providers … to meet mission requirements for payloads greater than 400 pounds" with a nearly billion-dollar contract whose pieces would be shared by the LA suburbs of Hawthorne, Auburn, El Segundo, and Huntington Beach, along with companies in Arizona, Texas, Colorado, and Alabama.[35]

In June of 2018 Northrop Grumman won a new contract to develop a new secure system for military satellite communications over the North Polar Region.[36] The failure to arrest rapid global warming is creating a whole new arena for military dominance contention up there, and the contractors are cashing in.

Three of the Big Five Head Over the Hills

For most people, Burbank, north of Hollywood, is known as a TV and film studio hub, the home of the Warner Brothers lot, the NBC lot and Disney's animation studios. But for almost 50 years this is also where Lockheed worked on its secret military projects, until Don Nakamoto got the news that they were shutting it down. During World War II the secret extended to the existence of the plant itself. To hide it from potential Japanese attack planes, the set designers of Hollywood covered the entire plant with camouflage netting over which they constructed a bucolic scene of houses and farms, complete with fake three-dimensional trees and rubber cars.[37]

Inspired by the stench of a chemical factory next door, and a moonshine still from the era's popular cartoon Li'l Abner, the plant acquired the colorful name of Skunk Works. During the Cold War it built such aircraft as the U-2 spy plane, the F-117 stealth fighter jet, and an early drone built to surveille nuclear test facilities in China.

Building secret military planes in a metropolitan area came with challenges, though, including the compromises to secrecy when your secret had to fly out over a residential area, sometimes announcing itself with a sonic boom. So, at the same time Lockheed ran Skunk Works in Burbank, the Air Force tasked it with developing a master plan for a Government-Owned Contractor-Operated

FIGURE 4.2 The tail end of a plane on display outside Plant 42 in Palmdale

Source: Photo courtesy of the author.

(GOCO) facility on a World War II-era Air Force base over on the far north side of the San Gabriel Mountains.

The resulting complex of buildings, under the colorless name of Plant 42, sits on 5,800 acres, has 3.2 million square feet of manufacturing space, and employs about 9,000 people, most of whom live in the adjoining town of Palmdale.[38] Various contractors have cycled in and out since then. But currently the main tenants are three of the four largest U.S. military contractors: Lockheed, Boeing and Northrop Grumman. Nowhere else in the country do they share the same space.

Rockwell (since acquired by Boeing) set up shop there to build the B-1 bombers that would drop nuclear weapons on the Soviet Union if the Cold War turned hot. Then, while the workforce at Plant 42 was swelling, the B-1 program became one of the most notorious political footballs of the Cold War.

Jimmy Carter ran for president calling the new bomber "an example of a proposed system which should not be funded and would be wasteful of taxpayer dollars."[39] President Carter's thinking was also influenced by his privileged knowledge that *another* bomber was on the drawing boards, a "stealth bomber" with theoretically greater capacity to evade surface-to-air missiles trying to shoot it down. In 1977 he canceled the B-1.

And the layoffs at Plant 42 began. While Palmdale has been through many of these boom-and-bust cycles since the 1970s, the blow to its economy when the B-1 was canceled is the one its economic development officials bring up most often. They describe it as "devastating to the economy."[40]

Boom and Bust: The B-2 bomber

Carter's election opponent built his campaign around the idea that Carter was "weak on defense." Exhibit A was his decision to cancel the B-1. By 1982 the

Reagan administration had Rockwell back in business building a hundred more B-1 bombers.

This was because the new "stealth" bomber was way behind schedule. Northrop Grumman had won the contract to produce the B-2 "Spirit" at Plant 42 with a variety of characteristics to make it "invisible" from the ground, including a coating that would deflect or absorb radar signals. As noted in Chapter 3, among the plane's litany of defects, this one stood out: as the *New York Times* put it, it couldn't go out in the rain.[41] Heat, humidity and rain deteriorated the stealth coating. Expensive new climate-controlled hangars had to be built to protect it from the elements.

As the process of fixing all that was wrong wore on through the 1980s, the costs approached the realm of the absurd. GAO calculated the total program price tag, including development and testing, at $2.1 billion per plane, or three times its weight in gold.[42] The usual arguments defended these costs, including the one that usually carries the day: Our National Security required it. As Floyd Spence, then chair of the House National Security Committee, put it, "Cost? What price tag do you put on freedom?"[43]

But the B-2's third problem was that it was built to drop nuclear bombs on the Soviet Union, which by the time it was finished no longer existed. The original plan to build 132 B-2s was whittled down to 21.

To demonstrate the value of its most spectacular, and pricey, weapons systems, flyovers at football games only take you so far. The real showcase is a hot war, and during the first part of the 1990s, there weren't any to speak of. (The B-2 wasn't ready for the Gulf War.) Finally, in 1997 the shrunken fleet of B-2s did drop bombs on Kosovo, and later Afghanistan. But the rationale for sending this fragile, exorbitant plane on such conventional missions, ones that cheaper, more resilient aircraft could readily cover, never added up. Secretary of Defense William Cohen had described the search for conventional uses for the plane as akin to sending "a Rolls-Royce down into a combat zone to pick up groceries."[44]

And the workforce at Plant 42 hit another bust. The economic adjustment strategy commissioned by Los Angeles County forecast that the B-2 cut would cost Plant 42 two thousand jobs. Rockwell had pulled out. Several of the Plant's sites lay vacant.[45] The Palmdale former director of economic development, Curtis Cannon, described making use of the unused space by recruiting the film industry to make movies out there. In his office hung a poster for "Hard Rain" a movie about a flood, with Morgan Freeman and Christian Slater. It required the hangar to be refitted with elaborate pumps and drains for continuous water flow.[46]

A few factors kept some military production going at Plant 42 during this period. First, as Cannon says,

> What's not usually talked about is that there's the production, but then there's almost always 20-plus year of maintenance…. The last time we were

out there a U-2 flew in. Seventy years old! They're still flying it. Not producing them, just maintaining. And upgrades, guts, computerized electronics.

The Plant's fleet of B-1 bombers are still maintained there. So are its successors,
the B-2s.

Lockheed's aircraft repair operations had been located east of LA, in the San
Bernardino Valley known as the Inland Empire. These operations were pulled over
the mountain to Palmdale. Most importantly, it brought Burbank's Skunk Works—
the Air Force's main incubator of secret projects. The name, which Lockheed
patented and zealously protects, now applies to all its operations in Palmdale, the
secret ones and the publicly known. The former complex in Burbank was torn
down, and in its place is a grab bag of businesses, including one dedicated to
Burbank's stock-in-trade: digital film post-production and sound mixing.

In 1996 came the news that a major new fighter jet program, the "Joint Strike
Fighter" or F-35, was in the works, and Plant 42 would be getting a decent-sized
piece of it.

Plant 42 Today

Military contractors in general like to impress the public with dazzling websites
convincing us, as Lockheed Martin puts it, that "Your mission is ours." Most of
the details they like to shield from prying eyes, a feature made to order for Plant
42. The extra secrecy of its "black box" operations extends to all the complex's
occupants. The vast spaces of Plant 42 are surrounded by razor wire fences, electronic sensors and surveillance from the skies. At one end is the Skunk Works
complex. At the other are a Boeing facility working mostly on guidance systems
for missiles and space vehicles, and Northrop Grumman's bomber projects.

The surrounding deserts also provide plenty of room for expansion. That is
what is happening. At Plant 42, Lockheed is planning to add a million square
feet to its complex to accommodate its new work, stretching out to the horizon,
on the F-35 and other "secret" projects like a new hypersonic spy plane (see
Chapter 7).[47] Across Plant 42's airfield, another mega-project—the successor to
the B-2—has come to town.

In a field next to Plant 42, tourists now stroll around Joe Davies Airpark, a showcase for the planes that have been built next door over the years. Boeing's gargantuan B-52 bomber is there: the "Stratofortress" assigned to drop nuclear weapons
on the Soviet Union during the Cold War, and still in use. So is Lockheed's F-104
fighter, referred to during the 1950s and 1960s as "the missile with a man in
it." So is Northrop Grumman's F-14 "Tomcat." Only the B-2 is absent, though
(stealthily) represented by a one-quarter scale replica of the real thing. Twenty-two
different models are on display now; they hope to bring that number up to 40.
Including an F-35.

Palmdale spreads out across the desert next to the Plant, on a grid of streets designated by numbers in one direction and letters of the alphabet in the other. Its economic development officials estimate that the military economy employs 25–30 percent of Palmdale's working population. Palmdale has struggled with its reputation for low incomes (beyond that 25–30%) and the attendant challenges of poverty. Mark Oyler, former Director of Economic and Community Development, mimics what he's heard: "Ooo, why would you want to go to that downtrodden place?" His team touts the successes they have had marketing this liability as an asset (reminiscent of Johnstown's pitch vis á vis Washington, DC): cheap land, cheap labor and a low cost of living, they say, make it an attractive business alternative to Los Angeles.

They are feeling bullish on the prospects for Palmdale's military economy. The contractors at Plant 42 are "talking about doubling" the total workforce out there. The formerly vacant spaces are full up. "Boeing took back the space that they'd leased out.… If anything changes, and Boeing is no longer there, we could lease that space [to other military contractors] in a second." Military drone builder General Atomics wants to move in, Cannon says. "It's a privilege to be there."[48]

The Hidden Drama at Plant 42

In Chapter 2 we looked at two mega-weapons programs—the F-35 and the *Columbia*-class submarine—on a collision course in a budget that can't afford them both. Add the B-21 bomber to the list.

As noted, Plant 42 sets a scene that exists nowhere else: three of the top four prime contractor competitors of the military-industrial complex operating cheek by jowl, sharing the same base. This seems a bit puzzling: In a place whose stock-in-trade is secrecy, these contractors don't seem particularly focused on protecting these secret projects from each other. According to Oyler, this works fine: "The[y] have worked side by side so well for so long, they [battle each other for the big contracts], let the dust settle and move on."

There is some truth to this.

Before the Pentagon picked its winner to head up its first big post–Cold War project, the F-35, all three contractors, plus a few more, threw themselves into the competition. Lockheed won. But Northrop Grumman became the project's most important subcontractor. At the other end of Plant 42, Northrop now manufactures the fuselages for the F-35. These get shipped to Fort Worth, Texas, where Lockheed installs electronics and attaches the wings, which are shipped in from England. Then Plant 42 gets the plane back for testing.[49]

But in the following decade, the Pentagon offered up a military-industrial prize to rival the F-35: the new bomber labeled the B-21. Two of Plant 42's contractors, Lockheed and Boeing, teamed up against the other one, Northrop. Lockheed had exited the bomber business in 1970 for fighter jets back in 1970 but was touted for its (decidedly mixed) record with "stealth" on the F-35. Boeing's record came from the B-1. On the "strength" of its (mixed, if you're being generous) record on the B-2, plus a promise to build the plane cheaper than the other team, Northrop won. And unlike the F-35, based in Fort Worth, this plane will call Plant 42 home.

Northrop has not invited its neighbors onto its B-21 team. Following standard practice for building political protection around major new weapons systems, in 2016 Northrop announced a partial list of subcontractors for the project, whose ties to members of key congressional committees involved in funding it are hard to miss.[50] Neither of its Plant 42 neighbors is among them.

Like Lockheed's, Northrop's footprint at the Plant is expanding, by 50 percent, with a million extra square feet. For a while the company housed its new hires in temporary trailers, on the way to expanding the workforce from 3,000 to 5,200. The *Los Angeles Times* described this development as "mark[ing] a sharp turn-around in the fortunes of the Southern California aerospace industry[,]" which had been assumed "would never again be home to a large aircraft manufacturing program and now it has one of the largest in modern history."[51]

As in Connecticut, the mega-projects of Plant 42 are headed for a more cutthroat political battle. The F-35 and the B-21, along with a new aerial refueling tanker, the KC-46A, that will allow these planes to extend their range, are the Air Force's top three aircraft priorities. It is exceedingly hard to see how the country pays for all three.

In 2016 one of the most widely respected U.S. defense budget analysts concluded that between fiscal years 2015 and 2023 the defense budget was on track to rise in real terms by 73 percent, and cited the Air Force's new aircraft programs as the biggest contributors.[52] The B-21 is the most expensive item in a trillion-plus-dollar plan to replace the nuclear triad. The F-35 program is projected to match or exceed those costs. The list of other aircraft programs that need to find space in the budget at the same time is long—a new combat rescue helicopter, the Global Hawk unmanned surveillance plane (also built at Plant 42), a new version of the F-15 fighter jet, among several others.

Recognizing that its expansive aircraft plans don't fit within its budget, the Air Force is trying to follow the Navy's example in raiding other Pentagon accounts. The Navy has had some success off-loading some of its budget, including the account for its nuclear submarines, into a defense-wide account called the Sea-Based Deterrent Fund.[53] The Air Force is trying a similar gambit, making the case for including its nuclear bomber and its new replacements for the intercontinental ballistic missiles (ICBMs) outside its own budget, in a separate, defense-wide Strategic Deterrence account.[54]

Referring to the Pentagon and all the programs that will be competing with the B-21, Jeffrey Lewis, a nuclear weapons expert at the James Martin Center for Nonproliferation Studies, said simply, "They don't have enough money."[55]

Something will have to give. And Plant 42 sits in the eye of this storm.

Buy American?

In this Mecca of Pentagon contracting that is Plant 42, churning out fighter jets and bombers and unmanned spy planes, sits one anomaly. This is Kinkisharyo, a Japanese company that set up shop in the hangar, where the B-1 bomber was once tested, next to the one where it used to be built. Kinkisharyo grabbed the space from Boeing in 2013, before full F-35 production and the B-21 bomber contract put facilities on Plant 42 at a premium. Here, more than 400 workers have been building electric light-rail cars for the city. They run all over LA, from Santa Monica to Monrovia to Long Beach to LAX airport, withholding tons of LA's prodigious carbon production from the air. Light rail, said one Metro board member, represented "the dawn of the new era when we finally decided to pull our heads out of the sand and build good alternatives to sitting in traffic."[56]

The company had previously manufactured its cars in Japan and then assembled them in places like Seattle, Dallas, and Phoenix. LA County worked out a deal requiring that after its cars had proved themselves on LA streets, the company would have to start actually building them in the area. "It was a huge leap to go to complete manufacturing—it was the first time Kinkisharyo had ever done that scope of work in the U.S.," says Steve Huckabay, the plant manager.[57] They salvaged and retooled four cranes in the ceiling from the B-1's production line, but not much else. The plan, said Huckabay in 2019, is that all future manufacturing for the U.S. market will be done at Plant 42. In 2020 the company completed its contract to deliver 235 rail cars to the city on time and on budget. If any of its defense contractor neighbors could claim that kind of record, it would be news indeed.

Further production has been on hold recently as California's budget problems, and the Trump administration's approach to mass transit (cut its funding) has slowed the progress of light rail projects. The Biden infrastructure plan would

FIGURE 4.3 Kinkisharyo at Plant 42

Source: Photo courtesy of the author.

turn this around. Meanwhile, in March of 2021 the Los Angeles Metro Board of directors awarded Kinkisharyo a $170 million contract to overhaul and upgrade its existing trains, locking in at least a hundred jobs at the Palmdale facility for the next four and a half years.[58]

How do those jobs stack up against the high salaries next door? Huckabay says they are competitive. And in 2020 a posting on Indeed.com from a Kinkisharyo Wire Assembly Technician suggested a somewhat altered standard, pegged to living wages and the societal value of the work: Under the heading "Pay good and we work a little more than 8 hours," it read "Good work[,] sometimes we work a little more time, but the work requires it[. We make] the means of transport that guarantee[s] the community of Los Angeles and all its surroundings."

Ten miles northwest of Palmdale in Lancaster sits the lone U.S. manufacturing site of a Chinese company called BYD (for Build Your Dreams). It is the world's third leading electric vehicle manufacturer (after Tesla and Volkswagen.) The 500,000-plus square foot Lancaster facility has produced more than 400 battery electric buses for LA County, among 14 states across the country, and has begun building and selling heavy-duty trucks here. And after a period of struggle over hiring policy and wage rates, it now offers high-paying union jobs.

Some in Congress have tried to block the manufacture of their mass transit vehicles in the U.S. on national security—espionage—grounds. But as the *LA Times* editorialized,

> [H]ow are trains and buses, which are built to public agencies' specifications, assembled on U.S. soil and inspected on a regular basis, more of an espionage threat than, say, the Chinese-assembled security cameras, phones, routers, computers and appliances in American homes and offices?[59]

Groups like the Alliance for American Manufacturing protest that American companies can't compete with Chinese companies like BYD making things on American soil.[60] Chinese manufacturers of electric vehicles, they say, have bene-fitted from government subsidies, as American companies have not.

This is true. While U.S. industrial policy has focused on its advantage in weapons production, and fossil fuels, China has focused strategically on growing the capability to produce affordable electric vehicles and solar panels. It is one of the paradoxes of climate change: China produces more greenhouse gases than any other country in the world, while doing the most to bring online the technologies to curb them. In other words, it is doing the most to create the problem and sim-ultaneously, the most to solve it. As of 2019, the world had about 425,000 electric buses, and about 421,000 of them were in China.[61]

China has nurtured its goal of a rapid transition to electrified transport with an industrial policy that combines subsidies, research incentives and national regulatory mandates. Its vertically integrated state-owned companies are not the American Way. But climate scientists keep foreshortening the time frames they say we have to act before the climate damage is irreversible. These facts make an urgent case for an American industrial policy focused less on the dazzling new frontiers of military technology and more on finding a way to get to net-zero emissions before it's too late.

Though BYD supplies most of the electric cars sold in China, it has so far not penetrated the U.S. market. Elon Musk heaps scorn on BYD ("Have you seen their car?") And some U.S. carmakers say the inner works of some of China's electric vehicles look suspiciously like ripped-off designs from U.S. models. But while Tesla has focused much time selling elaborately tricked-out electric cars in the upscale market, BYD has focused on building cars that most people can afford. If climate catastrophe is to be avoided, it is BYD's strategic focus, not Tesla's, that is more likely to make a difference.

In Antelope Valley, where Palmdale and Lancaster sit, you get to see what 80 years of a militarized industrial policy can look like. You also see, courtesy of Japan and China, a glimpse of what a different industrial policy could nurture there.

Southern California: "Aerospace Capital" or "Green Economy Capital"?

As we've seen, California led the way in drafting the essential outlines of such a new national industrial policy. CALSTART came into being to build something out of the aerospace collapse: It would link the state's severe air pollution problem to the development of a green industrial base that would tackle the problem while creating a new jobs base for laid-off aerospace workers. As we've also seen, these plans fell short of the necessary implementation. "We've been through a couple of peaks and valleys on this clean transportation technology industry," says Van Amburg, the CALSTART vice president. "We had a die-off for a while."

The reasons included piecemeal, insufficient, and fragmented government support for industrial transition; the resistance of the oil industry to green energy and transport initiatives, of major automakers to learning how to produce electric vehicles ("Who Killed the Electric Car?"), and of consumers to buy them; the technical challenges of battery life and charging; and the resistance of the majority of prime defense contractors to putting in the work of serious restructuring, retooling, and retraining for these new markets.

But California maintained its lead over the rest of the country in pushing the envelope on climate policy. In 2012 the Obama administration announced national fuel efficiency standards would be harmonized with California's more stringent ones. This gave automakers the signal that they could sell cars across the country, and internationally, built to the same higher standard. The carmakers' trade association embraced the change.[62] The carmakers were beginning to come around.

And when a new federal administration took over in 2017 committed to denying climate change and gutting climate policy, California became the leader of the resistance.[63] After the Trump administration withdrew from the Paris Climate Accords, California's governor convened a Global Climate Action Summit that extracted commitments from numerous states, cities and corporations to cut their own carbon production. National high-level delegations included China, whose joint agreement with the United States had enabled the Paris Accords. A Yale expert on Chinese environmental policy offered that "It almost is like China and the US … haven't missed a beat in this bilateral partnership on climate change because California has really stepped in to fill the role."[64] California itself committed to 100 percent renewable energy by 2045.

And when the Trump administration moved in 2019 to roll back the national fuel efficiency standard, and to undermine a voluntary fuel-efficiency agreement California had reached with four auto companies—Ford, Honda, BMW and Volkswagen—the governors of 23 states pledged their support to California's position.

By January of 2021 General Motors had announced it intended to go all-electric by 2035, and most of the rest of the automotive world was headed in the same general direction. The change of government then taking place surely had something to do with it.

At its Earth Day Climate Summit in April of 2021, the Biden administration pledged to cut U.S. emissions in half by 2030, with a "whole of government" approach to the task, with real money behind it. Electric cars are a big piece of the plan—to the tune of $174 billion, mainly to put electric charging stations all over America—as is funding for mass transit and the electric grid to run it on. And they want to institute a national clean power standard that would ratchet up the proportion of electric power coming from zero- or near-zero carbon sources. Also in the plan is significant spending on R&D: to create the technologies the president and others acknowledge we don't now have to get the job done. It can't hurt—though it also won't help—to acknowledge that had we shifted from a militarized to a green industrial policy back in the post–Cold War period, those solutions could have been in place by now.

The administration has outlined an industrial policy focused on propelling the kind of clean energy and transportation transition that could curb climate change's worst effects. Politics is currently acting to constrain these ambitions. And, as noted, what the Biden administration has *not* done is to dial back on the military industrial policy we already had.

Conclusion

CALSTART's membership keeps expanding, as does the scope of its work well beyond California's boundaries. At a 2020 summit of the international Clean

Energy Ministerial in Riyadh for example, nine countries from four continents and 80 government, city, industry, fleet and utility partners signed on to CALSTART's Global Commercial Vehicle Drive to Zero program designed to accelerate growth in the zero-emission commercial vehicle market. In 2021 CALSTART began administering for the California Air Resources Board a $165 million voucher program to boost sales of hybrid and zero-emission buses.[65]

But. Echoing developments at the federal level, California's aggressive push in the direction of the green economy doesn't mean it is reining in its commitment to the warfare economy. In 2018, for example, the governor's "California Competes" program gave its largest tax break *ever*—more than half of the total it had to give—to one company: Lockheed Martin, for its Skunk Works expansion in Palmdale. The company's response included a broad hint about what might have happened if the state had invested its money elsewhere. It celebrated "this partnership to create a competitive business environment which will enable our 75-year legacy of creating history-making aircraft here in California to continue."

The federal administration's push to get serious, finally, about climate change, if successful, offers places like California much more to build a jobs base on than they've ever had. And this state has a head start over all the rest. The question is whether the state and its manufacturers will prioritize this opportunity versus fiddling with exotic space travel and exotic weaponry, while the planet, and most definitely California, burns.

Notes

1 Office of Local Defense Community Cooperation, "Defense Spending by State: Fiscal Year 2020."
2 Allen J. Scott, *Technopolis: High Technology Industry and Regional Development in Southern California* (Berkeley: University of California Press, 1993) pp. 56–59.
3 Scott, pp. 60–62.
4 Michael Oden, Ann Markusen, Dan Flaming and Mark Drayse, "Post Cold War Frontiers: Defense Downsizing and Conversion in Los Angeles," Project on Regional and Industrial Economics, Rutgers University, 1996, p. 33.
5 Personal interview, June 20, 2019.
6 Ralph Vartabedian, "Lockheed Will Move Top Secret 'Skunk Works' from Burbank," *Los Angeles Times*, November 5, 1988.
7 Personal interview, Los Angeles, June 30, 2019, and subsequent email correspondence; Ellen Yan and John Chandler, "Job Cuts Infuriate Lockheed Workers," *Los Angeles Times*, May 10, 1991.
8 Daniel Flaming, Michael Beltramo and Associates, "Los Angeles County Economic Adjustment Strategy for Defense Reductions," Economic Roundtable, April 1, 1992, https://economicrt.org/publication/los-angeles-county-economic-adjustment-stategy-for-defense-reductions/.
9 Seth Mydans, "Displaced Aerospace Workers Face Grim Future in California Economy," *New York Times*, May 3, 1995.

10 Greg Bischak, "Defense Conversion," Institute for Policy Studies, January 1, 1997. https://ips-dc.org/defense_conversion/.

11 James F. Peltz, "Raytheon Acquires Hughes Wing in $9.5-Billion Deal," *Los Angeles Times*, January 17, 1997, www.latimes.com/archives/la-xpm-1997-01-17-mn-19465-story.html.

12 John Mintz, "How a Dinner Led to a Feeding Frenzy," *Washington Post*, July 4, 1997. www.washingtonpost.com/archive/business/1997/07/04/how-a-dinner-led-to-a-feeding-frenzy/13961ba2-5908-4992-8335-c3c087cdebc6/.

13 Rachel Weber, *Swords into Dow Shares* (Boulder, CO: Westview Press, 2018.)

14 Mintz, *Washington Post*.

15 Oden, Markusen, Flaming and Drayse, p. 13.

16 Author's personal knowledge.

17 "History," California Air Resources Board, https://ww2.arb.ca.gov/about/history; LA County Economic Adjustment Strategy.

18 Flaming, Beltramo et al., "Los Angeles County Economic Adjustment Strategy for Defense Reductions."

19 *Project California: A Blueprint for Energizing California's Economic Recovery*, discussed in Oden, Markusen, Flaming and Drayse, 1996.

20 Phone interview, July 1, 2019.

21 Phone interview, June 24, 2019.

22 William D. Hartung, *Prophets of War: Lockheed Martin and the Making of the Military Industrial Complex* (New York: Nation Books, 2012) p. 35.

23 The documentary "Who Killed the Electric Car?" (2006) examines this history.

24 Oden, Markusen, Flaming and Drayse, pp. 105–107.

25 "Aura: The Odyssey: "Star Wars to Sand Dunes," www.aurasystems.com/auragen.html.

26 Ted Johnson, "Aerospace Swords into Plowshares: Defense Contractors Convert to Consumer Goods and Brush Up on their Rusty Marketing Skills," *Los Angeles Times*, August 5, 1993, www.latimes.com/archives/la-xpm-1993-08-05-me-20751-story.html.

27 Potomac Institute for Policy Studies, "A Review of the Technology Reinvestment Project," January 30, 1999, pp. D-98 and D-99.

28 Jeff Gerth and Tim Weiner, "Arms Makers See Bonanza in Selling NATO expansion," *New York Times*, June 29, 1997. www.nytimes.com/1997/06/29/world/arms-makers-see-bonanza-in-selling-nato-expansion.html.

29 www.governmentcontractswon.com/department/defense/tarrant_county_tx_texas.asp.; OEA, pp. 12–13.

30 "San Diego's Military Community, Thomas Jefferson School of Law, www.tjsl.edu/military/san-diego-community.

31 Ronald D. White, "Full steam ahead for Nassco shipyard in San Diego, *Los Angeles Times*, July 3, 2011, www.latimes.com/business/la-xpm-2011-jul-03-la-fi-made-in-california-shipyard-20110703-story.html.

32 "The Changing Face of Aerospace in Southern California," LAEDC Institute for Applied Economics, p. 17.

33 Cubic.com.

34 City of San Diego, "Propel San Diego: Driving Defense Resiliency," Full Report, Released February 2018, https://future-iq.com/wp-content/uploads/2016/10/Propel-San-Diego-Strategic-Roadmap-Update.pdf.

35 U.S. Department of Defense *Daily Digest Bulletin*, January 13, 2021.

36 "Northrop Grumman Announces $429M Contract for Payload that will Provide Continuous Coverage of Polar Regions," https://news.northropgrumman.com/news/releases/northrop-grumman-awarded-429m-contract-for-payload-that-will-provide-continuous-coverage-of-polar-regions.

37 Kaushik Patowary, "How the Military Hid the Lockheed Burbank Aircraft Plant," Amusing Planet, Dec. 23, 2010. www.amusingplanet.com/2010/12/how-military-hid-lockheed-burbank.html.

38 "Air Force Plant 42, GlobalSecurity.org, www.globalsecurity.org/military/facility/afp-42.htm.

39 http://content.time.com/time/magazine/article/0,9171,919040-1,00.html.

40 Personal interview, Mark Oyler and Curtis Cannon, June 18, 2019.

41 Tim Weiner, "The $2 Billion Stealth Bomber Can't Go Out in the Rain," *New York Times*, August 23, 1997. www.nytimes.com/1997/08/23/world/the-2-billion-stealth-bomber-can-t-go-out-in-the-rain.html.

42 "B-2 Bomber: Cost and Operational Issues Letter Report, GAO/NSIAD-97-181," United States General Accounting Office (GAO), August 14, 1997. Retrieved: 13 December 2018.

43 Weiner, ibid.

44 Weiner, ibid.

45 Elizabeth Reid, "Recycling Defense Production Facilities," in *Los Angeles County Economic Adjustment Strategy for Defense Reductions*, Economic Roundtable, April 1, 1992, p. 279.

46 Personal interview with Curtis Cannon and Mark Oyler, June 18, 2019.

47 Joseph Trevithick, "Here's How Hypersonic Weapons Could Completely Change the Face of Warfare," The War Zone, June 6, 2017, www.thedrive.com/the-war-zone/11177/heres-how-hypersonic-weapons-could-completely-change-the-face-of-warfare.

48 Personal interview with Curtis Cannon and Mark Oyler, June 18, 2019.

49 Personal interview with Kathleen Dewhurst, June 17, 2019.

50 Dan Grazier, "Business as Usual Building a New Bomber," Project on Government Oversight, March 17, 2016, www.pogo.org/analysis/2016/03/business-as-usual-building-new-bomber/.

51 Ralph Vartabedian, W.J. Hennigan, Samantha Masunaga, "A top secret desert assembly plant starts ramping up to build Northrop's B-21 bomber," *Los Angeles Times*, November 10, 2017, www.latimes.com/local/california/la-fi-northrop-bomber-20171110-htmlstory.html.

52 Todd Harrison, "Defense Modernization Plans through the 2020s," Center for Strategic and International Studies, January 2016, p. 7. https://csis-prod.s3.amazonaws.com/s3fs-public/legacy_files/files/publication/160126_Harrison_DefenseModernization_Web.pdf.

53 Justin Katz, "Pentagon reprograms $208 million to National Sea-Based Deterrence Fund," Inside Defense, March 16, 2020. Https://insidedefense.com/insider/pentagon-reprograms-208-million-national-sea-based-deterrence-fund.

54 https://insidedefense.com/insider/pentagon-shifts-630-million-national-sea-based-deterrence-fund; Gertler, CRS, p. 13.

55 Ralph Vartebedian et al., *Los Angeles Times*, November 10, 2017.

56 Asia Morris, "Metro Says Goodbye to Old Blue Line Rail Cars after 27 Years of Service," *Long Beach Post*, June 21, 2017, https://lbpost.com/news/place/public-transit/metro-says-goodbye-to-old-blue-line-rail-cars-after-27-years-of-service.

57 Phone interview, September 30, 2019.
58 "Kinkisharyo lands deal for light rail vehicles," *Antelope Valley Press*, March 27, 2021, www.avpress.com/news/kinkisharyo-lands-deal-for-light-rail-vehicles/article.
59 Editorial: "Anti-China push in D.C. could cost 800 workers their jobs in Los Angeles County," *Los Angeles Times*, September 30, 2019, www.latimes.com/opinion/story/2019-09-27/china-byd-trade-war-congress.
60 Brian Lombardozzi, "Why China's CRRC and BYD Pose Such a Serious Threat to the United States." www.americanmanufacturing.org/blog/why-chinas-crrc-and-byd-pose-such-a-serious-threat-to-the-united-states/
61 Brian Eckhouse, "In Shift to Electric Buses, China is Ahead of US," *Bloomberg News*, May 15, 2019. www.bloomberg.com/news/articles/2019-05-15/in-shift-to-electric-bus-it-s-china-ahead-of-u-s-421-000-to-300.
62 Jody Freeman, "The Auto Rule Rollback Only Trump Seems to Want," *New York Times*, September 9, 2019. www.nytimes.com/2019/09/09/opinion/trump-clean-air-act.html.
63 E. A. Grunden, "California is gaining allies in its emissions standards war with Trump," thinkprogress.org, August 16, 2019.
64 Carolyn Beeler, "California emerges as a leader at climate summit," *The World*, September 14, 2018, www.pri.org/stories/2018-09-14/california-emerges-leader-climate-summit.
65 "California HVIP opening to new voucher requests; $165M in funding," greencarcongress.com. www.greencarcongress.com/2021/04/20210430-hvip.html.

5

PINE BLUFF

Foreign Policy Comes Home to Arkansas

We head back east now, from the West Coast to the South. For the second time we're coming from a Mecca of the military economy and landing in one of its backwaters. In this case we'll shift from focusing mainly on the private sector of this economy to its public sector, that is, the military's vast "empire" of bases.

Colonists built America's first bases—forts—to protect Europeans as they began their expropriation of Native American lands. World War I added about 30 of its own bases to the landscape but, like the rest of the military economy, the vast majority owe their existence to World War II, and their permanence to the Cold War. The Defense Department reports that its military footprint occupies nearly five thousand total sites around the world, more than 4,100 of them within U.S. boundaries: 148 are "large sites" defined as worth more than $2 billion; 89 are "medium sites" ($1–2 billion) and 3,208 "small" sites (worth less than $1 billion.) Apart from the coastal bases, most belong to either the Army or the Air Force.[1]

The spread of bases on U.S. soil includes the Naval Submarine Base at Kings Bay, Georgia, where the Connecticut-built *Ohio*-class nuclear submarines have their stealth properties refurbished with new "magnetic signatures." The largest aircraft "boneyard" in the world is outside Tucson, where a thousand planes that no longer fly sit lined up in the desert to rot and be harvested for parts. There are the missile testing sites, including one at White Sands Missile Range in New Mexico which, at more than a million acres, is larger than the entire state of Connecticut.[2] There are the nuclear missile silo sites in places like North Dakota and Wyoming. And there are massive bases like Fort Bragg in North Carolina, which houses more than 50,000 active-duty military personnel.[3] To name but a few of our base structure's myriad functions.

The other function of bases is economic. While every state has its bases, the highest concentration of them, beyond the coasts, is in the South, where the

DOI: 10.4324/9781003293705-6

money they bring in is most fervently sought.[4] Arkansas, however, is a distinctly minor player, near the bottom, at number 43.[5] California, as we saw, tops the list of destinations for U.S. military dollars.[6] DoD's Base Structure report lists 121 separate military bases in California, including training sites, fuel depots, and munitions arsenals. For Arkansas the report lists only four: two national guard bases, an Air Force base outside of Little Rock, and the Pine Bluff Arsenal (the one we'll focus on). It's a story of foreign policy change altering a backwoods corner of America.

The Pine Bluff Arsenal sits in the middle of acres of pine, here and there the scattered remains of timbering, a few houses and trailers, and not much else. Five more miles of similar scenery down the interstate gets you to the city of Pine Bluff. Forty miles in the other direction gets you to Little Rock. All of this sitting in the poorest quadrant of the state with the 49th highest median income in America.

But next door, rising into view from the woods like Oz, is "the best-kept secret in Arkansas," the National Center for Toxicological Research (NCTR). It's the Food and Drug Administration's only research lab outside of Washington, DC, a vast complex of 30 buildings on 500 acres, where about 600 people, nearly a third of them with PhDs, work in 132 separate labs running tests on the substances we eat, touch, and breathe. They've recently studied the effects of tattoos on the lymph nodes of the 36 percent of American young people who have them. They've investigated the cancer-causing properties of dioxin and myriad other pesticides. Whether the cheese sold at Walmart is safe. The toxic effects of the BP Gulf oil spill. And they train waves of visiting foreign scientists. A recent cohort took new food safety research methods back to places like Guyana, Hungary, and India.

Now for the obvious question: How did all this wind up in a neglected corner of Southeast Arkansas?

FIGURE 5.1 View from upstairs at the National Center for Toxicological Research

Source: Photo courtesy of the author, used with permission

Once the second-largest metropolis in Arkansas, Pine Bluff has now slipped into ninth place. Some of the reasons for this decline it shares with broad swaths of the rest of the country: manufacturing going away. Underfunded public schools. A downtown core hollowed out and blighted by the sprawl of strip malls outside town. And the scars of race.

Riots erupted in Pine Bluff and cities across the country the day in 1968 that Martin Luther King was assassinated in Memphis. The riots created the kind of charred and shattered landscape replicated on a larger scale in Washington, DC, and scores of communities across the country. In Washington, nearly all traces of the riots are gone. In Pine Bluff, they are everywhere, joining the slow decay of decades of poverty and neglect.

From Cotton to Chemical Warfare

We have to go back more than a century to get to Pine Bluff's Golden Age. Post-Civil War railroad construction converged in Pine Bluff and linked to the growing steamship traffic up and down the Arkansas River. Cotton went upriver, sometimes 800 bales at a time, and on the Cotton Belt Railway from East Texas to St. Louis, and planted seeds for Pine Bluff's emerging manufacturing base: a railcar construction factory and a rail maintenance shop in 1883, and a cotton compress business in 1884. By 1887 Pine Bluff's Board of Trade was posting cotton and grain stock prices hourly. Northern lumber interests came to town buying up great swaths of pine woods to feed sawmills and furniture-manufacturing enterprises. The population exploded from 3,000 to 10,000 during the last 20 years of the century, and Pine Bluff's look and sense of itself grew with its numbers and prosperity. Houses along the wide brick-paved streets began sprouting balconies, porticos, and Doric columns.

In the late nineteenth century, the city was sometimes referred to—and not just by its own residents—as the Paradise of the South. In Reconstruction Pine Bluff, slave-born Ferdinand Havis built enough wealth around his barber shop to buy 2,000 acres and one of the grand houses, and he was elected to represent Jefferson and three other counties in Congress. Another wealthy black businessman, Wiley Jones, got the franchise to build Pine Bluff's first mule-drawn streetcar line in 1886, on the east side of town. (A week after it began operating, a group of white men got another line up and running—on the west side of town.)[7]

By 1900 Pine Bluff had built an entertainment complex on the outskirts featuring a horse-racing track, baseball diamond, pavilion, and theater, all reachable by the new electric streetcar system. By this time, though, Jim Crow had also arrived, followed by Depression and then war. Pine Bluff joined communities all over the country, including all the places we've visited so far, in linking its economic fortunes to the war effort. The Arsenal became one of the military's eight sites for making its stockpiles of chemical and biological weapons.

Chemical Weapons: Their Legacy in Brief

On a spring day in 1915, Canadian and French-Algerian troops at Ypres in Belgium saw a yellow-green cloud wafting their way. German soldiers had opened canisters of chlorine gas by hand (a few of them died in the process) and let the prevailing wind take it across No Man's Land. As soldiers' lungs filled with foam and mucus, asphyxiation and lung tissue damage became new causes of death in the war that day. One witness described this as "death by drowning only on dry land."

It wasn't only the soldiers. The yellow-green clouds blew this horrific way to die beyond the battlefield into farms and towns. And they triggered a chemical arms race. Each of the "Great Powers" began developing its own better poisons and more creative ways to deliver them.

We should be clear that World War I was not the first time anyone had the idea of using poisons for mass killing. The records of a Chinese sect from the second century BC refer to bellows blowing smoke from burning mustard balls into tunnels occupied by an invading army. The Spartans tried something similar when they pumped sulfur smoke under Athenian walls. Leonardo da Vinci was also among those contributing ingenuity to this field: "Chalk, fine sulfide of arsenic and powdered verdigris," he wrote, "may be thrown among enemy ships by means of small mangonels [fifteenth-century missile launchers], and all those who, as they breathe, inhale the powder into their lungs will become asphyxiated." Fortunately, this remained one of his drawing-board projects. Until 1915.[8]

Why did so many countries hold off so long? Though the goal of war is winning, the fact that warriors through the centuries have mostly stuck to conventional weaponry, despite the lethal allure of unconventional kinds, shows that ideas of moral limits have complicated the goal.

By 1925 most of the world's countries had ratified the Geneva Protocol banning the use of chemical weapons in war. Invoking "the general opinion of the civilized world" in "justly condemn[ing] the use of "[a]sphyxiating, poisonous or other gases" in war, the Protocol declared that "the conscience and practice of nations" would be bound by "universally accepted … international law" to avoid them.

The United States was not one of those nations. Though our government had promoted the protocol, in the end it was one of the few that failed to ratify it. The same suspicion of internationalism that sank the League of Nations (plus lobbying from the American Chemical Society) blocked American participation in this concrete demonstration of what nations acting together could do. Fifty years later, in 1975, the United States finally signed on. By this time it had pioneered, and used, a new, exponentially more powerful weapon of mass destruction, whose role in the military economy we'll look at in the next chapter.

The Pine Bluff Arsenal

Here is where the woods around Pine Bluff enter the story. Since the law banned only the use, not the production or stockpiling, of chemical weapons, those countries preparing for the next war started piling up massive quantities of the stuff. The U.S. Army fenced in more than 18,000 acres in the woods north of town and, five days before Pearl Harbor, broke ground on the Chemical Warfare Arsenal. (A combination of security concerns and public sensitivities likely propelled the name change to Pine Bluff Arsenal, four months later.)

Over time the complex grew to include 900 buildings, fourteen miles of roads and five of track, moving raw materials and finished products in and out. Ten thousand civilians got jobs there. By the time the U.S. war effort was fully underway, production workers at the Arsenal were installing lethal gases and chemical compounds in bombs and artillery shells, and manufacturing smoke bombs. Next door they built a massive laboratory complex to come up with innovations that would keep the United States ahead of whatever the Axis Powers were up to.

In the end chemical weapons played almost no role in the most lethal war in history. (Roosevelt pledged the United States to no first use, but retaliation in kind.) Can the boundaries established by the Geneva Protocol claim the credit? Hermann Goring was asked at the Nuremberg trials why Germany didn't cross this line as it had in the previous war. He cited horses. Horse-drawn carts moved most supplies to the front, and the Wehrmacht had never been able to invent a gas mask a horse was willing to wear. Another possible reason: having experienced gas himself in the trenches of the previous war, Hitler didn't want to go there. The unspeakable irony of his use of the poison gas Zyklon-B notwithstanding.[9]

Why Pine Bluff? As we saw in Johnstown, the military economy often gets installed where politicians have maneuvered to get these job bonanzas sited in their districts. In Pine Bluff's case the answer is also because it's out in the middle of nowhere. If you're making and storing chemical warfare agents, that's where you want them.

After the war, Pine Bluff Arsenal joined the rest of the country in the about-face gyrations of peacetime to Cold-War. For a brief period, the Army worked on leasing portions of the property for private, civilian use. But in 1946 the Army reclaimed the Arsenal on "permanent status," and the chemical-weapons manufacture and storage mission was back in business. Over the years it became the second largest U.S. chemical agent stockpile, with about 3,850 tons of the stuff, including rockets and landmines containing the nerve agent VX and 3,700 one-ton containers of blister agent HD/HT behind chain link fence on the north side of the property.[10]

By 1953, as the world seemed to settle into a permanent Cold War new normal, operations at the Arsenal and its lab next door had added biological weapons to their repertoire. The Army's chief microbiologist figured out how to disseminate anthrax spores through the air, for example. And so "Project X1002" began stockpiling them at Pine Bluff. The Army also experimented with using mosquitoes as anthrax carriers. That's the project that sticks in a lot of people's minds.

John Mitchell is one of the thousands who have made a living at the Arsenal. After registering voters with the civil rights-organizing Student Nonviolent Coordinating Committee (SNCC) as a teenager, he took the employment route most widely available to African American men and joined the military service. Afterwards, he came home to a town where his skills as a Navy aircraft mechanic should have gotten him a job in the rail repair yard, except that the work had moved to Louisiana. Like numerous communities across America, Pine Bluff featured the local prison industrial complex as a top job prospect. But he decided that "being a prison guard would feel like I was in prison except I got to go home at night," so his choices narrowed to the Arsenal.

It was a job, he says, that paid enough so he didn't need two of them. Federal facilities like the Arsenal come with certain non-discriminatory hiring, working conditions and wage protections attached. For most of 19 years, he was in Shipping and Receiving. Big shipments pulled in and out of the base on their own rail line. The place was like a city unto itself, he says, with its own police force, fire department, and whole neighborhoods of housing for military brass, enlisteds, and civilians. On the north end, the igloos holding the munitions were segregated from the rest of the base behind razor wire and guard stations.

Did workers worry about getting in the way of some accidental contaminating event? Some did, some didn't. Brenda Doucey's father worked there for 30 years, and the family lived "a stone's throw away." She now runs the museum in the next town over, White Hall, whose display cases feature specimens of the gas masks and gas canisters produced on the base, as well as a large photographic display of the locally made, multi-colored smoke bombs in use in the Vietnam jungle (white for smoke screen, red to mark a casualty, etc.) She remembers the time her mother drove her father to the base infirmary after some chemical he was working with

FIGURE 5.2 John Mitchell

Source: Photo courtesy of the author, used with permission.

made him woozy. But when friends would ask her whether she was afraid to live there she always answered with cheerful fatalism, "No, I've lived here all my life, and if something were to happen, it wouldn't matter if you lived next door or miles away."

That possibility did weigh on John Mitchell from time to time: "Where would everybody go? Could I rent my house? That sort of thing." A sign posted in his building tried to find a little humor in the situation: "Please know where your gas mask is. Our chemicals work."[11]

Chemical and Biological Weapons Go Out of Business

Richard Nixon's presidency is a rich source of cognitive dissonance for American brains. Beside the virulent vindictiveness, the secret bombing of Cambodia and the Constitutional betrayals, we have to put legacies like the creation of the Environmental Protection Agency and the Occupational Safety and Health Administration. And, responding to public protest over napalm and Agent Orange in Vietnam, a year into his first term he announced that the United States would unilaterally end its biological weapons program. Publicly, of course, he framed the decision as setting an example that might "contribute to an atmosphere of peace and understanding between all nations." The Nixon we also feel we know said privately that if any country used biological weapons against the United States, he would nuke them.[12]

But "setting an example" turned out to be more than pious rhetoric. Five months later, the Soviet Union had dropped its objections to the Biological Weapon Convention, and it was completed. Between 1971 and 1972 the Army destroyed its stockpiles of biological agents at the Pine Bluff Arsenal.[13] The U.S. Senate ratified the Convention in 1974—a year before also finally ratifying the World War I era Geneva Protocol—and this treaty banning the first of the three "ABC" (atomic-biological-chemical) weapons of mass destruction was law.

In taking the United States out of the biological weapons business, Nixon also assigned a new mission to the chemical and biological weapons lab outside Pine Bluff. The scientists in the newly named National Center for Toxicological Research would no longer research ingenious lethal methodologies, but instead concentrate on figuring out what the chemicals in our own environment were doing to us. The new national focus on the scourge of cancer would now include determining what chemicals are carcinogenic, and what level of known chemical carcinogens in the environment is safe for humans. This mission would be purely research—no financial incentives to decide one way or another, and no regulatory function. Regulation it would leave to its new parent, the Food and Drug Administration (FDA). That is how what eventually became the National Center for Toxicological Research wound up way out in the pine woods of Arkansas.

And it's how the world managed to make biological agents illegal as weapons during the height of the Cold War. Getting this done for chemical weapons took another 20 years, and the ending of the Cold War. At a Geneva conference in 1992 the Chemical Weapons Convention (CWC), 12 years in negotiation, was signed. As the UN put it, this was "the first disarmament agreement negotiated within a multilateral framework that provides for the elimination of an entire category of weapons of mass destruction under universally applied international control."

This time, the United States was an early adopter: the Senate ratified it in 1993. By 1997 enough countries had signed on to put the treaty into force, and to create an international enforcement mechanism. The Organisation for the Prohibition of Chemical Weapons began setting up inspection protocols and timetables to oversee the destruction of chemical weapons stockpiles around the world. As of July 2021 the treaty binds 98 percent of the world's population, and has destroyed more than 98 percent of the world's declared stockpiles.[14]

This center hasn't always held, of course. President Obama was widely and somewhat unfairly criticized for drawing a "red line" against Syria's use of chemical weapons against its own people, and then passing up military action by striking a deal with Russia to remove 95 percent of the stockpiles out of Syria and institute inspections. The Syrian government has since violated these restrictions, as has Russia.[15] Yet the Convention holds together as a tool of force and influence over international events—imperfect, like the humans trying to use it—and a challenge to the world's nuclear powers to meet the CWC's standard for achieved disarmament.

Pine Bluff Arsenal Gets a New Mission

The Convention converted the Pine Bluff Arsenal to an about-face new task. It had been built to produce one thing, and now its job would be to reverse course and destroy that thing. A time to build up had become a time to break down.

Jim Bacon managed both sides of the process. He spent 17 years at the Arsenal, from 1979 to 1996, as the civilian assistant to the base commander, and then graduated to oversee the national chemical weapons destruction program in sites from Oregon to Colorado to Kentucky. He spent many hours during both periods testifying at congressional hearings, trying to calm the nerves of congressmen and their constituents with patient explanations of the safety procedures, EPA monitoring, and testing to see if machine parts could withstand "anything imaginable, even earthquakes. There were no chemical releases."

Then the one in 1968 in Toele, Utah, that killed sheep, but no people?[16] This was "an upset. There were no serious releases." Now retired from the government, Bacon is the pastor of the Center Grove Methodist Church and interim director of the Southeast Arkansas United Way. This seems quite different from his government work, he says with a chuckle, "but isn't." The work at the Arsenal and his current jobs both stem from "a love of human beings, taking care of their needs."[17]

By the beginning of 1999 a private contractor had begun constructing new buildings on the property where the destruction, mostly through incineration,

FIGURE 5.3 "Mission Complete"

Source: Photo courtesy of the author

of the entire stockpile of chemical weapons would take place. A few years later Arsenal workers were watching Russian scientists climb up on top of the one-ton vats they had formerly filled with blister agents, to verify that they were empty.

Some of the civilians employed to make chemical weapons got to keep their jobs, and some were replaced by private contractors. By 2011, it was mission accomplished. Since President George W. Bush's aircraft carrier escapade falsely declaring "Mission Accomplished" in Iraq may have put that slogan off limits for quite a while, the four-foot sign outside the Arsenal gates actually read: "Mission Complete." About 1,200 private and government employees worked on this project at its peak, but by 2010, 12 sets of "reductions in force" had cut this number nearly in half. And falling. The remaining workers who are not simply maintaining the base are still making things like phosphorus illuminating grenades. And they have turned their chemical weapons expertise into making equipment like hazmat suits, to defend against them.

Now What? Shut the Arsenal Down?

The Chemical Weapons Convention created new hope that the world could cooperate to control its most destructive impulses. It also threatened to put Pine Bluff's economic mainstay out of business. Ask about the Arsenal, and Pine Bluff residents get nervous. "You're not going to say anything bad about it, are you?" asks one after another. Pine Bluff sits in a part of the political landscape where suspicion of government, especially the federal government, practically courses through the bloodstream. The irony of these places is the passion that these residents feel for these federal institutions in their midst, on which they rely.

The military looks at closing bases as one good way of saving money for other military projects by removing its "excess capacity"—getting rid of facilities that exist by inertia rather than military need. Most members of Congress consider it their job to protect these bird-in-hand supports for their local economies. So, basing decisions were for a long time made through a Darwinist process of political power jockeying.[18]

But, remarkably, given what Congress is like now, in 1990 it devised a system for taking these decisions largely out of the realm of politics. That power was given to non-partisan commissions on Base Realignment and Closure (BRAC). In the past 30 years, five BRAC rounds have closed more than 350 installations for savings DoD estimates at $14 billion a year.[19]

Once a base appears on the closure list, the BRAC process prescribes a local committee made up of all community stakeholders to come up with a redevelopment plan, to be funded and assisted by the Pentagon's Office of Economic Adjustment (OEA), whose work has turned up in the three states we've visited so far. The Pine Bluff Arsenal has not actually closed, but the end of its mission has left it a shadow of its former self. So OEA came in to help the Pine Bluff community recover from the hit. In the cases we've seen so far, successes have been fairly marginal. Could Pine Bluff be different?

Most members of Congress have viewed such two-birds-in-the-bush efforts as less attractive than just keeping the Pentagon money flowing to their bases. Since the usual political horse-trading had been taken out of their hands, all that was left for them in influencing the BRAC process was to shut it down. Which, effectively, since 2005, they have done. Every year DoD testifies to its current excess base capacity; in recent years it has been upward of 22 percent. Pentagon officials talk about what they'd like to do with the savings. They ask Congress to authorize another BRAC round. Every year, Congress says no.

They do this even though studies keep on finding that communities whose bases have closed can come back stronger than they ever were when their base was keeping the economy afloat. Take the Philadelphia Naval Shipyard, which closed after the Cold War ended. It took 20 years, and many detours through corruption and lesser forms of wasted time and money, but it now supports more jobs than it did during its life as a military base, in a varied microeconomy of 145 enterprises that include retail, marine manufacturing, a clean energy incubator, an art museum, and a hospital complex.[20]

And the last BRAC round of 2005 produced cases like the Brunswick Naval Air Station in Brunswick, Maine. Like their counterparts in Philadelphia, Brunswick's redevelopers wasted a lot of time and money getting there but, in the end, they turned two million square feet of vacant buildings into a home for 150 businesses employing 2,500 people, branch campuses for Southern Main Community College and the University of Maine, a regional business airport, a technology business incubator, and the former base housing units full to capacity next to new housing under construction. And all the energy powering the site comes from renewable sources.[21]

OEA has identified numerous other cases in which converted bases have ultimately generated more civilian jobs than existed when the base was used for military purposes. They've been used for industrial parks, civilian airports, educational institutions, and public parks.

Base closure communities have some advantages in making the process work over communities facing the loss of private contracting. Closing bases are public institutions being turned over to local communities for their use. They are thus fairly immune from the suspicions ("Socialism!") visited on communities trying to work together to influence the course of private sector development.

A 2012 study by the Congressional Research Service (CRS) found that

> evidence from past BRAC rounds shows that local economies are, in many cases, more resilient after an economic shock than they expected.... Some communities came to regard the closing as an opportunity for revitalizing and diversifying their economies. Other communities found they were in stronger economic shape after several years than they thought possible on first learning their bases were closing.[22]

But CRS also points to Pine Bluff's reasons for fear. The plentiful examples of successful base conversion tend to cluster in or near urban areas, where land is at a premium. "Rural areas in particular can find the loss of a base and the revitalization of their communities especially difficult challenges." The Philadelphia Shipyard sits on one of the most valuable pieces of property in the country, at the heart of the Northeast Corridor. Pine Bluff, of course, doesn't.

Municipalities around military bases, urban as well as rural, have organized themselves into an Association of Defense Communities, mostly so they can work together to prevent a new BRAC. They have an energetic and well-populated Defense Communities Caucus in Congress to help them. If and when the Pentagon gets its way and successfully convenes a BRAC, these communities will of course be competing with each other to stay off the list.

Pine Bluff could serve as the poster child of the Pentagon's case for a new BRAC: Excess capacity to the tune of 3.5 million square feet of buildings, most of them quietly deteriorating, year after year, sitting on 14,000 acres of real estate, most of it lying fallow.[23]

The quandary for places like Pine Bluff is that land the Army controls but doesn't do much with doesn't do anybody much good. Of all the forms of Pentagon waste—gold-plated weapons systems that don't work; contracts that inflate their costs; redundant, gold-plated healthcare plans that retired generals don't need—excess base capacity is the one the military brass, at least, agrees should be cut. Most communities resist, having come to depend on this reliable source of "direct" jobs (employees at the base) and "indirect" ones (supplying the base's needs, including the dry cleaner and the pizza shop where "direct" employees take their business.) This includes those who traffic mightily in the rhetoric of complaint over the oppressions of federal intervention.

For years, this resistance has worked, blocking a new round of closures and realignments since 2005. And the Army continues to pay half a billion dollars annually to maintain scores of these underused buildings and properties across the country. These facilities quietly deteriorate, and the employment they provide shrinks as fewer and fewer people are needed to do less and less. The OEA process is supposed to help arrest this downward spiral.

Pine Bluff Stakeholders Convene

Enter Bryan Barnhouse, native Californian. Following public policy school at USC, he made the cross-country trek to Washington, DC. Signs of public policy heaven, in the form of organizations like his first employer, the International City/County Management Association, appear on building nameplates all over town. There he mostly helped with negotiations over environmental cleanup at closed and closing military bases. He met his future wife at one of the coed softball games on the National Mall that have launched a thousand DC romances. When she got her dream job in Little Rock, he followed, and his experience with military base transitioning landed him a job with the Economic Development Alliance of Jefferson County, in Pine Bluff.

Surrounded by the mostly vacant remains of Pine Bluff's downtown, The Alliance's compact new building sits on Main Street like a secular revival tent, staking its claim. There on Barnhouse's plate when he arrived in 2013 was the assignment to manage the grant from the Office of Economic Adjustment. He was now in charge of this effort to invent a new future for Pine Bluff.

We Americans like to tell ourselves that we're about confidence in fresh starts, unencumbered by the old arrangements. Slates wiped clean. But Jefferson County has a lot of old arrangements, including overlapping jurisdictions driving the way economic development is done here, and these aren't going away anytime soon. And just about nobody wanted to wipe the Pine Bluff Arsenal's slate clean. But the drastic job loss following the successful completion of the chemical weapons destruction mission forced everybody's hand to look for the opportunity in the crisis to figure out something new.

Following OEA's playbook, Barnhouse assembled a broad set of unusual suspects as stakeholders. About 150 of them showed up for the first meeting. Representatives of the Delta Regional Authority. The Commercial Innovation Center at Arkansas State University. County judges (who some say are the real local power brokers). The Governor's Dislocated Worker Task Force. The University of Arkansas at Pine Bluff. The National Center for Toxicological Research (NCTR). The Arsenal. A few state senators. Local business leaders (Automatic Vending of Arkansas; Entergy Arkansas; C&L Electric Cooperative) and the Little Rock Chamber of Commerce.

At first the big tent generated the buzz of unfamiliar faces throwing new curves into the conversation. Jeanne Anson, then the executive officer of the FDA research lab, says sitting next to a representative of the timber industry was eye-opening. She'd been driving past all that timber on her way to work for years and had never talked to anyone making a living managing this key piece of the local economy. To build in a sense of movement, of shaking things up to see what ideas could be dislodged, they moved, literally. One meeting took place out at the Arsenal. Another in Dumas, about 50 miles south of Pine Bluff deeper into Mississippi Delta country. A third at Southeast Arkansas Community College.

The old arrangements included food. For a breakfast meeting early on, Barnhouse, the California/DC guy, ordered up a menu featuring fruit, nuts and yogurt. It was made clear to him that in future traditional Southern breakfast foods along the lines of biscuits and grits needed to appear.

David Dempsey, representing one of these local economic power players, wryly labeled the process "*in*teresting." OEA's "fast-talking consultant" from New Jersey helped them walk through "some neat sectoral strategies." But the process was all about meetings and, after 35 years in the business, Dempsey has decided the definition of a good meeting is: "No such thing." It was mostly "pie in the sky stuff" and he didn't see any pies being delivered from on high.

About 60 of the original 150 attendees were still there at the end of the process–unfortunately not always the same 60. The question was: Could this gumbo of interests align, and then stick with each other long enough to make something work?

The OEA consultants assembled them into teams: "Technology and Infrastructure." "Entrepreneurship, Innovation and Commercialization." "Talent Development." And the fourth: "Sustainability," which meant: Once they had a plan, who and what was going to be around to make it happen? They did their "SWOT" brainstorming to identify community Strengths, Weaknesses, Opportunities, and Threats. And they identified the region's main industry clusters—like healthcare, chemical manufacturing, biotechnology, machining, and sustainable agriculture and food processing—and tried to figure out which ones could be made to grow. They also called out their infrastructure deficit: Pine Bluff's need to be connected to economic lifelines like new interstates and rail lines, a deeper port, and twenty-first century broadband.

The craft of economic development takes three basic forms: Attract (businesses from elsewhere). Retain (the ones you have). Grow (new ones). Most communities traditionally rely on the first two. The bidding wars among them to attract and retain big companies have intensified in recent years, as we saw for example with California's massive subsidy to Lockheed. The deal-sweeteners—"Come here and pay no taxes for the first five years!" "No, come *here* and pay no taxes ever!"—have the obvious downside of draining city treasuries of money for other things, not to mention that between communities they are a zero-sum game.

In 2014 the Arkansas' governor upped the usual ante to lure a familiar name—Lockheed Martin—into the state to build the Army's replacement for the Humvee, called the Joint Light Tactical Vehicle. Beyond the run-of-the-mill tax abatements, the governor offered Lockheed $87 million out of the state's general fund to finance the factory itself. Critics included the libertarian Koch Brothers, whose Americans for Prosperity Super PAC called this "a multi-million-dollar, debt-financed giveaway to a single corporation." "Arkansas taxpayers," the Kochs said, "should not be fronting the money for one of the largest and most successful companies in the world." In late August of that year the Army announced that, these extreme enticements from Arkansas notwithstanding, the contract was going to Oshkosh Trucks in Wisconsin. And by 2021, their eyes turning to so-called Great Power Competition, the Army and Marines were planning to reduce their buys of a vehicle that is not in fact very light, and was built for the Middle East.

Tasked with finding wagons other than the Arsenal to hitch to, Jefferson County's planning exercises kept circling back to NCTR, the potential gold mine for a Life Sciences cluster.

The Bioplex

Locals had been kicking around the idea of a "Bioplex" on two parcels of land on either side of the Toxicological Research lab, at the north end of the Arsenal. The idea was to add the title of "economic engine" to NCTR's portfolio to unlock its potential as a source of commercial opportunity for a region that could really use some. Their plan was to take ownership of the land from the Arsenal and develop a cutting-edge biotechnology park there, with NCTR as its idea factory as well as ideal anchor customer: a multi-million-dollar enterprise, right next door.

Companies housed at the Bioplex, they thought, would find the business opportunities hidden in the treasure chest of NCTR research. Working with NCTR, a company called Vivione did develop a technology that cuts the time from days to hours needed to detect e coli in a chicken breast. Other companies could become convenient suppliers of the lab's research tools: Zebrafish, it turns out, can often serve as a functional, cheaper alternative to lab rats. Why not use Arkansas's expertise in aquiculture—catfish farms are very big in the state—to provide NCTR with all the fish it could use?

The "blue-sky thinking" exercises produced a flip chart worth of ideas. Commercialize NCTR technology to detect air-borne toxins. Find spin-offs from NCTR's status as the only licensed primate lab in the country. Expand the idea of growing zebrafish for NCTR experimentation to supply places like the National Aquaculture Research Center in Stuttgart, 50 miles away. Companies at the Bioplex could produce vaccines and antidotes, which the FDA could simply walk over from next door to inspect. Eventually these operations could expand into the broader pharmaceutical world.

At the final meeting, after the OEA consultants walked through their recommendations, Barnhouse asked everybody who was ready to put organizational skin in this gameplan to stand. A few stood immediately. Then a few more. Uncomfortable seconds went by. In the end everyone stood, and applauded, and it was over. Barnhouse sensed that southern sociability and peer pressure were lifting as many of those people to their feet as was a commitment to anything that would last once they all pulled out of the parking lot.

The OEA consultants saw the same thing. Embedded in the largely upbeat final report were warnings that overcoming the old arrangements "can be a massive and complex effort" that required "approaches that might push the region's "comfort zone." "Success," they wrote, "will depend upon working together differently than ever before."

And the double-edged sword of these OEA-orchestrated planning processes lurked in the back of many minds: If you show that the community can do fine without the base, you might be more likely to find yourself on the BRAC list.

The comfort zone won. Because the commitment in that standing ovation was more socially manufactured than real, the long-term governance and administration system for economic development they'd nominally agreed to didn't materialize. There wasn't money, Barnhouse said, to do the kind of comprehensive outreach and marketing for these plans that OEA's final report warned would be necessary to keep the momentum going. Barnhouse was pulled back into the more conventional attract-and-retain economic development tasks, and to Pine Bluff's centuries-old mainstays of agriculture and timber.

But with the prodding and cheerleading of a local power lawyer with political connections named Jack McNulty, Barnhouse also threw himself into another push for the Bioplex. He almost got there. Offering to custom-design the space to the company's specifications, he got Vivione, the company whose "Rapid-B Scanner" could find e coli (and many other pathogens) in record time, to sign up as the anchor tenant. The University of Arkansas at Pine Bluff (UAPB) was interested in moving its Zebrafish Research and Production Facility there. Plans included a "globally connected" conference center that NCTR's director said would "facilitate the growing global outreach of our scientific programs." UAPB also agreed to move its supercomputer there to speed the transfer of data from NCTR to Washington, DC.

Then Vivione backed out. McNulty's congressional lobbying to get the property turned over from the military for private development didn't quite succeed. Standing in the way was Armed Services Committee member John McCain. He didn't like the idea of deeding away military property but went along with a 25-year lease that specified "only for a facility known as The Bioplex."

McNulty didn't see a problem with this arrangement. He does now. To attract financing to build the Bioplex, they needed a commitment from an anchor tenant, but prospect after prospect shied away from committing their enterprise to space they might, down the road, have to give back to the Army.[24]

Then financing from the Commerce Department's Economic Development Administration (EDA) was held up in a classic chicken-and-egg stalemate: Vivione needed the money to commit, and EDA needed their commitment to the space to give them the money. Other concerns surfaced about the available workforce's lack of technical skills. And to attract people who did have those skills, you had to face the hurdle of getting people to relocate to the middle of nowhere.

What exists now is a nice colorful "Bioplex" sign, and a fine piece of pristine asphalt leading nowhere with a county road sign naming it "Jack McNulty Road." And, as the honoree himself puts it, "Weeds and ticks."

And Beyond the Bioplex?

Creating a Life Sciences Cluster around NCTR would require connecting the Middle of Nowhere to somewhere. While this project hung in the balance, Pine Bluff made a pitch for a new highway link to Louisiana. But Arkansas politics tends to divide along the points of a compass, and the southeast quadrant is often on the losing end. State powerbrokers steered highway funds to the northeast instead, where Walmart's headquarters in Bentonville exerts a powerful pull.

Pine Bluff's piece of infrastructure action could include a high-speed rail system linking it to areas of economic dynamism like Atlanta and New Orleans. Reconnecting Pine Bluff's economic future to its past could involve reviving its preeminence in building rail cars. The Biden administration's plans include a mandate to steer investment toward neglected corners of America. Pine Bluff should be able to lay claim to a top spot on this list.

In 2017, as the OEA-sponsored process was losing steam, the city's residents and business interests were launching a somewhat similar process of their own. The first sentence of its Strategic Plan to "Go Forward Pine Bluff" pulled no punches on what they were up against, referring to media characterizations of the place as "a town full of crumbling buildings," "the worst place in America to live." The plan laid out numerous ambitions and artists' renderings for leafy downtown squares and convention centers, plus Land Bank financing to tackle the blight of 450 abandoned buildings. They now have some forward movement to point to—a new library and an aquatic center—and a long way to go.

At the moment though, the biggest job creator in town follows the economic development trend across the country of bringing jobs for some and financial ruin for others: legalized gambling. A gargantuan casino opened in 2020 run by the Quapaw tribe and featuring two acres of gaming space. Referring also to the town's new medical marijuana operation, the former director of economic development for Jefferson County said wryly, "I never thought my swan song would be gambling and marijuana."[25]

Doubling Down on the Military Economy

Meanwhile plans for the Arsenal now focus mostly on finding new ways to make it look indispensable to the Pentagon. While the OEA process was paying lip service to the goal of diversifying this mission beyond defense, the governor, Asa Hutchinson, was pushing in the opposite direction. Though the state has only four significant military installations—compared, again, to California's 121—the first sentence of his Economic Development Commission's 2016 report announced that "Arkansas has been a leader in the military and defense sector for decades." It committed to "position Arkansas as a priority state in our national defense plan."

The way to do that, according to the report, was to figure out how to "increase the military value of Arkansas military installations, to invite more mission opportunities, and to minimize and mitigate the state's defense-related weaknesses."[26]

Several pages were devoted to assessing the likelihood of, finally, a new BRAC. Getting new military missions assigned to the Arsenal seemed like the key to staying off the list, if and when there was one. Deep in the report were the numbers that explained this: While excess capacity across all U.S. bases is pegged at 22 percent, that number climbs to 33 percent for Army bases, and to 36 percent for arsenals specifically.

The mayor of the nearby town of White Hall, Noel Foster, has thrown himself into this task. White Hall, population 5,000, "exists because of the Arsenal," he says. "It grew up around it" to accommodate the huge World War II influx of workers. This modestly self-described "old country boy without much education" has learned the craft of lobbying, working with the state's congressional delegation and undertaking the requisite pilgrimages to Washington. Last year this work yielded an increase in the appropriation for smoke bomb projectiles that only the Arsenal makes. And he has reeled in a Texas company called Ready One that is on track to renovate one of the Arsenal's many unused buildings, where disabled workers will sew clothing designed to protect soldiers from chemical or biological attack.

But such projects don't actually amount to an indispensable mission for the military. The governor envisions consolidating the nation's "Joint Logistics Distribution for Chemical and Biological Defense" there. That is, the Arsenal would become the hub for supplying the country, and "ultimately" the world, with the tools to withstand chemical and biological attack. Standing in the way is the requirement mentioned for this role, as for most of its alternatives: a modern surface and air transportation network. The Pine Bluff area doesn't currently have one.

The other problem is the competition over such military missions. "When the Blue Grass Army Depot" in east central Kentucky "found out we were trying to get language put into the [National Defense Authorization bill] about this idea," says Foster, "Mitch McConnell began firing off letters." The BRAC process is designed to take base closing decisions out of politics. When there isn't one, parochial politics has plenty of room to operate.

People like Foster are not giving up on building economic prosperity around the Arsenal. He is overseeing a state-funded study to figure out "compatible" uses for the plentiful vacant land around it. (Like what? They haven't gotten that far.)[27]

The Arsenal is not in danger of closing any time soon. It has, for one thing, Senator Tom Cotton on the Senate Armed Services Committee, perhaps the most aggressive advocate for increased spending for the Pentagon, and for Arkansas' military facilities, in its corner. But it is in real danger of limping along in its current state. The governor's report found that in 2016 it was operating at only 57 percent of its capacity in 2009, more than a decade after the chemical weapons stockpiling mission began to shut down. The Arsenal's problem, articulated succinctly in the report: "No anchor mission."

Conclusion

This struggling corner of backwoods Arkansas built an economic revival of sorts around chemical weapons, and then had cast about for something to take its place. Now they are back to hanging on to the remnants of that mission, in addition to preserving the state's "best-kept secret" next door. That Arkansas "secret" successfully converted the chemical weapons mission into life-and-health saving research for America and the world. But what brought the chemical weapons mission to Pine Bluff—the asset of being in "the middle of nowhere"—became its chief liability when the mission went away.

In 2019 the governor cut the ribbon on some newly refurbished lab space for the National Center for Toxicological Research, and the broadband has finally been upgraded. To the extent possible following a Covid-induced slow-down, the Center launched new research into topics such as the effects of opioid exposure on prenatal development, and the means of controlling salmonella contamination. The energy put into the Bioplex, though, was the highwater mark, for the time being, of the effort to create commercial activity around NCTR's research.

As we will see in the next chapter, some of the country's federal labs have focused considerable attention on seeding private-sector enterprises with their research. This is not the case at NCTR; tech transfer is not its priority. And while the budget for the FDA headquarters outside of Washington, DC, has grown in recent years, NCTR's budget has stayed flat. Bryan Barnhouse, the DC-transplant who ran the OEA process back in 2015, calls it "an underutilized asset for the state."[28]

In 2021 the Arkansas legislature passed a resolution commemorating NCTR's fiftieth anniversary.[29] While mostly focusing on its contributions to consumer protection and scientific collaboration, the resolution mentions the Arkansas

Research Alliance and its mission to develop "job-creating research" in the state. Barnhouse, who now runs this Alliance, mentions an NCTR scientist who figured out a way to enable saliva samples to be assayed with greater accuracy for viral agents. The technology has been licensed—but to a company in Boston. Any similar ventures fueling economic development for the local area? He wishes. He's "trying every day."[30]

Notes

1 "Base Structure Report – Fiscal Year 2018 Baseline," Department of Defense. www. acq.osd.mil/eie/Downloads/BSI/Base%20Structure%20Report%20FY18.pdf.
2 247wallst.com/special-report/2018/09/06/americas-largest-military-bases/11/.
3 Catherine Lutz, *Homefront: A Military City and the American 20th Century* (Beacon Press, 2001).
4 Stephanie Savell and Rachel McMahon, "Numbers and Per Capita Distribution of Troops Serving in the U.S. Post-9-11 Wars in 2019, by State; *Costs of War Project.* https://watson.brown.edu/costsofwar/files/cow/imce/costs/social/Troop%20Numb ers%20By%20State_Costs%20of%20War_FINAL.pdf.
5 "Defense Spending by State: Fiscal Year 2019," U.S. Department of Defense Office of Economic Adjustment, released January 13, 2021. https://oea.gov/defense-spending-state-fiscal-year-2019.
6 "Defense Spending by State: Fiscal Year 2019," U.S. Department of Defense Office of Economic Adjustment, released January 13, 2021. https://oea.gov/defense-spending-state-fiscal-year-2019.
7 This history comes from James Leslie, *Pine Bluff and Jefferson County: A Pictorial History* (Virginia Beach, VA: The Donning Company Publishers, 1981.)
8 Max Boot, *War Made New: Technology, Warfare, and the Course of History: 1500 to Today* (New York: Gotham, 2006).
9 "History of Chemical Warfare," Wikipedia, https://en.wikipedia.org/wiki/History_of_chemical_warfare.
10 Russell Bearden, "Pine Bluff Arsenal," *Encyclopedia of Arkansas*, https://encyclopediaofa rkansas.net/entries/pine-bluff-arsenal-2927/.
11 Personal interview, March 25, 2015.
12 Francis J. Gavin, *Nuclear Statecraft: History and Strategy in America's Atomic Age* (Ithaca, NY: Cornell Studies in Security Affairs, 2012).
13 Jonathan B. Tucker and Erin R. Mahan, "President Nixon's Decision to Renounce the U.S. Offensive Biological Weapons Program," National Defense University Press, https://ndupress.ndu.edu/Portals/68/Documents/casestudies/CSWMD_CaseSt udy-1.pdf.
14 "The Future of the Global Norm Against Chemical Weapons," Arms Control Association, July/August 2021, www.armscontrol.org/act/2021-07/interviews/future-global-norm-against-chemical-weapons-interview-susanne-baumann-german.
15 Joby Warrick, *Red Line: The Unraveling of Syria and America's Race to Dismantle the Most Dangerous Arsenal in the World* (New York: Doubleday, 2021).
16 Lorraine Boissoneault, "How the Death of 2,000 Sheep Spurred the American Debate on Chemical Weapons," *Smithsonian Magazine*, April 9, 2018. www.smithsonianmag. com/history/how-death-6000-sheep-spurred-american-debate-chemical-weapons-cold-war-180968717/.

17 Phone interview, March 10, 2015.

18 "Base-Closing Plan Survives Assaults by Some on Hill," *Congressional Quarterly*, Washington, D.C.: CQ Almanac 1989, 45th ed pp. 470–473.

19 United States Department of Defense, *Base Closure and Realignment Report*, 2005.

20 www.politico.com/magazine/story/2016/07/philadelphia-what-works-navy-yard-214072.

21 Steve Levesque, "Maine Voices: Redevelopment efforts firmly on path to realizing vision for former Brunswick Navy base," *Portland Press-Herald*, June 26, 2021.

22 https://fas.org/sgp/crs/natsec/RS22147.pdf.

23 *Department of Defense, Base Structure Report*, FY 2018 Baseline.

24 Personal interview with Jack McNulty, March 26, 2015.

25 Phone interview, Bryan Barnhouse, 11/7/19.

26 "Arkansas Military Installations Impact Analysis," November 2016.

27 Phone interviews with Noel Foster, 12/9/19 and 12/10/19.

28 Phone interview, November 7, 2019.

29 HR 1047.

30 Phone interview, April 30, 2021.

6

LOS ALAMOS, NM

Weathering a Midlife Crisis

What's There

More than a million years ago, volcanos created the Rockies, including New
Mexico's Jemez Mountains at the southern end. The Jemez volcanos deposited horizontal layers of rock on the mountains' western side, forming New Mexico's iconic
tabletop mesas. Erosion then carved deep canyons into one mesa, creating what Los
Alamos locals call a handful of fingers reaching down toward the desert flats.

Up on top are the 800 buildings across 35 square miles of the Los Alamos
National Laboratory, where the Nuclear Age began, and is being perpetuated.

The views up there are stunning. J. Robert Oppenheimer, director of the
Manhattan Project, would lift the hard feelings of a bad day's work by looking at
the beauty and peace around him. The climate is exquisitely temperate, with about
three hundred clear and sunny days a year.

Rising up behind the town and the Lab is federally-protected National Forest.
On the way up there to a ski resort—close enough for Lab employees to hit
the slopes on their lunch hours—you pass large swaths of this forest that remain
denuded and charred by the wildfires of 2011 and 2013. Since a 2000 wildfire
spread to buildings at the Lab and surrounding homes, highly sophisticated and
well-resourced fire departments have so far protected the Lab and the town. The
Lab's director acknowledges that the future ravages of climate change will make
this task more challenging.

The Human Geography

Los Alamos County has about 19,000 residents, two-thirds of them in the town
itself and most of the rest in the bedroom community of White Rock, about five

DOI: 10.4324/9781003293705-7

FIGURE 6.1 Up above Los Alamos

Source: Photo courtesy of the author.

hundred feet down the mesa. 71 percent of them are white. At the base of the mesa lies Rio Arriba County, population 40,000, 90 percent of whom are Hispanic or members of one of the county's several sovereign nation pueblos.

The economic tale of these two counties is startling. Census figures put Los Alamos County residents near the top of America's list in per capita income. *Forbes Magazine*'s latest reckoning pegged the county at number three nationwide.[1] Rio Arriba's residents scrape the bottom of the list. Espanola, Rio Arriba's largest town, struggles to shed its reputation as the heroin overdose capital of America.[2] The trip from the bottom to the top of the canyon, in other words, traces one of the most extreme wealth divides in America.[3]

Los Alamos's relationship to New Mexico as a whole replicates the disparity. Los Alamos schools are generally agreed to be excellent, while a 2021 ranking of state school systems put New Mexican schools overall dead last.[4] In 2019 the state's poverty rate missed dead last—Mississippi occupied that spot—by two-tenths of a percent.[5]

Los Alamos doesn't look like one of America's richest places. Though some spacious homes perch on its outer mesas, the central core looks more frontier town than wealthy enclave. Its hidden wealth comes from the Lab's high salaries. While the highest are naturally reserved for upper-echelon scientists and administrators, the workforce as a whole takes home substantially more than the region's non-governmental economy can offer.

If you are seized by the calling to explore the fundamental facts of the universe through physics or chemistry, going to work at Los Alamos might be tempting. Your entry-level salary would easily exceed what you could make in academia. Attracting "the best minds" to this remote spot requires extra salary inducements.

The salary available to you in private industry could be competitive. But it's easier to think of yourself as a scientist, rather than a weapons maker, at Los

Alamos than, say, at Lockheed Martin. Sitting in the center of town next to Ashley Pond—an actual pond named for a Mr. Ashley Pond, whose ranch school was commandeered for the Manhattan Project—former Los Alamos physicist Minesh Bacrania describes the pleasures of intellectual cross-pollination at the Lab, which have attracted scientists since 1942:

> It was nice to be able to say, I have this idea, let me go find an expert in [a related field]. You start asking around and somebody says, "Oh go talk to whoever," and it turns out they're an expert in it.[6]

Every day a major human migration occurs up and down "The Hill," as the locals call it. Only 40.0 percent of the Lab's workforce lives in Los Alamos. Some choose a 25-mile commute from Santa Fe and its cultural offerings and amenities. But also: there simply isn't enough room for all of them up there.

The barracks and Quonset huts of the Manhattan Project had to be converted to permanent housing when the Cold War turned this wartime encampment into a major Cold War fixture. Much of this housing was eventually converted to privately-owned apartments; some retain their barracks-like look. But Los Alamos can't manufacture more flatland. One result is, as former physicist Bacrani says, the housing prices are "ridiculous." Which is another reason why most Lab workers don't live there and why those who do put Los Alamos on the *Forbes* list of richest counties every year.

Its chronic housing shortage is about to get worse: For the last few years the Lab has been hiring about five hundred extra people a year to fulfill the Energy Department's new mandate to invest massively in nuclear weapons.

How All This Came to Be Here

In places like Chicago, New York, and Berkeley during the late 1930s, as momentum crested toward war, nuclear physicists exploring the new world of the atom's interior realized that atomic fission could yield unprecedented explosive power. They knew such work was also going on in Germany. In a letter delivered personally by Albert Einstein, a few of them helped persuade President Franklin D. Roosevelt to approve a secret crash program that would assemble U.S. scientists, including many European emigres, to build a nuclear bomb.

Though Oppenheimer and his military overseer, General Leslie Groves, wrangled their way through the three years it took to get this done, they agreed immediately on Los Alamos as the place to do it.

A ranch school for boys tucked high up into the Jemez Mountains reminded Oppenheimer of a happy summer he'd spent nearby as a teenager, overcoming a sickly childhood with exhilarating physical pursuits. Groves saw a place close enough to railroads to provide a decent supply line, but remote enough, and geographically obscured enough, to have a chance of keeping the enormous operation a secret. Using its wartime powers, the Army took over the school, and moved a few ranchers and pueblo dwellers out, making way for construction equipment to move in. The conception of what they needed kept growing, until by August of 1943 20,000 construction workers were up there putting together what eventually became the Project's 268 separate buildings.[7]

Oppenheimer had little trouble recruiting most of this new scientific frontier's leading lights for what was officially dubbed "Project Y." They had been working remotely, in tandem, pushing toward radically new understandings of the basic structures of the universe. Now they could accelerate their discoveries by collaborating side-by-side with their peers. The younger scientists would get to work with the stars of their field.

The Project was a hotbed of different teams pursuing different theories. They were used to operating in obscurity, their head-in-the-clouds reputations personified by the woolly-headed Einstein. Now they were key players in the war effort, even if many didn't know the project's goal until July 16, 1945, when the "Trinity" test in the desert 210 miles south of Los Alamos revealed it, three weeks before the "practical use" of an atomic bomb on Hiroshima.

Disquiet over whether it *should* be achieved was present from the beginning.

A few of the physicists whose discoveries made the Manhattan Project possible, most notably Niels Bohr and Leo Szilard, recognized the full destructive potential of their discoveries long before the Project was conceived. But as we saw in Chapter 4, technological advances in lethality can get billed as the way to end all wars. When a new kind of war becomes capable of destroying humankind in a matter of hours, it becomes impossible to wage. And, so, according to this line of thought, establishing international control of this capability becomes the only sane way out.

As Szilard's colleague, Eugene Wigner, put it,

> We realized that, should atomic weapons be developed, no two nations would be able to live in peace with each other unless their military forces were controlled by a higher authority. We expected that these controls, if they were effective enough to abolish atomic warfare, would be effective enough to abolish also all other forms of war.[8]

The risk of the Manhattan Project, though, was that the weapons would be developed but the international controls would not. Two forces propelled its scientists to take the risk: the danger that Germany would win the war by building the bomb first, and the drive to push the frontiers of their science.

Oppenheimer summed up the latter motive this way:

> When you see something that is technically sweet you go ahead and do it and you argue about what to do about it only after you have had your technical success. That is the way it was with the atomic bomb.

The White House press release announcing the bombing of Hiroshima called the bomb "the greatest achievement of organized science in history."[9] The night before the Trinity test, the creator of the first chain reactions, Enrico Fermi, imagined an upside if the bomb failed: it would demonstrate to the world that if its best scientists couldn't make an atomic explosion, it couldn't be done.[10]

As doing it approached, various arguments not to do it were also raised, and pushed aside. It became clear that Germany had abandoned its bomb project. Then Germany surrendered. As it became clear that the Los Alamos bomb *would* be built, the argument shifted to: build it, but don't use it. Then: demonstrate its use, but not on human populations, at least not until the Japanese had the chance to consider surrendering, knowing what was about to happen to them. And, to lay the groundwork for international control, share the information with the world.

Weeks before the Trinity test, Szilard circulated a petition to President Harry Truman, signed by some of the Project's physicists, looking ahead:

> The development of atomic power will provide the nations with new means of destruction. The atomic bombs at our disposal represent only the first step in this direction, and there is almost no limit to the destructive power which will become available in the course of their future development. Thus a nation which sets the precedent of using these newly liberated forces of nature for purposes of destruction may have to bear the responsibility of opening the door to an era of devastation on an unimaginable scale.[11]

In a remarkable denial of his own agency, Truman confided to his diary: "I fear the machines are getting ahead of the morals." Then he gave the order to let them. Nationalist power politics, safeguarded by secrecy, had guided the Project from its inception and remained in control at the end.

The incineration of hundreds of thousands of humans, most of them civilians, in Hiroshima and Nagasaki followed. And the United States bears the responsibility for setting the world on the path to enable its own extinction. International control remains elusive.

Cold War Los Alamos

Beyond the idea of ending the war, Truman ordered the devastation of Hiroshima and Nagasaki to gain the upper hand in postwar geopolitics. Following Japan's surrender, he ordered up an arsenal of new bombs.

Some, including Oppenheimer, tried to contain a nuclear arms race, and actively opposed Los Alamos' first Cold War project—developing a hydrogen bomb.

In a meeting with Oppenheimer in September 1945, Truman opined that the Soviets would never be able to build a bomb.[12] But by August of 1949, the Soviets had, helped by spies who breached Los Alamos's wall of secrecy. The United States tested its first hydrogen bomb in November of 1952. The following year, the

Soviets did the same. France and Britain soon started their own nuclear weapons programs, and by 1974, China and India had joined them.

The one-off use of the Los Alamos mesa to build a nuclear weapon turned into an enduring enterprise. The facility began expanding toward its current total of more than 13 thousand employees. As the Lab grew, its bombs shrank. By miniaturizing nuclear warheads so that many could be delivered by a single missile, while increasing their explosive yield, the two superpowers could now visit nuclear devastation anywhere in the world within half an hour. "Civil defense" drills putting schoolchildren under their desks (I was one of them), and the "security" of Mutually Assured Destruction (MAD), became the abnormal Cold War normal. Once the world acquired enough weapons to destroy humankind many times over, the competition turned to acquiring more overlapping systems—subs, planes and silos—to deliver them at ever greater speeds, as well as the ever-receding goal of building "shields" to defend against them.

The Soviet Union's implosion of 1989–1991 raised the possibility of ending the nuclear nightmare through negotiated disarmament. As we'll see, Los Alamos National Laboratory, along with the rest of the nuclear complex, thought it might need to stave off its own extinction by dreaming up new reasons for being.

This period of reimagining didn't last long. Los Alamos was soon back to its core business of "improving" the nuclear arsenal. That's where we are now.

What Los Alamos Does Now

Los Alamos is the first and largest of the eight key facilities spread around places including: Oak Ridge, Tennessee; Hanford, Washington; and Aiken, South Carolina (more on them later)—that design, build and test components for the U.S. nuclear arsenal.

Its history infuses the place. The main road up the Hill becomes Trinity Drive when it gets to town, and crosses Oppenheimer Drive on the way. A couple of streets over is the national park where a few of the Ranch School cabins are preserved, and its carefully curated history told. There's a street named for Bikini Atoll, where tests of Los Alamos's hydrogen bombs blanketed a seven-thousand square mile area of the Pacific with radioactive dust and rendered the island permanently uninhabitable.

Was it black humor or blithe denial that led Albuquerque's minor league baseball team—"The Isotopes"—to erect statues of characters from The Simpsons in their ballpark? The show's recurrent anti-nuclear theme once featured Homer, nuclear power plant employee, narrowly averting a nuclear meltdown by pure luck.

As for what goes on inside, the Lab remains guided by the secrecy imperative baked in from the beginning.

A cohort of the leading original bombmakers, including the project director himself, argued that guarding the secrets of this new weapon would kill us all: that only creating an open system of internationally shared information and control over nuclear materials would prevent a nuclear war that no one could win. Pieces of such a system exist, most notably the on-going efforts to make the Nuclear Nonproliferation Treaty live up to its promise, and the inspectorate regime of the International Atomic Energy Agency (IAEA). In January of 2021 the first comprehensive Treaty on the Prohibition of Nuclear Weapons went into force, but without the support of the nine nuclear weapons states themselves (United States, Russia, France, China, United Kingdom, Pakistan, India, Israel, and North Korea). For them, the norm of guarding their own arsenals, and cloaking information about them, remains.

Secrecy

A "need to know" standard compartmentalized the participants in the Manhattan Project from each other. The standard endures. A couple of the Los Alamos Lab's shuttle-bus drivers invoked it to explain why they can't divulge anything about their route. Or their own names. Or anything that might jeopardize the "roof over our heads" that a Lab job provides.

For the scientists and technical people, this compartmentalization is codified into an elaborate hierarchy of security clearances. In *Nuclear Rites*, the anthropologist Hugh Gusterson describes the Lab as "an enormous grid of tabooed spaces and tabooed topics."[13]

By many accounts, Los Alamos's penchant for secrecy seems strangely to have *increased* after the Cold War's nuclear danger *decreased*. During the Cold War, one anonymous researcher said,

> Scientists had much more of a sense than they do now that they were free agents; they could talk to whoever they wanted to. Nowadays scientists are much more likely to say "I need someone's permission to talk." Or they'll say, "Don't come to Los Alamos, come to Santa Fe," or they'll say "Please don't write to me on my lab account, write to my gmail." Never used to happen.[14]

Why the tightened grip of security at the Lab? It may have several causes. The 9/11 attacks extended new "national security" controls far and wide over American life. And at Los Alamos in the years since, various scandals—involving both successful Russian spying and nuclear accidents—have given constricting the flow of information extra appeal.

Los Alamos's practices partake of a broader national problem. It is widely agreed, even in the upper reaches of the military, that the classification system has gotten out of hand. During the Trump administration the vice chairman of the Joint Chiefs of Staff described the penchant for over-classification as "just unbelievably ridiculous."[15] It also goes back a long way. For many years the number of rolls of

FIGURE 6.2 Minesh Bacrani

Source: Photo courtesy of the author, used with permission.

toilet paper used at Oak Ridge was classified, because Soviet agents might deduce how many people worked there.[16]

The Lab's secrecy, particularly in its core-weapons work, affects the quality of the science. Gusterson quotes one Los Alamos scientist acknowledging that once you start doing classified research, "the scientific community loses sight of you," because you can't discuss your findings. As the philosopher Sissela Bok says, "neither the [Lab scientists'] perception of a problem nor their reasoning about it then receives the benefit of challenge and exposure."[17]

Former Los Alamos physicist Minesh Bacrania agrees that "sometimes peer review is not as rigorous [in the weapons work]. The attitude is, 'We're working on this, it's a secret, we're asking for two million dollars.' But it may or may not be a good idea." In non-nuclear research, he says, "You're always struggling for money.… With the weapons work we'd always joke that they could just get a line item from Congress and they could do whatever they want."

Gusterson adds that the climate of secrecy provides nuclear scientists with psychological protection against questions raised about the utility or morality of their work. They can simply say when challenged: "You just don't know what I know."

Los Alamos' Nuclear Weapons Work

"It is essential that Los Alamos continues to lead the world in nuclear science," says its strategic plan. It is doing so now, in the sense that 75 percent of the current U.S. stockpile of nuclear warheads was designed there.[18]

U.S. nuclear strategy is based on the Triad, that is, on maintaining the capacity to deliver massive numbers of nuclear weapons by land, sea or air. The Lab supplies each of the three legs, including the B61 gravity bomb, designed to be dropped from a variety of fighter jets and bombers; the W76 and W88 design, to be launched from the Navy's Trident missile submarines; and the W78, to be carried to its targets by the Air Force's ICBMs. Each Trident II missile can carry as many as 12 W88 warheads, each of them over 30 times more powerful than the bomb that destroyed Hiroshima.[19]

Behind the Lab's deepest layers of security is a 233,000-square-foot building in a technical area called TA-55, where the United States processes its plutonium into weapons-grade material. This building "was constructed to withstand 200-mile-per-hour winds, and any credible seismic event."[20] (Los Alamos sits on a seismic fault line.) There are also facilities researching and testing improvements in the high explosives that trigger the bombs.

When the United States decided to end its Cold War underground nuclear testing, the Lab was handed a new mission: ensure the weapons work without exploding them. This Stockpile Stewardship program allowed LANL to vastly increase its supercomputing power to crunch experimental data and compare it with the calculations of computer modeling. By 2030, according to the current strategic plan, "scientific computing will be increasingly pervasive in all aspects of the LANL mission."[21]

Most scientists at the Lab like to think of themselves as researchers and designers, leaving the bomb-making to other parts of the nuclear complex. But their government is now requiring the Lab to get much more deeply into the production side. The United States now has a crash program to replace the plutonium cores, or pits, of the existing stockpile. While South Carolina's Savannah River facility will do the majority of the production, Congress is requiring Los Alamos to produce 30 new cores a year by 2026 and 80 by 2027. The Lab's own "Vision" for 2030 says meeting these goals will require "breakthroughs in plutonium production science … and related successful operations involving integrated criticality, safety and waste disposition."[22] Most independent experts are skeptical that Congress's mandate is feasible; even the Lab's management is hedging its bets. Compared to LANL's other achievements, they say, "the development of modernized efficient production capabilities … has been less successful."[23]

The production proceeds because those in charge assume the United States should be replenishing its stockpile of weapons of mass destruction—an assumption that needs far more scrutiny than it is getting. As does the question of whether the breakneck pace is necessary. In 2006 the elite JASON group of Pentagon scientific advisors estimated the life of the existing pits at a hundred years, meaning that our oldest pits would need replacing in 2090. In 2019 a team at Lawrence Livermore Lab extended the estimated timeframe to 150 years.[24]

Yet money for this "urgent" priority will be (almost) no object. The Biden administration's first 2022 budget request said the Lab needed $1.2 billion more than in fiscal year 2020, boosting its budget by almost a third to $3.8 billion.[25] More than 70 percent of this budget is devoted to preserving and enhancing the capability of the United States to wage nuclear war.

Nuclear Non-proliferation Work

A little over 10 percent of the budget is devoted to preventing such war. There are two ways to approach the non-proliferation task. You can work cooperatively with other nations to dismantle the world's nuclear arsenal. Or you can focus on preventing other countries from having them. LANL does the latter.

Nonproliferation became a bigger part of the Lab's public mission after the Cold War. Los Alamos styles itself "the premier national laboratory for nuclear nonproliferation," and that means nuclear detection, both remote and onsite. The Lab's pitch: "It takes a weapons lab to find a weapons lab."[26]

The Lab's search for more sensitive and powerful detection devices reaches to the heavens. As we'll see in the next chapter, space-based nuclear weapons are prohibited by treaty, but since detection devices are not, the Lab is mounting detectors on satellites. The detection mission also reaches into the earth: When North Korea tests its weapons, the ground shakes and the Lab feels it. The Lab also sends teams overseas to help the IAEA monitor suspected and verified nuclear sites. Lighthouse Directional Radiation Detectors scan potential radiation fields and track the prohibited movement of radioactive materials.[27]

Since the Lab is in the technology business, its approach to nonproliferation stays in that lane. Developing technologies to locate nuclear materials leaves the problem of what to do about them to politics and diplomacy. The U.S. commitment to disarmament under the Nuclear Nonproliferation Treaty has, to put it mildly, stalled.[28] So a strategy of preventing other countries from acquiring nuclear weapons is faced with the obvious limitations of "Do as I say, not as I do."

Beyond Nuclear Research

Not all of LANL's scientists work on nuclear matters. The non-nuclear research "has to be related to the mission of national security," says former LANL physicist Bacrani, though "It's a loose kind of thing." Since energy independence is a national security priority, he says, LANL has a modest project to improve solar energy technology. And the Lab got involved in addressing the Deep Water Horizon spill because "there were technical measurement skills that we had that other people didn't."

The Lab has applied supercomputing to other non-military priorities. It has, for example, built comprehensive databases for HIV gene sequencing, and in May of 2020 it announced that its work on an HIV vaccine would be shifting to a COVID-19 vaccine.[29]

The Bradbury Science Museum in town is devoted to showcasing LANL's current projects and achievements. The majority of the displays feature non-weapons projects.

But the Lab's budget tells a different story. Its budget for nuclear weapons work is climbing at the expense of those other priorities. Its Energy Efficiency and Renewable Energy portfolio now makes up 0.01 percent of the Lab's budget—a smaller portion than is devoted to Fossil Energy and Carbon Management. And the Science fund from which DoE money for the Lab's non-weapons research comes now accounts for 1.7 percent of its work.[30]

The nuclear weapons work is wholly funded out of Congress' appropriation to the National Nuclear Security Administration. Non-nuclear weapons research, though, usually requires fund-raising—from places like the National Institutes of Health and the National Science Foundation. As Bacrani puts it, to do the non-nuclear work "you're always struggling for money."

Contamination

The Manhattan Project scientists knew something about the damage their bomb would do. One of them mused before the final test that "Owing to the spreading of radioactive substances with the wind, the bomb could probably not be used without killing large numbers of civilians, and this may make it unsuitable as a weapon for use by this country."[31] Yet despite the proof provided by Hiroshima and Nagasaki, bomb-making at the site went into high gear in the Cold War. Though post-war bombs were tested far away in the Pacific, and later underground, radioactive waste also piled up around the Lab over the years.

For three decades this waste was simply dumped and covered over with dirt at a constellation of sites—some 2,100 of them, from small pits to large landfills. They stretch down the mesa from Los Alamos all the way to the Rio Grande. Finally in 1989 the Energy Department began cleaning them up, focusing first on burying the waste deeper, then on shifting toward carting more of it away. Three decades later, they're acknowledging that the cleanup process is barely half done.[32] In August of 2021, the Energy Department announced that for one of the Lab sites they were going back to an older, cheaper cap-and-cover strategy.[33]

Addressing the Lab's responsibilities for environmental safety, Lab director Thomas Mason says, "When unexpected things happen, we take responsibility for learning from that so we don't have a recurrence." He owes his job primarily to a series of "unexpected things" that got previous managers replaced.

In 2011, mishandling of plutonium rods at the manufacturing facility came close to sparking a nuclear chain reaction and subjecting workers to deadly radiation. A group of engineers in charge of ensuring nuclear safety at the Lab quit in protest of "what they considered the lab management's callousness about nuclear risks and its desire to put its own profits above safety." What was originally intended as a brief curative shutdown of the Lab's plutonium pit production facilities wound up lasting until 2018. That year, in DoE's nationwide safety report card on the nuclear weapons complex, Los Alamos alone did "not meet expectations."[34]

Also in 2011, a large forest fire came within three and a half miles of some of the many piles of "legacy waste" at the Lab. DoE and the state of New Mexico reached an agreement to speed up the hauling of waste to the Waste Isolation Pilot Plant (WIPP) in Carlsbad.

In 2014, inside WIPP's underground repository, one of the drums holding Los Alamos waste exploded, contaminating the facility and closing it for nearly three years. A *Los Angeles Times* reporter estimated the accident's cost at over $2 billion.[35] The DoE concluded that the wrong kind of material had been used to soak up liquid in the drum. A researcher who interviewed people directly involved in the accident has a more systemic explanation: the expedited schedule caused a variety of safety shortcuts.[36] Speeding up the removal of radioactive wastes from your neighborhood seems like a good idea, until you hear about haste making waste.

The Lab sits on top of a regional aquifer providing drinking water to Los Alamos, Santa Fe, Espanola, and the San Ildefonso Pueblo. The National Conference of State Legislators' Nuclear Legislative Workgroup reports that "hazardous chemicals, mainly tritium, have been found in surface waters and aquifers beneath LANL."[37] The chemicals spread in stormwater runoff from the mesa down the canyons. The current system for preventing such spread: Rain triggers a warning monitor, and engineers temporarily reroute the Rio Grande to avoid contaminating it further.

Joseph Maestas, Espanola's former mayor, and later a Santa Fe council member, says "When I was on the council, we had active policy statements against cap and cover. We want the legacy wastes removed."[38] But at a community meeting in 2019, the contractor responsible for the cleanup dampened these hopes, citing "safety, equity and economic issues." Safety: Digging it all up could cause leakages of radioactive materials, or accidents during transport. Equity: where does it all go? No one wants this stuff, as the protracted political fight over putting nuclear wastes from power plants as well as weapons facilities in Yucca Mountain makes clear.[39] Economic: Moving it all may not be cost-effective. How clean is clean enough? That's hard to know.

The gist of the Serenity Prayer—learning to live with what we can't change—sums up the philosophy of many Los Alamos residents. A docent at a Los Alamos museum says "There's industrial waste all over," citing Cleveland's once-burning Cuyahoga River. Gallows humor helps: the owner of a local frame shop says, "We tell each other, 'Let me know if I start glowing.'" Living in a place still struggling to contain its radioactive waste, says anthropologist Joseph Masco, requires navigating between paranoia—What are they not telling us? What will the effects be?—and numbness.[40]

In 2018, the same year it replaced the Lab's management, DoE signed a ten-year $1.3 billion "Los Alamos Legacy Cleanup Contract." One of the Lab's shuttle drivers mentions "a lot of safety protocols" instituted by the new management, Triad Security. People cut the grass around the Lab's administration building wearing suits and masks, he says, which "might be overkill."

But things keep happening. DP Road starts down the mesa a couple of blocks from Los Alamos's main supermarket. The businesses on one side have cheap rents because they sit across the road from one former waste dump and up the street from another one, where cleanup is underway. The site across the street has been turned over to the county for development, but on Valentine's Day 2020, excavation uncovered metal and glass contaminated with both uranium and plutonium. This was "a surprise," the National Nuclear Security Administration (NNSA) administrator said, but there was "no immediate threat to anyone out there right now." NNSA has locked the site, covered it in tarps, and commenced an investigation.[41]

Then in August of 2021 the Lab announced it had found 45 barrels of radioactive waste so potentially explosive that it would be too dangerous to move them. This followed a 2020 report from the Defense Nuclear Facilities Safety Board that hundreds of such barrels could be on the site.[42]

The DP Road site, where trucks continue to haul away contaminated material deemed safe to move, is to be zoned commercial and industrial. Next door to the other site, the one that was supposed to be clean, construction had begun on two apartment complexes, one for low-income people and the other for the elderly. In Los Alamos's housing crunch, all available land—even this land, at least for some groups—is being pressed into service. More contaminated waste was discovered at DP Road in 2021. Construction on the housing complex continues.[43]

Compounding the Lab's space problems is its time crunch to produce new plutonium pits. Considering the prolonged hiatus in pit production, Kingston Reif, Director of Disarmament and Threat Reduction at the Arms Control Association, says "there's no way they're going to achieve [the goal] by 2030."[44]

FIGURE 6.3 Joseph Maestas

Source: Photo courtesy of the author, used with permission.

But the pressure is on. In April of 2020, New Mexico's two senators urged the Lab to give watchdog groups and citizens a little more time to comment on the plans for accelerated pit production. NNSA responded that "a two-month extension of the comment period would have a severe adverse impact on the detailed planning and coordination" of the schedule.[45]

Former mayor Maestas notes the area residents' "conundrum." Efforts to push for more cleanup, or to question the plans to ramp up weapons manufacturing, face one enduring fact of life: The Lab is the biggest employer in Northern New Mexico. A high school diploma gets you a good $20–30 per hour government job, with benefits, doing, for example, environmental cleanup. Writing about the scandal surrounding the 2014 nuclear waste explosion, anthropologist Vincent Ialenti reported, "Multiple times I heard about a [cleanup] worker who, voicing safety concerns, was told something like: 'If you have a problem, there are plenty of people out there who would love to take your job!'"[46]

Jobs

On the side of the road connecting Santa Fe to Los Alamos sits the Buffalo Thunder Casino. Walking through its flashing neon hoopla gets you to a ballroom in the back where the Lab holds its monthly Community Conversation. This is part of a broader DoE effort to demonstrate the commitment of its nuclear-weapons facilities to the communities around them.

On a morning in early March 2020, every place setting on the round banquet tables includes a glossy brochure touting the "Economic Impact On New Mexico: Los Alamos National Laboratory." Lab director Thomas Mason begins his remarks citing the estimated $3.1 billion the Lab generates per year, supporting a total of 24,169 jobs, including people the Lab employs directly, plus the employees of its subcontractors, plus the jobs of people the employees create by spending money in their communities.

The extreme economic disparity makes this "a peculiar place," says Callum Bell, CEO of a small biotech spin-off from LANL technology, but, "Without the Lab Northern New Mexico would be a very depressed place.… If it wasn't there, there wouldn't be that injection of money into the economy."[47] The jobs figure is going to grow, Mason points out, to build the staff for pit production.

The report finds that the state as a whole gets more in taxes from the Lab and its employees than it provides the Lab in services. But an economic disparity turns up when this calculation is done for the northern region. Counties like Los Alamos that do substantial business with the Lab come out ahead. Those, like Rio Arriba at the bottom of the mesa, that aren't big Lab suppliers but have to provide support services for Lab employees, come out behind.

The Lab is trying to do more local subcontracting. Leading the discussion at one table is Eric Brown, LANL's division leader for Explosive Science and Shock Physics. He says there's a lot of talk at the Lab about how to "build capacity" in northern New Mexico, including for the construction projects the new pit pro-duction work will require, rather than relying on "companies brought in from Albuquerque and farther afield." The hope is to "have a broader relationship with those businesses, not just one-off contracts," to enable them to invest in equipment and training.

Ben Sandoval, who runs youth programs for the Espanola YMCA, says that they have five of their kids involved in robotics and connected to the Lab. But, "I have to be honest now," he says, "I believe there's a lot more subcontractors in the Los Alamos County area. We're not getting that growth in Rio Arriba County.… I'm struggling with why we're not building infrastructure in Espanola."

Mason talks about some ways they're trying. In 2019 the Lab gave a $500,000 grant to the Regional Development Corporation, an Espanola-based private non-profit whose goal is to "facilitate job growth and diversify the economies" of the surrounding counties. They offer business advice and micro-grants and no-interest loans for local manufacturing and technology companies. The "Economic Impact" brochure claims more than seven thousand projects with New Mexican small businesses. One wonders why it only mentions one: a Santa Fe start-up that "turns cremated ashes into alabaster-looking stones."

The Lab needs machinists, and it touts a program it has sponsored to train them. That program will be down in Santa Fe. The Lab's partnership with the University of New Mexico to train more mechanical engineers will be in Los Alamos. Its program to train Radiological Control Technicians—to try to prevent the accidents that keep happening as they ramp up their handling of plutonium—will be at Espanola's Northern New Mexico College.

Mason also says LANL's match for its employees' giving campaign will incen-tivize donations to the local area. And he mentions LANL scientists contributing to STEM education in the community. For fiscal year 2021, though, the line item in the LANL budget for Workforce Development for Teachers and Scientists—$532 million in 2019—was zeroed out.

Diversification

The Los Alamos National Laboratory is, to repeat, by far the largest source of jobs in northern New Mexico. Among economic development professionals, though, it is axiomatic that putting all your eggs in one basket isn't the right recipe for eco-nomic health. Communities need to diversify their economies beyond depend-ence on one thing. As Joseph Sanchez, vice president of Hacienda Home Centers in Espanola and past president of the local Major Subcontractors Consortium, puts it, "The last thing we want is for northern New Mexico to become so dependent on the laboratory that it's not creating a diversified economy."

While the Lab has put some money behind its rhetorical support for diversifi-cation, the scale has not made much of a dent in the economic disparity. Former mayor Maestas says the "contrast between Los Alamos and Rio Arriba counties has never really changed ... since the Manhattan Project." One local business owner at the Community Conversation also notes that, in one respect, the Lab gets in the way of diversification. "We train people for our businesses, and then they end up going to work at [Los Alamos] because the Lab can offer better benefits than a small business can."

"The Labs suck the talent out of local businesses," adds Greg Mello, who runs the Los Alamos Study Group, a local activist alliance. Mello mentions hearing from the manager of a local newspaper about someone he had just trained to lay out ads, who then quit "Because the Lab will pay him three times as much as [the newspaper] can."

LANL has one major asset to put behind spreading the jobs base beyond its own enterprise: a vast repository of research—of intellectual property—some of which could be transferred outside the Lab to seed businesses in the area.

Back in 1974 legislation created a system of Cooperative Research and Development Agreements (CRADAs) enabling the federal labs to work with entrepreneurs in commercializing lab technology. The idea was that some of the trillions of taxpayer dollars spent on military R&D should be turned to productive use outside the military's world. Periodic legislation since then to strengthen the success of technology transfer from the labs is one indicator that these good intentions have a way to go to live up to their promise. As does a 2020 New Mexico law creating a tax credit for the state's labs to give them a financial incentive to get more involved in technology transfer to local small businesses.[48]

The Federal Labs Consortium claims as members more than three hundred federal research and development facilities scattered around the government. The Consortium has ramped up its activities in recent years—tech transfer trainings, competitions for most successful CRADAs, and so on. A representative bulletin from August 2021 advertises shared research between NIH and an Army Research Institute on hearing loss from explosive devices, and a project from the Pacific Northwest National Lab purporting to transform kelp and fish waste into carbon-neutral diesel-like fuel.

When you ask northern New Mexico locals about technology transfer, two poster children come up over and over: two local companies founded by former Lab scientists making use of Lab-originating technologies. The first is Pebble Labs, a biotech company in Los Alamos developing disease-resistant, genetically modified agriculture. A $4 million state economic development grant in 2019 enabled Pebble Labs to expand its operations and envision a workforce of 230. Los Alamos County gave the company two parcels of land to build a job-creating biotech campus adjacent to its lab. By March of 2020, however, the company announced its first layoffs due to "soft investment" and, in August of 2021, announced plans to cancel the agreement to build the biotech campus.[49]

The other poster child is Descartes Labs based in Santa Fe, which collects and analyzes geospatial data for purposes such as detecting levels of methane in oil fields and the effects of weather and soil changes on agriculture. The company is valued at $200 million,[50] supported by venture capital as well as state and local development funding.

"We want to see more spin-offs," but beyond those two, Maestas says, the examples are "few and far between."

The Lab did pioneer one of the most significant scientific advances of the modern age. In researching the effect of radiation on DNA, Lab scientists developed the concept of sequencing the human genome. Until 1992 it was home to the national database, called Gen Bank. That year, Gen Bank moved to the campus of the National Institutes of Health in Bethesda, Maryland. New Mexico's senior senator at the time made sure that a piece of the project stayed in the state. The National Center for Genomic Research is in Santa Fe, though its workforce has declined to 20.

The day before the Community Conversation, New Mexico's Department of Economic Development holds an "Innovate New Mexico Technology Showcase" at the Sandia Golf Club in Albuquerque, with panelists like the CEO of Descartes Labs and exhibitors from other local tech companies. Jon Clark, formerly at LANL, represents the Department. One problem with trans-ferring technology from the labs, he says, is that too often they're just licensing technology to out-of-state companies rather than developing them here. (The DC-area and Silicon Valley are major destinations.) The Department is working on a five-year science and technology plan to keep more of this technology gold mine in-state.

One of the exhibitors from a local biotech company talks about why LANL has less of a "footprint" in the state through successful technology commercializa-tion than does Sandia National Laboratories, the state's other nuclear weapons lab. He agrees that "A lot of what [LANL does] gets exported to basically DC." And he sees the two labs as having very different cultures: "Trying to get intellectual property out of Los Alamos is a nightmare.... Compared to Los Alamos, Sandia almost gives it away.... Sandia interacts with the community more, so develops more collaborations that way.... And there's more involvement with the Small Business Administration here."

Part of this comes down to proximity. Sandia Lab is in Albuquerque; getting to LANL means that long drive up the Hill. Conceding the point that Sandia outperforms Los Alamos in technology transfer, a source close to LANL's man-agement also notes that, because LANL focuses more on research and Sandia on engineering, Sandia's work has a head start toward commercialization.

And finally,

> At Los Alamos you have to jump through all their security hoops. There's an extra shell outside of Los Alamos.... You go through security and then through intermediate security areas. Whereas at Sandia, you're still in a security area, but the lab is probably there in the same building.

Lawrence Livermore Lab, the third nuclear weapons lab in the Complex, outside of San Francisco, likewise has focused more on technology commercialization. According to a source long familiar with both labs, Livermore looked at the protocol requiring potential industry partners to wait an hour for a badge and an escort as a problem that needed to be solved. In 2020 they opened an advanced manufacturing research facility right next door to the Lab, to facilitate commercial collaborations.

LANL's technology transfer effort is coordinated by its Richard P. Feynman Center for Innovation (named for one of the Manhattan Project's pioneering physicists). Though its website lists many technologies ripe for the picking, the Feynman Center is less forthcoming with examples of those that have been picked, or what they have accomplished in the real world. It highlights one in September 2020: An "Air Evacuation Bridge" that "would potentially enable hospitals to adapt, utilize, and re-purpose existing and otherwise infrequently used equipment in the fight against COVID-19." How, is not described. The Lab was "seeking a commercialization partner."[51] A year later the post has not been updated; in other words, no partner has apparently been found. As this book went to press, no new photographs had joined it. The Lab posted its last overall progress report on its technology-transfer effort in 2018. Inquiries to learn more were not returned.

Whatever the fate of the U.S. commitment to nuclear weapons, the technology repository at Los Alamos might be useful in fueling an economy for purposes beyond nuclear weapons, building prosperity for a region and a state that could really use some. It hasn't happened yet.

The fiscal year 2022 budget for the Lab's Office of Technology Transitions is $50,000, down from $55,000 in the last Trump budget.[52] For fiscal year 2021 the budget for its technology transfer effort, housed at the Richard P. Feynman Center, is $10.3 million, or three tenths of one percent of LANL's total. The budget for its Community Partnership Office in 2020 was $2 million, down from $2.3 million the previous year. LANL's economic outreach seems largely sincere. The funds applied to it, though, matched against the scale of the region's economic disparity problem, also bring terms like "drop in the bucket" and "window dressing" to mind.

The latest Big Think economic development proposal is the idea of an Innovation Triangle: Santa Fe's director of economic development, Richard Brown, speaks enthusiastically about a masterplan linking housing, transportation, cultural amenities, and high-tech employment in Los Alamos, Santa Fe, and Albuquerque. He acknowledges that it is as yet mostly a glimmer in the eyes of a few economic planners.[53] Joseph Maestas wonders why Espanola isn't part of it.

The Nuclear Complex

The whole of which Los Alamos is a part has over the years generated an enormous literature—historical, technical, and political. No matter how inured to the

Nuclear Age we get, the Complex's larger meaning—the capacity nuclear weapons bestow to extinguish life on earth on any given day—keeps people thinking and writing. Here I'll only try to lay out the basics.

Responsibility for what is now officially called the Nuclear Security Enterprise is shared by the Energy Department, which oversees the making and maintaining of the weapons themselves, and the Defense Department, in charge of the multiple systems—planes, submarines, and land-based missiles—poised to get them where they're pointed. The term nuclear complex refers to the sites around the country that collectively produce nuclear materials, fabricate nuclear and nonnuclear components, assemble and disassemble nuclear warheads, test them, integrate weapons and DoD's "delivery vehicles," and deal with the environmental consequences of it all. The federal government owns them, and contractors operate them (they are therefore "GOCOS").

In the beginning was Los Alamos. It maintains its flagship status today, commanding the most employees and largest budget in the Complex, a role that plutonium production will grow. During the Manhattan Project it was supplied with enriched uranium by the Y-12 plant in Oak Ridge, Tennessee. and with plutonium by the Hanford Engineering Works near Richland, Washington.

Oak Ridge still produces and stores all the Complex's enriched uranium—for the "secondaries" that combine with the "primary" plutonium pits to make a nuclear weapon. Hanford provided the "primaries" until it was shut down in the years before the Cold War ended. The cleanup of "severe" contamination there is projected to last until 2060 and cost a total of $100 billion.[54] This will be followed by "indefinite long-term stewardship," that is, we broke it, we own it.

To accommodate the Cold War demands for a massive U.S. nuclear stockpile, the Complex rapidly expanded. In 1949 it added Sandia laboratory, which would engineer the designs that Los Alamos produced. The Complex is now also responsible for the "systems integration" of the weapons into the delivery vehicles. Also that year, a former production plant for World War II Navy fighters was converted into the Kansas City Plant (now the Kansas City National Security Campus), which manufactures most of the nonnuclear mechanical and electronic components for the weaponry.

Then in 1951 came the Pantex Plant in Amarillo, Texas, a new facility solely dedicated to assembling the weapons. Also that year, the United States began its atmospheric testing of the weapons within the continental United States at the Nevada Test Site, taking up a space nearly the size of Connecticut. In 1992, the year a series of post-Cold War test ban treaties shut atmospheric testing down, the United States broke ground on the Savannah River Site near Aiken, South Carolina, where five reactors began producing plutonium and tritium. A year later, contamination from the reactors shut these reactors down, and the site began focusing mainly on remediation and the recycling of tritium from dismantled warheads. Now, however, the site has been assigned the primary responsibility, shared with Los Alamos, for restarting the production of plutonium pits.

By 1952 the Complex had added a third lab into the mix: Lawrence Livermore, which designed most of the nuclear weapons not assigned to Los Alamos, including the first warhead for a U.S. submarine-launched ballistic missile.

And, finally, as part of its on-going struggle to deal with the radioactive legacy of its nuclear complex, in 1999 the federal government established the Waste Isolation Pilot Project (WIPP) in Carlsbad, New Mexico. In addition to serving as Los Alamos's repository, WIPP is now home to waste shipped from Livermore, Rocky Flats, Savannah River, and Hanford, among others. As we've seen, this mission has not gone smoothly.

How Many, What Kinds, for What Reasons, at What Costs?

By 1955 the Complex was going full-tilt piling thousands of nuclear warheads a year onto the stockpile. At the time of the 1960s Cuban Missile Crisis, the pile held about 25,000 warheads. At the peak, in 1965, the United States was sitting on 31,255 warheads.[55] The question, "Once your weapons can destroy the world many times over, why do you need more?" has never received much of an answer.

The U.S. postwar dreams of keeping its new weapons to itself had been quickly supplanted by the USSR's intentions, and capacity, to keep pace. This parallel buildup produced the first deterrence doctrine: Mutually Assured Destruction (MAD), as in: Having enough weapons to ensure that nobody would be crazy enough to use them, knowing they would themselves be obliterated. As scholar Joseph Masco puts it, "[D]uring the Cold War living on the brink of nuclear combat quickly became naturalized as the very foundation of national security."[56]

But almost as soon as the arms race got underway came the efforts—from the foreign policy elite to the grassroots—to find a way out of it. Deterrence doctrine now had a complement: international nuclear arms control. A series of bilateral negotiations—"détente" and SALT (Strategic Arms Limitation Treaty) talks in the 1970s, START (Strategic Arms Reduction Treaty) talks in the 1980s—began to take big chunks out of the stockpiles. Yet the ones that were left retained their ability to end life on Earth in a matter of hours. Grassroots movements began pressing governments to stop the arms race in its tracks and move beyond arms control to nuclear disarmament. The largest was the Nuclear Freeze movement, which, in June of 1982, held what was then the biggest demonstration in history —a million people crammed into New York's Central Park.[57]

The most important of the treaties connected arms control and disarmament. The Nonproliferation Treaty (NPT) went into force in 1970. It bound, and still binds, nearly all of the world's nonnuclear states never to acquire nuclear weapons, and the declared nuclear powers, including all members of the UN Security Council, to pursue nuclear disarmament toward ultimately eliminating their arsenals. Fifty years on, though, the nuclear states have not disarmed, and since President Obama's inspiring 2009 speech in Prague, they have stopped talking much about doing so.

The United States has roughly 3,800 warheads, 1,750 of them deployed, the remainder held in reserve, plus about 2,000 retired and waiting to be dismantled—enough to blow up the world many times over. They include several warhead designs for each leg of the nuclear triad: about 400 of them deployed on Intercontinental Ballistic Missiles sitting in silos, with roughly 900 Trident missiles cruising the world attached to submarines, and about 450 bombs ready to be loaded on B-52, B-2 and soon B-21 bombers based in the United States and Europe.[58] These numbers are approximations because in 2018 the Trump administration began classifying them. And while the Biden administration's introductory National Security memorandum promised the highest standards of transparency, as of 2021 these numbers remain classified.

During the time the United States has been reducing the numbers of its nuclear weapons, it has been increasing their explosive power and speed of delivery. The majority of the stockpile is located in two places: Kirtland AFB, near the Sandia lab in Albuquerque, and in Kitsap, Washington. Conventional wisdom holds that deterrence requires hanging on to some of them.

There are significant dissenters. One of the Air Force officers who spent time during the 1970s in a Minuteman ICBM silo waiting for the order to launch, Bruce Blair founded the organization Global Zero in 2008 with a plan to get rid of them. Global Zero has assembled a large cadre of international experts and political leaders promoting a series of steps leading to the elimination of world nuclear stockpiles. Organizations large and small around the world push the same goal with a range of tactics from research to lobbying to civil disobedience.

Frustration with the decades-long failure of the Nonproliferation Treaty to get the world any closer to abolition launched the International Campaign to Abolish Nuclear Weapons (ICAN) that same year. It claims more than five hundred partner organizations in more than a hundred countries. In 2017 ICAN won the Nobel Peace Prize for successfully steering the United Nations to pass the Treaty on the Prohibition of Nuclear Weapons. The treaty went into force in January of 2021, when 50 countries had ratified it; none were nuclear powers.

In his Prague speech, Obama declared "clearly and with conviction America's commitment to seek the peace and security of a world without nuclear weapons." The path he outlined ran through arms control. The new Strategic Arms Reduction Treaty his administration negotiated with the Russians prescribed further stockpile reductions—the preview, he said, to further cuts and negotiations to bring all the nuclear states toward abolition. Integral to the plan was bolstering international control.

But when it came time to ratify the treaty, Obama had lost his congressional majority. To get the cuts in each country's stockpile, he agreed to a (devil's) bargain: in exchange the United States would commit to replacing almost its entire nuclear arsenal, warheads and delivery systems and all. Under this scenario, a win for arms control requires a trillion dollar-plus win for the arsenal's military industrial interests.

Then the Trump administration's Nuclear Posture Review reversed the Obama plan to reduce the role of nuclear weapons in the country's national security strategy. Whereas Obama's replacement deal traded off massive new costs for reduced numbers of warheads, Trump began an assault on the structures of arms control—the Intermediate-Range Nuclear Forces Treaty, New START, the Open Skies Treaty, flirting with the idea of restarting testing, building a low-yield, destabilizing, "usable" nuclear weapon—while goosing the budget. In 2020 the Air Force's chief of nuclear operations described the replacement program not in terms of preventing nuclear war but as giving the United States the edge to compete and win in war.[59]

One long-standing idea for heading in the opposite direction, toward a smaller role for the arsenal in the U.S. defense strategy, is to cut out one of the legs of our nuclear triad. This would reduce both the overkill in our capacity to start a nuclear war and the dangers that we will do so inadvertently. It's generally agreed that the best leg to choose would be the land-based Intercontinental Ballistic Missiles (ICBMs), because they are most vulnerable to attack. The Pentagon appeared to take this idea off the table in September of 2020 by signing a $13.3 billion down payment contract with Northrop Grumman on an $85 billion project to build a whole new set of ICBMs. The contract is sole source, meaning not competitively bid, and will be spread across numerous states, including Utah, Alabama, Colorado, California, and Maryland.[60] The Pentagon has projected total costs for the program over decades at $264 billion.[61]

While the replacement plan is underway, its purpose as a path to deep stockpile reductions is, as yet, not. The Biden administration *has* reversed its predecessor by recommitting to the New START framework limiting U.S. and Russian stockpiles for another five years. And it has ordered a new review of U.S. nuclear policy to be completed in 2022, including a commitment to again reduce the role of nuclear weapons in U.S. security policy, and to see new arms control agreements with Russia and China.

Costs

The price tag for replacing the whole stockpile and its multiple delivery systems was initially estimated at more than $1 trillion, and has been on the way to doubling since then.[62] It included costs such as $100 billion for the B-21 bomber, whose operations we visited in Palmdale, and $350 billion for the new and refurbished nuclear weapons themselves, as well as a successor to the Minuteman missile and 12 new *Columbia*-class nuclear submarines currently costed out at $109.8 billion.[63]

In addition to closeting information about how many weapons our nuclear arsenal holds, the federal government has never released a comprehensive accounting of what they cost. An intensive effort by a team at the Brookings Institution in 1998 produced *Atomic Audit*, which assessed the total expenditures during the first 50 years since the Manhattan Project, including the costs of the environmental cleanup. They arrived at the figure of $5.5 *trillion*, noting that since some costs were classified, this was unquestionably a conservative estimate.[64]

How much is enough to constitute a deterrent? The Brookings group quoted retired Army Chief of Staff General Maxwell Taylor, arguing in 1960, when the U.S. strategic arsenal already had about 7,000 warheads, that "a few hundred missiles" (presumably armed with a few hundred warheads) "would satisfy deterrence." A few years later, when Secretary of Defense Robert McNamara pegged the equivalent of 400 megatons as sufficient for Mutually Assured Destruction, the stockpile contained about 17,000 warheads.[65] The extreme disparity between needs and expenditures equals waste, extreme overkill, and increased danger, and it continues.

The Trump administration's fiscal year 2021 budget request increased the previous year's spending on the total replacement plan by 19 percent. Spending on nuclear weapons specifically got the biggest boost, increasing by 25.0 percent. In its plan for the outyears, the nuclear budget would absorb an increasingly large percentage of total military spending through the early 2030s.[66]

In addition to promising his government would reduce the role of these weapons in U.S. security policy, Candidate Biden promised to reduce our "excessive expenditure" on them. So far, he has not. His budget continues the overall Trumpian trajectory, both on funding and on the architecture of the replacement program.[67] In May of 2021, the Congressional Budget Office costed out the program up through 2030 at $634 billion, an increase of $28 billion from its estimate two years before.[68] The new Nuclear Posture Review, due in 2022, would signal whether Biden's promise to change this trajectory will be kept.

It Could Have Been Different

Following the death of the Soviet Union, the negotiated START I agreement cut U.S. nuclear warhead stockpiles almost in half (from 10,000 to 6,000). And, as mentioned, U.S. military spending dropped by almost a third from its Cold War peak. The new bilateral Cooperative Threat Reduction program began providing funding and technical assistance to the former Soviet states to secure, dismantle, and remove the nuclear weapons and fissile material stockpiles from their territory.

Congress commissioned a small federal agency called the Office of Technology Assessment (OTA) to scope out how the United States should adjust to these extraordinary developments on the home front. Before being shut down in 1995 by the new Republican congress, OTA produced two landmark reports. The first, *After the Cold War: Living With Lower Defense Spending*, looked at the role of federal, state, and local governments in helping workers, communities, and businesses adjust by "finding productive civilian uses for the resources and people formerly devoted to the Nation's defense."

The second, *Defense Conversion: Redirecting R&D*, focused mostly on the three nuclear weapons labs.[69] This report began, "The end of the Cold War frees the Nation to turn more of its energies into building a stronger civilian economy." It examined ways to strengthen the mechanisms of technology transfer from the labs to create jobs in the private sector, particularly the CRADAs between lab scientists and private companies. In looking at the options for the labs, including radically downsizing them, the report argued that, "As public institutions, the labs' existence is best justified if they serve missions that are primarily public in nature."

The end of the Cold War offered the country an opening to turn these R&D institutions toward national challenges beyond exercising military power—those that have clear benefits to human welfare but need pre-competitive R&D investment. They could be a place where R&D on non-military national needs could be pursued to a stage when private enterprise would be ready to seize them. The final section of the report focuses on an illustrative example: the role these institutions might play developing such advances in clean transportation as low-emission cars and high-speed rail—like the ones we saw Southern California was pursuing.

Civil society also got involved in seizing this opening to rethink the Labs' post-Cold War mission. From academia, the Project on Regional and Industrial Economics (PRIE) at Rutgers University published a year-long study in 1995, "*Coming in from the Cold: The Future of Los Alamos and Sandia National Laboratories.*" The report noted that the Labs' budget had expanded by 60 percent during the 1980s, and then declined only 12 percent after the Cold War ended. Based on two independent assessments by nuclear scientists, it concluded that the deterrent could be maintained while reducing the nuclear weapons work by two-thirds. One-third, they argued, could be shared by deficit reduction, environmental remediation, dismantlement and an expansion of the non-proliferation mission. And the remaining one-third they recommended dedicating to new non-nuclear missions in energy, environment, health, and transportation.

The researchers pointed to capabilities the Lab already had in these areas but described them as scattered and marginal. The challenge would be to focus on missions that were clearly in the public interest, were similar in scale to the nuclear mission, and drew on capabilities the Lab was uniquely suited to provide.

> [N]on-nuclear missions … will be easier to fund and protect for the long run if they are bundled together to address major national needs … it will require considerable entrepreneurship on the part of Lab managers to shape these into new broad mission areas and defend their location at the Labs.

The researchers outlined reforms to the then-anemic efforts at technology transfer that could turn a strengthened program of non-nuclear research into economic diversification for the region.

The Los Alamos Study Group produced its own study in 1992: "*The Conversion of Los Alamos National Laboratory to a Peacetime Mission: Barriers and Opportunities.*" They examined the pros and cons of four scenarios: (1) the status quo; (2) shifting the Lab's research agenda toward the non-proliferation mission, with a smaller budget; (3) the lab would become a "Critical Technologies" lab and turn toward more research on alternative energy sources; (4) it would become a "Disarmament Lab" with a smaller budget devoted to overseeing the downsizing of the stockpile to a number necessary for a deterrent while supporting cooperative global security measures.

Amid talk that Los Alamos's mission might be obsolete, its employees wondered whether they'd have a job the next year. The editor of the *Santa Fe Reporter* remembers a "weaponeer" describing the Lab as

> a charging rhino. Its target is gone, but it has too much momentum to stop, too much poundage for quick turns. Meanwhile, lab workers cling to the back of the beast, not knowing where they will be at the end of the ride.[70]

Looking back from years later, one writer from Oak Ridge remembered worrying that an

> obviously debatable line of thought held that the national laboratory system, which was considered by many a Cold War appliance for winning the nuclear arms race, was obsolete. Even less-informed ideas were gaining traction, such as applying military base-closing criteria to the labs, or arbitrarily reducing the system by 25 percent.[71]

These worries further gained traction when the federal government itself began entertaining ideas of radical restructuring. In 1994 the Secretary of Energy convened a Task Force on Alternative Futures for the DoE National Laboratories, unofficially called the *Galvin Report* after its chair, the former CEO of Motorola. But in the end the task force members' conception of alternatives leaned heavily toward the status quo. Their idea of post-Cold War change was to shift the Labs from building and explosively testing new nuclear weapons to "stewarding" the existing stockpile and preventing other countries from acquiring them.

The task force mostly side-stepped questions of closures, consolidations, and budgets. And they were mostly skeptical of the Labs' efforts to help commercialize their technologies, particularly through CRADAs. They did urge the Department of Energy to give higher priority, with "a heightened sense of urgency," to the cleanup. They admonished the labs not to go scrambling for new missions, but rather to stick with what they were good at, defined as national security, energy, and environmental remediation.

Remarkably (or maybe not, given its corporate leadership), the task force trained its greatest rhetorical enthusiasm on this "bold" idea: "The principal organizational recommendation of this task force is that the laboratories be as close to corporatized as is imaginable." They cast the government in this scenario as the customer, saying "world-class commercial customers do not tell their suppliers how to do things." Management of each lab could be "formed with many of the basic principles and criteria of a conventional commercial corporation." Major savings, they envisioned, could follow this move to the "higher standards of self-initiated … quality service to customers that are being perfected in the private sector."

One brief section of the report gestures toward a genuinely alternative mission for the labs:

> The Task Force generally believes that the highest priority research areas by the Department [of Energy] and the laboratories are in the areas of energy efficiency, conservation, renewable energy sources (including photovoltaics, biomass, wind, geothermal and hydrogen) and more efficient recovery of gas and oil resources.

But pursuing this research, they hasten to add, depends on close coordination and consensus building with the energy-supply industry (which could be counted on to be less than cooperative.)[72]

DoE declined to fully "corporatize" the labs. They have been managed by a revolving succession of profit and nonprofit structures over the years, involving universities and commercial and military contractors. (Currently, Los Alamos director and the CEO of its management overseer, Triad Security, are the same person.) But the labs' missions have remained largely the same, as their budgets have gradually climbed. While each of the non-nuclear mission areas proposed by government and civil society has a presence at Los Alamos, it is more of a foothold than a focus.

The Federal Laboratories Consortium continues to highlight a grab bag of technology transfer efforts, as does DoE's own Office of Technology Transitions. But with a total budget of $19 million to cover the entire federal laboratory system, it isn't going to turn the labs into significant engines of growth for the civilian economy.[73]

During the post-Cold War period, DoE did expand its focus on alternative energy development, opening an Office of Energy Efficiency and Renewable Energy (EERE), and ARPA-E, an energy-focused research agency modeled after the Defense Department's Defense Advanced Research Projects Agency (DARPA). The 2021 budget request gave these initiatives the back of its hand: it cut ARPA-E by 173 percent and EERE by 75 percent.[74] It also cut funding for the National Renewable Energy Laboratory (NREL)—the only national lab focused on renewable energy—more than in half.[75] And it increased the nuclear weapons budget by 25 percent. In keeping with its both-and approach to budgeting, the first Biden budget reverses the cuts to renewable energy without cutting spending on nuclear weapons. It is one step in the right direction, but not the kind of change that pushed the labs during the post-Cold War period to rethink their nuclear missions.

And It Must be Different

But the story isn't over. Periodically, we are pushed to reexamine what we mean by national security and how we should be achieving it. The end of the Cold War gave us one such push. The climate crisis—accelerating toward irreversibility, visible, felt and well-documented—is giving us another. In considering possible missions for the labs beyond nuclear weapons, the Galvin Commission urged the labs to stick with what they knew—that is, energy. Had this charge been embedded in an industrial policy, with the resources to back it up, focused on converting our economy to run on clean-energy sources, a new economic base for northern New Mexico might have been born. As it is, the pieces of such a policy are modest, and scattered. The nascent plan for an Innovation Triangle in northern New Mexico that would seed the economy with commercialized lab technologies so far looks like what economists call "technology push"—building businesses out of anything that will sell, rather than building manufacturing hubs around national needs.

The means to lift the New Mexico economy are pulling in two directions: toward the heavens, and the earth. Its wide-open flat spaces are ideal as a launching pad for massive solar and wind installations, but also for exotic space travel. National need favors one, and tech mega-fortunes the other.

Conclusion

Many observers are skeptical that, as Jay Coghlan, the activist director of New Mexico Nuclear Watch, put it, the leopard can change its spots.[76]

Nor does it seem to want to. In late April of 2021, Los Alamos director, Thomas Mason, held another Community Conversation, on zoom this year rather than in a ballroom. He walked through the bullet points of LANL's community engagement, including $413 million in contracts to small businesses (we are "contractually obligated" to increase these, he said), a lot of jobs, and individual staff members' donations and service hours to local nonprofits. After parrying such customary topics as the latest toxic cleanup problems and why the Lab was back in the plutonium-pit production business, he was asked why, to address its chronic shortage of space, LANL recently expanded to Santa Fe rather than Espanola, where there would be "more economic impact"? His response was to say, that's where the vacant office space was.

Someone else mentioned the new Energy Secretary's promise to turn her department toward more investment in renewable energy. Would that mean less money for its nuclear weapons mission? The question hearkened back to the post-Cold War period, when Los Alamos took tentative steps toward reimagining itself for a denuclearized world. But while leaving open the possibility of doing more on renewables if that's the way the budgetary winds blew, Mason noted pointedly that record funding for the nuclear weapons mission "has bi-partisan support."

At the end of the hour someone raised again the elegantly simple question that has hung over the Lab unsettled since its scientists first arrived on top of the mesa: "What does Los Alamos do for New Mexico?"

His face settling into a look of resignation, Director Mason started over on his bullets.

As for what Los Alamos does for the rest of the world, year by year it has become clearer that dabbling around the edges with solar energy research projects is not enough. The daily and accelerating ravages of climate change require a massive mobilization, and as the most-highly resourced national laboratory in the country, Los Alamos should be part of it.

Notes

1 Andrew DePietro, "The Richest Counties in the U.S. by State," *Forbes*, March 8, 2021. www.forbes.com/sites/andrewdepietro/2021/03/08/the-richest-counties-in-the-us-by-state/.

2 Claire Provost, "Atomic City, USA: How once-secret Los Alamos became a millionaire's enclave," *The Guardian*, November 1, 2016, www.theguardian.com/cities/2016/nov/01/atomic-city-los-alamos-secret-town-nuclear-millionaires.

3 Paul Toscano, "America's Biggest Wealth Gaps," CNBC, March 29, 2012, www.cnbc.com/2012/03/29/Americas-Biggest-Wealth-Gaps.html?page=6.

4 Adam McCann, "2021's States with the Best and Worst School Systems," wallethub.com, July 26, 2021, wallethub.com/edu/e/states-with-the-best-schools/5335.

5 "Quick Facts," U.S. Census Bureau, 2019, www.census.gov/quickfacts/fact/table/MS,NM,US/PST045219.

6 Personal interview, March 5, 2020.

7 Richard Rhodes, *The Making of the Atomic Bomb* (New York: Simon and Schuster, 1986), pp. 490–491. This is generally considered the definitive work on its subject.

8 Quoted in Rhodes, p. 308.

9 Quoted in Rhodes, p. 735.

10 Account of General Groves, quoted in Rhodes p. 664.

11 Quoted in Rhodes, p. 749.

12 Nuel Pharr Davis, *Lawrence and Oppenheimer* (New York: Simon and Schuster, 1968), quoted in Steve Sheinkin, *Bomb* (New York: Roaring Brook Press, 2012) p. 216.

13 Berkeley: University of California Press, 1998, p. 70.

14 Personal interview, February 14, 2020.

15 Aaron Mehta, "'Unbelievably ridiculous': Four-star general seeks to clean up Pentagon's classification process," *Defense News*, January 29, 2020. www.defensenews.com/pentagon/2020/01/29/unbelievably-ridiculous-four-star-general-seeks-to-clean-up-pentagons-classification-process/.

16 Gusterson, p. 69.

17 Quoted in Gusterson p. 92.

18 www.lanl.gov/science-innovation/_assets/docs/science2030.pdf.

19 Joseph Masco, *The Nuclear Borderlands: The Manhattan Project in Post-Cold War New Mexico* (Princeton: Princeton University Press, 2006) p. 75.

20 "TA-55 PF-4," Los Alamos National Laboratory Fact Sheet, www.energy.gov/sites/prod/files/2018/02/f49/NNSA%202016_TA-55-factsheet.pdf.

21 "Los Alamos 2030: A Vision for Science," Los Alamos National Laboratory, www.lanl. gov/science-innovation/_assets/docs/science2030.pdf.

22 Los Alamos, p. 13.

23 Los Alamos, p. 4.

24 Sharon K. Weiner, "Reconsidering U.S. Plutonium Production Plans," *Arms Control Today*, June 2020, www.armscontrol.org/act/2020-06/features/reconsidering-us-plutonium-pit-production-plans.

25 Office of the Chief Financial Officer, "Department of Energy FY 2022 Congressional Budget Request: Laboratory Tables Preliminary," June 2021, www.energy.gov/sites/default/files/2021-06/doe-fy2022-budget-laboratory.pdf.

26 "Emerging threats and opportunities," Los Alamos National Laboratory, www.lanl. gov/mission/emerging-threats.php.

27 "Protecting Against Nuclear Threats," Los Alamos National Laboratory, www.lanl.gov/mission/nuclear-threats.php.

28 Assessing Progress on Nuclear Nonproliferation and Disarmament: 2016–2019 Report Card, Arms Control Association, www.armscontrol.org/reports/2019/assessing-progress-nuclear-nonproliferation-disarmament-2016-2019-report-card.

29 "HIV vaccine-research team shifts to SARS-CoV-2," Los Alamos National Laboratory, www.lanl.gov/discover/publications/connections/2020/2020-05/science.php.

30 Nuclear Watch New Mexico, "Budget and Economic Information: Los Alamos National Lab FY22 Budget Chart," https://nukewatch.org/resources-and-information/economic-information (accessed August 4, 2021).

31 Rhodes, p. 325.

32 Leah Cantor, "The Waste That Remains," *Santa Fe Reporter*, August 23, 2019, www.sfreporter.com/news/2019/08/23/the-waste-that-remains/.

33 Scott Wyland, "Energy Department: Cap rather than clean up Los Alamos lab waste," *Santa Fe New Mexican*, www.santafenewmexican.com/news/local_news/energy-department-cap-rather-than-clean-up-los-alamos-lab-waste.

34 Patrick Malone, "Repeated safety lapses hobble Los Alamos National Laboratory's work on the cores of U.S. nuclear warheads," Center for Public Integrity, www.sciencemag.org/news/2017/06/near-disaster-federal-nuclear-weapons-laboratory-takes-hidden-toll-america-s-arsenal.

35 Ralph Vartebedian, "Nuclear Accident in New Mexico Ranks among the Costliest in US History," *Los Angeles Times*, August 22, 2016, www.latimes.com/natin/la-na-new-mexico-nuclear-dump-20160819-snap-story.html.

36 Vincent Ialenti, "Waste makes haste: How a campaign to speed up nuclear waste shipments shut down the WIPP long-term repository," *Bulletin of the Atomic Scientists*, 2018 Vol. 74, No. 4, pp. 262–275, https://thebulletin.org/2018/06/waste-makes-haste-how-a-campaign-to-speed-up-nuclear-waste-shipments-shut-down-the-wipp-long-term-repository/.

37 www.ncsl.org/research/environment-and-natural-resources/los-alamos-national-laboratory.aspx.

38 Personal interview, March 4, 2020.

39 www.usatoday.com/story/news/politics/2018/06/03/yucca-mountain-congress-works-revive-dormant-nuclear-waste-dump/664153002/.

40 Joseph Masco, *The Nuclear Borderlands* (Princeton, NJ: Princeton University Press, 2006.)

41 Tris Deroma, "NNSA investigates radioactive discoveries," *Los Alamos Monitor*, March 1, 2020.

42 Scott Wyland, "Report: Some Los Alamos hazardous waste too dangerous to move," *Santa Fe New Mexican*, August 2, 2021, www.santafenewmexican.com/news/local_news/report-some-los-alamos-nuclear-waste-too-hazardous-to-move/article.

43 Scott Wyland, "More radioactive contaminants found at Los Alamos housing site," *Santa Fe New Mexican*, July 23, 2021, www.santafenewmexican.com/news/local_news/more-radioactive-contaminants-found-at-los-alamos-housing-site/article.

44 Phone interview, May 1, 2020.

45 Scott Wyland, "New Mexico's U.S. senators request more time for comment on LANL pit production," *Santa Fe New Mexican*, April 22, 2020.

46 Ialenti, p. 267.

47 Personal interview, March 2, 2020.

48 "New Program helps New Mexico small businesses bring tech to market," Los Alamos National Laboratory Community Connections, April 9, 2020, www.lanl.gov/discover/publications/connections/2020/2020-04/econ-dev.php.

49 Ron Davis, "NM bioscience company plans expansion in Los Alamos," *Albuquerque Business First*, July 10, 2019, www.bizjournals.com/albuquerque/news/2019/07/10/nm-bioscience-company-plans-expansion-in-los.html; Maire O'Neill, "Pebble Labs lays off 13 employees," Los Alamos Reporter, Mary 11, 2020, https://losalamosreporter.com/2020/03/11/pebble-labs-lays-off-13-employees/; Carol Clark, Pebble Labs Seeks to Terminate Economic Development Agreement with Los Alamos County," *Los Alamos Daily Post*, July 19, 2021, https://ladailypost.com/pebble-labs-seeks-to-terminate-economic-development-agreement-with-los-alamos-county/.

50 Ingrid Lunden, "Descartes Labs snaps up $20M more for its AI-based geospatial imagery analytics platform," techcrunch.com, October 11, 2019, https://techcrunch.com/2019/10/11/descartes-labs-snaps-up-20m-more-for-its-ai-based-geospatial-imagery-analytics-platform/

51 www.lanl.gov/projects/feynman-center/techsnapshot-content/5efa199c0aae160bd801c5b7/5efa199c0aae160bd801c5b7.pdf. Retrieved September 7, 2021.

52 "FY 2022 Congressional Budget Request: Laboratory Tables Preliminary," Department of Energy, June 2021, www.energy.gov/sites/default/files/2021-06/doe-fy2022-budget-laboratory.pdf. The table actually lists the appropriation for LANL's Office of Technology Transitions (OTT) at $275 million, and for the entire department at $50 million, clearly an error. The Budget Justification documents put the request for the Department's OTT at $19 million, a 10% increase over enacted FY 2021.

53 Personal interview, March 4, 2020. www.santafenewmexican.com/news/business/innovation-village-aims-to-combine-tech-sector-housing-in-santa-fe/article_b44033e8-8b35-11eb-9289-a7ccf8c64ed8.html.

54 This history is derived primarily from "The U.S. Nuclear Weapons Complex: Overview of Department of Energy Sites," Congressional Research Service, Updated September 6, 2018, https://crsreports.congress.gov.

55 Robert S. Norris, "The History of the U.S. Nuclear Stockpile 1945-2013," Federation of American Scientists, August 15, 2013, https://fas.org/pir-pubs/the-history-of-the-u-s-nuclear-stockpile-1945-2013/.

56 *The Nuclear Borderlands* (Princeton: Princeton University Press, 2006), p. 48.

57 Katrina vanden Heuvel, "Our nation needs a wake-up call to the nuclear threat," *Washington Post*, July 7, 2020, www.washingtonpost.com/opinions/2020/07/07/our-nation-needs-wake-up-call-nuclear-threat/.

58 Hans M. Kristensen and Matt Korda, "United States nuclear forces, 2020," *Bulletin of the Atomic Scientists* vol. 76, pp. 46–60, www.tandfonline.com/doi/full/10.1080/00963402.2019.1701286.

59 Robert Burns, "Air Force awards $13.3 billion contract for nuclear missiles," *Washington Post*, September 8, 2020, www.washingtonpost.com/world/national-security/air-force-awards-133-billion-contract-for-nuclear-missiles/2020/09/08/e0167fb2-f22a-11ea-8025-5d3489768ac8_story.html.

60 Burns, "Air Force awards $13.3 billion contract."

61 Anthony Capaccio, "New U.S. ICBMs Could Cost Up To $264 Billion Over Decades," *Bloomberg.com*, October 3, 2020, www.bloomberg.com/news/articles/2020-10-03/new-u-s-icbms-could-cost-up-to-264-billion-over-decades.

62 Jon Wolfstal, "The Trillion Dollar Nuclear Triad," Middlebury Institute for International Studies at Monterey, January 7, 2014, www.nonproliferation.org/us-trillion-dollar-nuclear-triad/; "FY 2021 Defense Spending Briefing Book," Center for Arms Control and Nonproliferation, February 11,2020, https://armscontrolcenter.org/fiscal-year-2021-defense-spending-briefing-book/.

63 Congressional Research Service, "Navy Columbia (SSBN-826) Class Ballistic Missile Submarine Program: Background and Issues for Congress," Updated September 14, 2021, https://sgp.fas.org/crs/weapons/R41129.pdf.

64 Stephen I. Schwartz, *Atomic Audit* (Washington, DC: Brookings Institution Press, 1998), www.brookings.edu/book/atomic-audit/.

65 Schwartz.

66 "Surging U.S. Nuclear Weapons Budget a Growing Danger," Carnegie Endowment for International Peace Issue Brief, March 19, 2020.

67 "Budget Overview: Fiscal Year 2022," National Nuclear Security Administration, www.energy.gov/sites/default/files/2021-06/20210608%20NNSA%20Budget%20Overview.pdf.

68 "Projected Cost of U.S. Nuclear Forces, 2021 to 2030," Congressional Budget Office, www.cbo.gov/publication/57130.

69 https://ota.fas.org/reports/9202.pdf.

70 Janet Bailey, "Laboratory without a Cause," *Santa Fe Reporter*, August 17–23.

71 Bill H. Cabage, "1990s panel blunted 'surplus labs' claim," *ORNL Reporter*, November 6, 2018.

72 www2.lbl.gov/LBL-PID/Galvin-Report/Galvin-Report.html.

73 "Department of Energy FY 2022 Congressional Budget Request: Laboratory Tables Preliminary," June 2021, www.energy.gov/sites/default/files/2021-06/doe-fy2022-budget-laboratory.pdf.

74 www.energy.gov/sites/prod/files/2020/02/f72/doe-fy2021-budget-in-brief_0.pdf.

75 www.energy.gov/sites/prod/files/2020/02/f72/doe-fy2021-laboratory-table_1.pdf.

76 Personal interview, March 5, 2020.

7

NEW FRONTIERS FOR MILITARISM

Militarization of the Border

"Build a wall." It started out as a mnemonic concocted by campaign aides to make sure their candidate's speeches turned again and again to riffing on "Mexican rapists" and "terrorists" violating our southern border.[1] As it became a centerpiece of U.S. policy during the Trump administration, the theme also served to showcase another: "rebuilding" our "decimated" military. Active duty and National Guard troops, as many as five thousand of them at a time, along with their tools of warfare, began massing at the border. While the Department of Homeland Security (DHS) remained nominally in charge, it was clear that the military was taking on new roles in border enforcement. Deployed in such roles as monitoring camera systems from command-and-control rooms, and installing more razor wire, they freed up members of the regular border patrol to hunt down more people in the desert.[2]

The Guard's presence sparked a Constitutional crisis, since it violated norms going back to 1878, when the Posse Comitatus Act barred the use of the U.S. military for domestic law enforcement. The administration cited the military's authority to go after drug smuggling; DHS helpfully designated the entire southern border of the United States as a drug-smuggling "corridor."[3] President Trump's strategies for funding the wall included shutting down the federal government and declaring a national emergency—moves that launched their own budget/constitutional crises.[4]

Building a wall had appeal as a simple solution to a very complex challenge, and as a focus for xenophobia. To a military-industrial complex accustomed to promoting costly, high-tech bells and whistles for Great Power competition, though, it wasn't a great fit. It would focus resources on a technology hearkening back to

DOI: 10.4324/9781003293705-8

medieval times that the big contractors had no special expertise in making. Not to mention that twenty-first-century wall violators have had little trouble cutting through it with low-tech tools.[5]

As we'll see, the defense contractors managed.

The "build the wall" border policy became the most visceral symbol of Trump policy cruelty when images of small children being torn from their parents' arms and put in cages began appearing in the media. But the Trump administration didn't militarize the border; it just took a long-militarized policy to grotesque extremes.

During the Vietnam War the U.S. military had installed heat and motion surveillance sensors to establish the "McNamara line" between North and South. In the waning days of the war, this technology also appeared on the southern U.S. borders. The Reagan administration began expanding its fleet of military helicopters and fixed-wing aircraft to hunt down and intimidate border crossers with aerial spotlights and loudspeakers, resorting to the same drug-interdiction rationale later used by the Trump administration. As the first President Bush was celebrating the dismantling of the Berlin Wall, his administration was building another one—the first section of steel barrier on the San Diego–Tijuana border.

The idea was to suppress the flow of immigrants by pushing border crossings from urban areas to more remote and dangerous places. The Clinton administration turned this germ of an idea into an elaborate strategy of "Prevention through Deterrence." Its innovations did not focus on wall-building, but on widening the border zone with multiple layers of high-tech cameras and enhanced sensor systems extending a hundred miles out into the desert.[6]

The policy's logic of deterring immigration by making it ever more dangerous and deadly remains in force today, though its decades-long result is not deterrence but at least 30,000 deaths in the desert between 2014 and 2018 alone. In separating (and caging) families, the Trump administration was simply looking for a new, even crueler way to make the price of immigration too high.

After 9/11, in rough tandem with overall military spending, the budgets to pay for all this soared. By 2003 the new Department of Homeland Security (DHS) had become the largest federal law enforcement agency in the United States, or, as one constitutional scholar called it, a new "standing army on American soil."[7] Though its charge focused on terrorism and weapons of mass destruction, most of its work focused on immigration enforcement. The combined budgets of the new Customs and Border Protection (CBP) agency and Immigration and Customs Enforcement (ICE) had increased over their predecessor agencies to $9.9 billion, a 1,000 percent increase over ten years. By the time Trump took office, this figure had doubled.

BOX 7.1 ACADEMIA AND THE MIC

Among the partners contributing to the border militarization project has been American academia. The mission statement of a DHS-funded consortium, calling itself the Center of Excellence on Borders, Trade, and Immigration, promises "to establish a coordinated, university-based system to enhance the nation's homeland security" by producing tools, technologies, and research for homeland security use. The consortium includes the universities of Houston, Arizona State, Virginia, West Virginia, North Carolina, and Minnesota, plus Texas A&M, Rutgers, American, and Middlebury.

World War II kickstarted this alliance of academia and the Military Industrial Complex (MIC). In a 1946 memo to the War Department, General Eisenhower touted the "invaluable assistance" during wartime of "Scientific and Technical Resources as Military Assets.... This pattern of integration must be translated into a peacetime counterpart."[8] That same year Congress created the Office of Naval Research for this purpose. (This research partially funded my own college education, through my academic mathematician father's summer contracts to do extremely abstract math research that the Navy thought might someday find a military application.) The other service branches soon got their own counterparts.

As the Cold War shifted the nature of warfare, universities in places like California were well-positioned to adjust. The California Institute of Technology in Pasadena had been marrying technological research to new military projects for years. During the war its Guggenheim Aeronautical Laboratory was renamed the Jet Propulsion Laboratory, laying the groundwork for the Cold War aerospace merger of aircraft and spacecraft. The engineering schools at academic powerhouses UCLA and USC joined Cal Tech in training the scientists and engineers for the region's new aerospace industry.

Between 1960 and 1986 the Department of Defense (DoD) spent $20 billion (in constant 1987 dollars) on academic research, topping out at $1.1 billion in 1986. During the Reagan years academia's share of DoD's basic research funds climbed from 39.8 percent to 54.5 percent. By 1986, 54 percent of federal funding for computer sciences came from DoD, as well as 35 percent for math and 60 percent for electrical engineering.[9]

Throughout the post–Cold War period, DoD handed out more R&D funding than all other agencies put together and, during the post–9/11 military buildup, the gap widened even further.[10] Also during this period, academic institutions began to increase the pressure on their faculties to bring in outside money. As DoD stood, and stands, uniquely ready to provide, so the pressure increased on faculty to adapt their research to military categories. While this arrangement has funded valuable research in fields including breast cancer, PTSD and tropical diseases, the nation's overall research efforts are distorted when they need to line up with DoD priorities. In perhaps the most notorious case in recent years, the anthropology profession was rocked by the disclosure that the military was paying anthropologists to help them win hearts and minds in the Afghan War.[11]

As at Google, academics have mounted resistance from time to time against the militarization of their institutions. During the 1980s, for example, the MIT biology department voted not to accept money from DoD because of its biological weapons research.[12] In 1990, 64 percent of the University of California faculty voted to recommend that the university end its relationship with the Los Alamos and Lawrence Livermore labs.[13]

This didn't happen, though. Beyond the University of California, places like Johns Hopkins, MIT, and Texas A&M now share in the management of the nuclear weapons labs. In July of 2019 the National Nuclear Security Administration (NNSA) showcased more than $65 million in grants to universities for research supporting "Stockpile Stewardship." And with such grants, plus training programs and fellowships, the NNSA lays down the pipeline developing its future workforce. A 2019 report by the International Campaign to Abolish Nuclear Weapons (ICAN)—the 2017 Nobel Peace Prize recipient—detailed the involvement of 50 American universities in the nuclear weapons complex.[14]

Beyond acts of resistance, the antidote to the creeping militarization of U.S. academic research is an overhaul of federal R&D funding priorities. The Biden administration has made a promising start by increasing the proportion of non-military R&D funds in its budget, and by including this goal in his frameworks for economic renewal. Real reform will require further shifts in the federal agenda with cuts to the budget for military R&D as well.

Academia has an invaluable role to play in urgent national priorities beyond military force. Chapter 4 cited a post–Cold War joint effort by Cal Tech, USC, and UCLA to set up collaborative teams developing the technologies of hybrid vehicles, fuel cells, alternative fuels, solar-power systems, and advanced batteries, and transferring them for use by commercial manufacturers.[15]

The distortions of federal funding toward military objectives have held that kind of work back. Now more and more universities are getting involved in it. We have no more time to waste in getting them the support they need.

The Obama administration set up shop with plans to pursue the ever-elusive goal of comprehensive immigration reform, including a clear path to citizenship for undocumented immigrants. Like the Clinton administration before them, they saw "strengthened" border enforcement as the price they had to pay to clear that path. The closest they came was in 2013: The "Border Security, Economic

Opportunity, and Immigration Modernization Act," which passed in the Senate but not the House, would have provided a qualified form of legalization for the undocumented. It would also have added $46 billion to border militarization, including earmarks for to specific corporations.[16] While the Customs and Border Protection (CBP) budget lost about a billion dollars during Obama's term,[17] the total border enforcement budget rose to almost $20 billion.[18] Deportations increased, along with new remote and mobile surveillance systems and a new fleet of drones.

Along with his wall obsession, Trump repudiated the citizenship goal, while inflating the goal of the whole border-security operation. By 2018 the budget for border enforcement as a whole had risen to nearly $24 billion.[19]

Then came the Biden administration. While struggling with an accelerated flow of migrants over the southern border, it has dismantled the worst of Trump administration border cruelty. But this does not include dismantling the web of military technology that is installed there. In his first speech to Congress, Biden assured the members that his budget had "a lot of money for high tech border security." And the growing swarm of companies showing up at expos around the world showcasing such technology will be working hard to convince U.S. procurers that continuous technological innovation will be key to getting our border policy right.

The Big Pentagon Contractors Cash In

Though the border enforcement budget is only about 3 percent of the military's budget, or about 6 percent of its procurement budget, U.S. military contractors had been watching this pot grow steadily over decades, and could spot a market opening when they saw one. Since the military technologies of the Vietnam War began to be deployed at the U.S. border, the contractors had also watched border security become more and more enmeshed with the high-tech bells and whistles of militarized national security.

So they had positioned themselves as border-security experts, using their usual suite of persuasive strategies. The specific corporations earmarked in the 2013 bill had spent more than $11 million on political campaign contributions since 2009, donations that included every Senate co-sponsor of the bill.[20] Corporate lobbying also intensified during the two months leading up to the vote.[21]

The list of the 14 biggest border contractors from 2005–2019 includes all of the Big Five military primes. During that time Boeing received 17 contracts for planes ICE uses for deportations and a land surveillance system. General Dynamics secured 111 contracts to build surveillance towers. Lockheed Martin got $1 billion for, among other things, surveillance planes. Northrop Grumman got $340 million for biometrics, border screening and radar surveillance. And Raytheon supplied the CBP with surveillance and radar systems for maritime drones.[22]

The Big Five's commanding position over government contracting in general has also given them a competitive advantage in some of the low-tech (and lowdown) dimensions of Trump's border market. In 2017, for example, General Dynamics got $4 billion from the Department of Health and Human Services Office of Refugee Resettlement to provide "infrastructure services for the shelter care of unaccompanied children."[23]

Two more of the top contractors should be mentioned here: First, General Atomics, the San Diego-based company we met in Chapter 3. It developed its Predator drone for use in the Afghanistan War, and then sold this "combat-proven" product to the CBP; teamed up with Northrop Grumman's radar systems, this drone can detect people from a height of 25,000 feet. In 2018 General Atomics got a $275.9 million contract to maintain its fleet of border drones.[24]

The second U.S. border contractor worth noting outside the Big Five is Elbit Systems, Israel's largest military contractor. As we've seen, the United States is accustomed to spreading its high military technology around the world. In the case of militarizing the border, it had plenty to learn from its Middle East "ally." Israel has honed its capabilities on some of the most heavily militarized borders in the world, building physical and technological fortresses around the Palestinian territories. Then it sold that expertise to the United States, constructing most of the towers in Arizona that feed surveillance data from infrared cameras and ground-sweeping radar to command-and-control centers.[25]

In 2006, on the strength of its reputation as a "systems integrator" of complicated military projects, Boeing was awarded a multi-billion-dollar contract for the most ambitious surveillance system yet, to cover the entire border. Drawing on its military experience, the company also knew how to inflate costs and timelines in the course of contracting to build things that it would eventually be clear it didn't know how to build. The system didn't work, and after five years DHS cancelled the contract "due to concerns about the price, timeline, and 'effectiveness of the technology.'"[26] Such costly failures don't keep the big primes down for long, however. Though each of them has paid numerous penalties for contracting fraud over

FIGURE 7.1 Drone at the border

Source: Kletr via Adobe Stock

the years, they are always welcomed back into the game.[27] By 2016 a Boeing subsidiary had a contract to build border-patrolling drones.[28]

The military contractors' embrace of the border market had its limits. President Trump's obsession with squeezing the money out of Congress to pay for his wall did not sit well when he seemed willing to trade higher-tech parts of the budget to do it. In May of 2019 a Pentagon document surfaced indicating its intent to redirect, to the wall, $1.5 billion Congress had designated for projects including a nuclear intercontinental ballistic missile system and even the F-35.[29]

Members of Congress worried about their spending prerogatives. "We look forward to hearing your views on how you intend to repair the damaged relationship between the defense oversight committees and the Department [of Defense]," three members of those committees complained.[30] For their part, of course, the military contractors worried about their cash cows—the ones they could have without having to compete with ordinary construction companies.

Breaking into the Club

By continuously cultivating a revolving door of relationships—linking their executives and lobbyists to Pentagon officials and key congressional committee chairs—the big prime contractors try to make sure their line of work remains a club that's hard to join. The strategy has succeeded remarkably well.[31]

Silicon Valley is one of the principal insurgencies trying to break in. The militarized border has been integral to this effort. Sometimes border contracts become entrées to the big leagues over at DoD. Sometimes, working the other way around, military wares get imported for border use.

Venture capital has been Silicon Valley's comfort zone, and it has been used to scale the walls of the MIC. One leg up has been a venture capital fund called Founders Fund. Set up by Peter Thiel, the Stanford whiz kid co-founder (with Space-X's Elon Musk) of PayPal, it has backed a portfolio of defense technology start-ups. Thiel used this vehicle to fund his own company, called Palantir, and to cultivate such military officials as H.R. McMaster, Michael Flynn, and James Mattis—contacts that yielded contracts providing software to U.S. military units in Iraq and Afghanistan. By 2011, ICE was using Palantir's "FALCON analytical platform and Integrated Case Management (ICM) system" to track down migrants at the border.

These early moves ramped up as the Trump administration—where these contacts became high-ranking officials—began boosting military spending and intensifying its focus on the border. Thiel had also cultivated the relationship that now mattered most. His $1 million campaign donation got him a Trump Tower office and a seat on the transition team executive committee, which he used to help staff the administration's technology policy posts with his friends.

The traditional defense powerhouses, including Raytheon, Lockheed Martin, and Northrop Grumman, had been competing for an $876 million contract to build a real-time intelligence system for the Army. Palantir sued to be included, and in March of 2019, Palantir beat out the primes and won the contract.[32]

Other start-ups have been backed by Thiel's Founders Fund to follow suit. Anduril, for example (its name, like Palantir's, an homage to *The Lord of the Rings* trilogy), opened its doors in 2017. By September 2018 it had already secured a $5 million CBP contract to build an integrated drone and surveillance tower system in the San Diego area. This led to another contract with the Marine Corps to build autonomous 'counter intrusion' and surveillance systems at its bases, some of them on the Arizona–Mexico border.[33] It is also parlaying the technology into the arms export market, via contracts with the UK military.[34]

As the company was ramping up, one of its founders got himself appointed to DoD's Defense Innovation Board. This allowed him to write recommendations on the Pentagon's software acquisition policy while marketing software to the Pentagon.[35]

The Defense Department is attracted to the idea of innovation—it would be hard to miss the attraction of military men to their high-tech toys. But DoD is skittish about betting big on unproven companies and technologies. Palantir and Musk's Space-X are as yet the only two venture-capital-backed multi-billion-dollar military companies. (During the same period China has launched about a dozen such companies.)[36]

Silicon Valley's push to join the club continues. Besides waging court battles (which of course the primes also wage with each other) the Palantirs of the world seek membership in the traditional ways: a raft of political contributions, for example, by its executives and lobbyists to the Defend America PAC, whose largest contributors are the big primes.[37]

The Valley's mega-players—Google, Amazon and Microsoft—have also been jumping into the game, most conspicuously, as noted, with the fight between Microsoft and Amazon over the rights to build the Pentagon's $10 billion cloud computing infrastructure. With $480 million from the Army, Microsoft is also outfitting soldiers in the battlefield with virtual reality headsets.[38]

The Military's New Frontiers

The Wall itself has not been a winner for the MIC, to the extent it diverted money from the MIC's more favored projects and into the pockets of Trump's construction company cronies. The virtual wall on the other hand—the complicated web of surveillance technologies extending a hundred miles out from the Wall—has been a better fit.[39]

But in the scheme of overall spending on military hardware, the border project is small potatoes. The real prizes are locked up with the technological push toward a new Cold War, that is, toward Great Power competition with China and Russia.

Here are the major elements of this technology push. They are all connected.

Hypersonic Weapons

In the mid-fifties the nuclear terror surged into high gear with the arrival of Intercontinental Ballistic Missiles (ICBMs) that could reduce the timing of a nuclear strike to a matter of minutes. Hypersonic weapons now present the prospect of an array of different delivery vehicles carrying conventional and/or nuclear weapons, following less predictable and therefore harder-to-detect flight paths.

The United States has been tinkering with this capability since the early 2000s. Two years before Reagan and Gorbachev signed the Intermediate-Range Nuclear Forces Agreement (INF) limiting the range of ICBMs (until the Trump administration killed it), Sandia Lab had already made the first breakthrough in hypersonic weapons and has been at it ever since.

The project, pushed to the back burner by post 9/11's counter-terrorism mission, is back in front. Though these weapons remain in the prototype-phase, the pursuit of them in recent years, and the funding increases to go with it, have surged. The 2018 National Security Strategy calls them one of the key technologies enabling the United States "to fight and win the wars of the future," in part because military planners see hypersonic weapons being too fast for an enemy's air and missile defense systems.[40] That same year the Pentagon's head of R&D, Michael Griffin, identified the development of hypersonics as his number one priority. And in April of 2020 the Army's director of hypersonics warned, "We need to accelerate the pace of testing.... Fourth quarter FY23 is when the Army builds [this weapon]; that time is coming really fast."[41] Hypersonics, Griffin said, are "not an advantage that we can concede to people who wish to be our adversaries."[42]

Namely the Russians and the Chinese. Russia began accelerating its hypersonic weapons program *in response to U.S. missile defense deployments* and to the 2002 U.S. withdrawal from the Anti-Ballistic Missile Treaty.[43] According to Putin, the maneuverability of hypersonic weapons would be the only way to evade

FIGURE 7.2 Air Force testing new hypersonic weapon

Source: Department of Defense via Defense Visual Information Distribution Service

U.S. missile defenses to get nuclear weapons to their targets. China has developed an operational hypersonic weapon.[44] The other countries trying to get into the game include Japan, Australia, India, France, Germany, and North Korea. It looks like a classic arms race in the making, only with more countries than were involved during the Cold War.

These weapons come in two basic types. The first, known as boost-glide, uses a conventional rocket to get the weapon to hypersonic speed, after which the "glide body" carrying the warhead separates from the rocket and coasts, from a point near the upper limits of the atmosphere, to its target. The other prototyped version uses a cruise missile design, flying lower, with more maneuverability, but has air friction problems the boost-glide model doesn't.[45]

All the services want in on this next big thing. The Pentagon has assigned to the Navy the task of building the rocket booster while the Army builds the glide-body of a weapon all the services are intended to share. The Air Force wants to adapt these weapons to launch from planes, the Navy wants them launched from submarines, and the Army from trucks. The newest military technologies will be melded with the oldest: One of the Army's artillery pieces being developed to carry hypersonic missiles is labeled the "Giant Cannon."[46]

The big difference between the hypersonic plans of the Russians and Chinese versus the United States: Some of the Russian and Chinese models are built to accommodate nuclear warheads. The U.S. models, so far, are not. With an overlayered nuclear triad as a backstop, the United States seems to be focusing its hypersonic weapons planning more on gearing up for a Great Power war, most notably in the South China Sea. Griffin, the R&D director, said that without its own hypersonic weapons, if "the Chinese started throwing hypersonic missiles at American bases in the Pacific and sinking carrier strike groups," the only options for the United States would be "to let them have their way or go nuclear."[47]

In April of 2020 the Pentagon announced that it had set up a "war room" to ramp up mass production of both boost-glide and cruise missile types. For this they are working out the needs of a "hypersonics industrial base" built from the prime contractors all the way down to the small, specialized suppliers.[48]

So begins the push to expand the budget to pay for all this. R&D funding for hypersonics rose gradually during this century but stayed in the millions of dollars until the new push to move toward production. The FY 2022 budget increased Trump administration spending on hypersonics to $3.8 billion, up from $3.2 billion in fiscal year 2021.[49] Appropriations for the Army and Navy nearly doubled from the previous year. Assuming the plans for mass production proceed, these amounts will look like a modest down payment.

The services, and their contractors, would all be happy if this spending were simply added on top of the previous menu of weapons programs. But in 2020 then-Defense Secretary Mark Esper began talking about the need to cut some "legacy" programs to make room for this "modernization". Budget trade-offs are not what the MIC has in mind. Making sure that hypersonic weapons are loaded onto legacy platforms like artillery pieces is one way to attach the latter to the modernization agenda.

A Raytheon vice president stated the obvious to his fellow contractors at a meeting of the National Defense Industrial Association in December of 2018: "From a pure business perspective, there is a significant opportunity in the hypersonic domain."[50] Four of the big primes—Lockheed Martin, Boeing, Raytheon, and Northrop Grumman—are getting significant pieces of the action, with Lockheed, as usual, more equal than the others. In February of 2021 DoD awarded Lockheed and another contractor, Dynetics, a contract to build a ground-launched hypersonic weapon by the end of the year, and get into production in 2023.[51] Whether these timelines will be met is, of course, unknown.

The director of Skunk Works in Palmdale pronounced Lockheed's hypersonic technology "mature" in 2017. Banner ads are running widely with taglines like: "It's too late to start thinking about hypersonics. That's why we're already one step ahead"; and "Lockheed Martin: the integrated solutions you already trust, now at hypersonic speeds." Back in 2013, in a remarkable display of chutzpah, Lockheed's former CEO Marilyn Hewson portrayed $1 billion for a single prototype as a bargain: "[W]e're proving a hypersonic aircraft can be produced at an affordable price. We estimate it will cost less than $1 billion to develop, build and fly a demonstrator aircraft the size of an F-22."[52] Note that the previous year the United States had decided the F-22 was an unaffordable plane, and stopped buying it.

The fifth prime, General Dynamics, will have a lesser role, but will be loading these weapons on some of the submarines its subsidiary Electric Boat builds in Connecticut, and on parts of its fleet of ground vehicles. Also as usual, these companies are teaming up when they're not competing: Northrop Grumman and Raytheon revealed a formerly secret hypersonic cruise missile program in 2019.[53]

Missile Defense

The principal attraction of hypersonic weapons to U.S. war planners is, again, that with their speed and maneuverability they'll be able to get through an adversary's defense systems. But, of course, if ours can do this, the adversary's probably can too. U.S. R&D spending has heavily favored developing the offensive weapons themselves over the defensive systems to counteract them: $3 billion in fiscal year 2021 for offense, $206 million for defense. But the Pentagon's R&D chief predicted that the United States would field systems capable of defending against hypersonics by the middle of the decade.

Of course, this is the sort of promise DoD has been making since the Reagan administration hatched the idea of a technological shield over America blocking all incoming missiles. After decades of effort and billions of dollars to realize Reagan's dream of a Strategic Defense Initiative, DoD abandoned the idea of making the United States invulnerable to intercontinental ballistic missile attack.

They have lowered their sites to defeating medium- and intermediate-range ballistic missiles.[54] The contractors responsible for this decades-long record of repeated failure—including Lockheed, Boeing, Raytheon, and Northrop—now all have contracts promising to figure out how the rudimentary missile defense systems currently in place might fend off hypersonic attacks. According to physicist and nuclear expert James Acton, it is not plausible that these systems, designed to defend small areas, could protect the entire continental United States.[55]

In March of 2021, DoD announced that Lockheed and Northrop would split a nearly $4 billion contract for the Next Generation Interceptor. In a nod to the decades of missile defense failure, the contract includes the equivalent of "Let's just see how this goes":

> Allowing a technology development phase will help ensure that the NGI is an efficient and effective part of an integrated Missile Defense System solution by permitting the department to further analyze requirements and make necessary adjustments in preparation for the product development phase.[56]

The Congressional Budget Office estimates the cost of the current missiles defense plan over the next decade at $176 billion, a 40 percent increase over its estimate in 2017.[57] Add this to the pile of military programs we have encountered on the tour—including the F-35, the B-21 bomber, and the *Columbia*-class submarine—that current spending plans cannot conceivably accommodate.

Yet, while still trying and failing to make a ground-based interceptor to function reliably in real-world conditions, the Pentagon claims it needs more money to build a massive new system that *this time* will work. In August of 2021 an Air Force General told the Space and Missile Defense Symposium that what they really need is a space-launched system that sees "everything, characterizes everything that goes on on this planet, from a missile perspective, all the time, everywhere." With the salesmanship that has launched a thousand military projects ultimately going nowhere, he assured his audience that "we should be able to get there quickly because that technology is not difficult."[58]

Lacking the means to protect the country from a long-range nuclear attack, the Pentagon (and the contractors) are promoting these systems as speed bumps—additional war-making options—short of nuclear war. This presumes, though, there would be time to exercise those options. In the course of the Nuclear Age, near-miss errors bringing one or the other superpower to the brink of launch have been averted by humans pulling them back. Hypersonic weapons reduce the time for humans to judge and act in this way. In the foreshortened timeframe, some analysts also say they could escalate a crisis *toward* a nuclear war if an adversary detecting a hypersonic weapon with an unpredictable flight path can't be certain it is not nuclear-armed.[59]

Artificial Intelligence

Though historically the idea of creating "thinking" machines has been pursued mainly outside the military, there was no way it would stay there. The Pentagon's interest in Artificial Intelligence (AI) includes a range of applications, from human-controlled robots on the battlefield to autonomous weapons systems that "once activated, can select and engage targets without further intervention by a human operator."[60] AI is heavily involved in the operations of the Cyber Command, as well as in processing the intelligence data that is being generated at such accelerated rates that it threatens to overwhelm the capacity of humans to understand and use it.

And, as with hypersonic weapons, the military's interest in AI has been spurred by the actions of the Russians and Chinese. In 2017 China pushed the Americans' competitive buttons by announcing its intentions to seize the global lead in AI by 2030, including by acquiring U.S. AI companies. They are exploiting the architecture of their extensive domestic surveillance operations for military purposes and are working on building autonomous vehicles for military operations on land, sea, and air. In classic arms-race fashion, the Chinese are said to be feeling the pressure to match U.S. developments in the field. The Russians are likewise active in the field, with a particular focus on robotics.[61]

Sandia Lab has parlayed its contributions to hypersonic weapons technology into a focus on militarized AI. They have set their sights on using AI to speed up hypersonic flight plans and adjust them during flight. In 2019 they convened the first Autonomy NM conference, where researchers from eight universities discussed how this might get done by 2024, and what civilian applications—to fields like manufacturing, transportation and agriculture—are most plausible.[62]

In contrast to the military's natural dominion over aircraft at hypersonic speeds, the innovations in AI have come mainly out of the commercial sector built around Silicon Valley. This represents a challenge to both the military and its traditional contractors. All the big primes have been given pieces of this new technological prize,[63] along with numerous other traditional defense contractors including Leidos and L3 Technologies. But they are now competing with, and having to team up with, a host of unfamiliar AI powerhouses and startups.

In 2020 the Defense Department reportedly had over 600 active AI projects going at once.[64] So far, their share of the official line-item accounting in the Pentagon budget amounts to less than a billion a year.[65] But much more money is hidden in the allocations for the AI components within larger systems. The prospect of incorporating AI into military operations from logistics to autonomous weapons makes this a major focus of most defense contractor growth plans.

To establish control over this hotbed of traditional contractors and Silicon Valley upstarts, the Pentagon created the Joint Artificial Intelligence Center (JAIC). It is supposed to approve the AI research undertaken by the individual service branches and sort out such problems as the divide between the world used to the speed of venture-capital financing and the protracted procurement cycles of defense contracting. JAIC is housed within the Defense Advanced Research Projects Agency (DARPA), the Pentagon's central research arm for new technologies.

JAIC has discovered obstacles of other kinds—cultural and ethical—to its goal of mining Silicon Valley's talent for the military's purposes. In 2019 the National Security Commission on Artificial Intelligence found that the stars of AI tend to worry that working in the DoD enterprise would lack a "compelling sense of purpose" as well as "a technical environment … that would maximize their talents."[66] The Obama administration tried, with limited success, to lure this talent for temporary assignments in the Pentagon by setting up a Defense Digital Service—a "tour of duty for nerds," as its former director called it.[67]

Disquiet within the ranks of the traditional primes over the ethics of what they are doing is, at least publicly, exceedingly rare. This has not been the case with the new entrants from Silicon Valley. JAIC's first National Mission Initiative—called Project Maven—became a showcase for the cultural and ethical disconnects. JAIC contracted with Google to install AI in drones to enable more sophisticated surveillance and targeting on the battlefield. Three thousand Google employees signed an open letter to their CEO asking him to cancel the contract, painting the issue with a broader brush: "We believe that Google should not be in the business of war"—and asking the company to declare "that neither Google nor its contractors will ever build warfare technology."[68] Going ahead with the work, the petition read, "will irreparably damage Google's brand and its ability to compete for talent. Amid growing fears of biased and weaponized AI, Google is already struggling to keep the public's trust." It would violate the company's core values, the petition went on, putting Google in the company of the likes of Raytheon and General Dynamics. They also mentioned Palantir, whose AI surveillance work on the border is now finding broader application within the Pentagon's technology designs.

In a milestone in the history of ethics in corporate behavior, Google walked away from the contract, and AI weaponry in general. Two factors complicate this picture, though. First, with an eye on vast military market beyond Project Maven, Google declared that it would continue to work with the military "in many other areas."[69]

And, second, the Pentagon, of course, simply found new contractors. Sharing the new one was Anduril, which has made an aggressive case that U.S. national security requires a deep dive into AI for military use. Its co-founder said this:

> We have to realize that countries like China are weaponizing artificial intelligence and using it not just to create totalitarian police states in their own countries but exporting that technology to other countries that are going to use it to build their own totalitarian police states.[70]

New Frontiers of Danger

The military does deploy some unmanned vehicles for purposes that save lives, such as detecting and dismantling landmines and Improvised Explosive Devices (IEDs) and cleaning up contaminated environments. Its moves to incorporate "Sea Hunters"–unmanned and AI-controlled ships—rather than larger destroyers in its plans for naval warfare, which could save American lives and will probably save some taxpayer dollars.[71] But we elevate the risks of miscalculation and escalation, threatening ourselves and the world, when we enable our weapons to deliver destruction at hypersonic speeds and hand over the decisions to use them to machines.

When AI systems fail, their failures can be exponentially more consequential than the ones committed by humans. While humans tend to make individual mistakes, AI failures tend to self-replicate with far more potentially destructive effects.[72] Experts also refer to "technical debt," that is, to the escalating dangers when AI systems are deployed to interact with other systems.[73]

The most obvious danger in giving decision-making power to machines is that adversaries will appropriate it. Unlike, say, the parts for a fighter jet, sources point out to the Congressional Research Service, "stolen software code can be used immediately and reproduced at will."

The Pentagon promises that humans will always be involved in the ultimate life-and-death decisions of armed robots. Yet war and peace scholar Michael Klare observes that the technology is moving in the direction of less and less human control. Ceding that control entirely, he says,

> could occur as a deliberate decision, such as when a drone is set free to attack targets fitting a specified appearance ("adult male armed with gun"), or as a conditional matter, as when drones are commanded to fire at their discretion if they lose contact with human controllers.[74]

The most serious danger created by these new technological frontiers is their potential to escalate a conventional conflict to nuclear war. The Trump administration's push to beef up U.S. nuclear capabilities included billions more for the B-21 bomber project underway in Palmdale, the *Columbia*-class ballistic missile submarine, and the newly designed ICBMs—that is, every leg of the nuclear triad. But the largest item in its nuclear modernization budget was designated for the electronic systems governing decision-making over a nuclear strike: NC3: Nuclear Command, Control and Communication. The Congressional Budget Office projects that this part of the modernization effort will cost $77 billion over ten years.[75] Movies from *Dr. Strangelove* to *The Terminator* have dramatized what can go wrong (nuclear annihilation) when the machines get out of hand.

During the Cold War, military strategists worried about so-called Catalytic Nuclear War, that is, a third state-or-non-state actor sparking a nuclear war between the United States and the Soviet Union. In 2021 a fellow at West Point's Modern War Institute and the author of *Artificial Intelligence and the Future of Warfare; The USA, China, and Strategic Stability*, analyzed the ways that AI made this prospect more likely.[76]

With their embrace of hypersonic weapons, the assurances of Pentagon planners that this won't happen in real life become less reassuring. When weapons, which may or may not be nuclear armed, can travel at hypersonic speeds, U.S. leaders detecting an attack have even less time to decide what to do. Investing in military AI, its advocates say, will help by giving them more information, sifted and integrated and accompanied by a menu of cyber-generated response options. In 2019 two scholar/practitioners of nuclear policy and deterrence theory generated controversy and alarm by writing that "America Needs a Dead Hand," that is, the kind of fully automated detection-and-response nuclear strike system Russia is said to possess.

> It may be necessary to develop a system based on [AI], with predetermined response decisions, that detects, decides, and directs strategic forces with such speed that the attack-time compression challenge does not place the United States in an impossible position.[77]

Asked whether he agreed that "America needs a Dead Hand," the director of JAIC said he didn't. Yet, in a classic arms race, the competitors cannot be trusted to be transparent about what they are doing—to each other or to their own citizens. This applies to China and Russia (The plot of *Dr. Strangelove* turned on Russia's secret automated nuclear strike system that nobody could turn back), but applies to JAIC's professed commitment to full transparency as well.

The Militarization of Space

The militarization of space got its semi-official kickoff during the summer of 1957, when Americans stood on their lawns watching Sputnik cross the night sky. The United States hurried its space program along in response and, while tending to frame it in peaceful terms, also tagged it as Cold War competition a little over a decade later by planting the American flag on the planet's only moon. Through the remainder of the century, space as a warfare arena was openly discussed mainly in the likes of the *Star Wars* fantasies, and in the largely failed "defensive" efforts to build space-based shields against nuclear missiles.

But the uses of space have multiplied in the new century and now penetrate deeply into what now feel to us like the essential structures of American life. United States satellites—numbering nearly a thousand, more than any other country—now control some operations of our power grid, for example, of our ability to perceive the patterns of weather and climate, and of our communication and navigation networks.

The U.S. military has increasingly come to rely on its satellites for its own functioning—surveillance, communications, and weapons targeting, including for one of the military's two designs for hypersonic weapons. And, contemplating what we risk if our satellites are attacked, the military has begun to work on ways to protect these satellites, including with what is termed "orbital warfare." Though most of this work is classified, a partially declassified space drone, resembling a miniature space shuttle, is in orbit testing, according to the military, "capabilities necessary to maintain superiority in the space domain."[78]

In arms-race fashion, the Russians and Chinese accuse the United States of militarizing space, and so are developing their own military "solutions." In July of 2020 the U.S. military accused Russia for the first time of firing a projectile from a space satellite. Back in 2007 China inadvertently showed the world its own antisatellite missile capability when it shot down its own weather satellite, sending more than three thousand pieces of wreckage into space. The head of U.S. space operations says the Chinese are "training specialized units with weapons that can blast apart objects in orbit." A 2019 Defense Intelligence Agency assessment reported that both China and Russia had reorganized their militaries to put more emphasis on their space operations.[79]

As with its interest in developing hypersonic weapons, the U.S. military's thinking about space as a domain for military dominance was temporarily sidelined by its focus on 9/11. This thinking resumed behind the scenes, but in 2018 debuted as official national policy when the Trump administration's new National Security Strategy declared space for the first time as "a warfighting domain." Turning the cinematic fantasy versions of this idea into reality became one of the former president's shiny object preoccupations. This one has actually come true, in the sense that the U.S. military now has its first new service branch since the Air Force was created in 1947, the U.S. Space Command.

The Space Force does have a serious rationale: to better coordinate the space-based military programs that are littered across multiple service branches and other agencies. Recall, though, that creating the Air Force did not mean it got all the aircraft—the other branches now have their own models. This centripetal-centrifugal dynamic is likely to extend itself into space.

Congress did insist that the new branch's personnel come from reassignments within the existing force—about 16,000 of them according to the current plan—rather than adding to the total. Adding a new branch means creating a new bureaucracy, however. In specifying no more people, Congress did not say no more money. The Congressional Budget Office estimates the Space Force's initial set up costs in the range of $3 billion, plus $1 billion for new management and administrative positions. Its overall budget for 2021 is $15.4 billion, projected to grow by $2.6 billion over the following five years.

Government watchdogs call this a down payment on what this new bureaucracy will cost. The military contractors are certainly looking at the Space Force as a major growth opportunity.[80] The Government Accountability Office warns that rather than reducing fragmentation and inefficiency, the new force may exacerbate them. Like military contracting in general, GAO says, current space projects routinely go billions over budget and years beyond schedule.[81]

Some proponents of the Space Force see it as the underpinning of an "open international system" in space. But until a new National Security Strategy appears, official U.S. policy undermines this goal by committing to achieving U.S. military dominance over space.

Stopping a New Arms Race on the Frontiers

These dimensions of the new frontier—hypersonic weapons and militarized AI and the increased militarization of space—all suggest that we are ramping up a new Cold War. The solution is arms control: international treaties that verify transparency and compliance to contain the dangers of this new technological arms race. During the Trump administration the U.S. lost valuable time by focusing instead on dismantling most of the existing architecture of nuclear arms control. The crucial work of repair and progress must include extending the architecture of arms control to include these new frontiers of the nuclear danger.

The Center for a New American Security (CNAS), a prominent Washington, DC, national-security think tank, has been spending a lot of time and energy thinking about AI. Its task forces and reports focus mostly on "cementing" America's lead in the AI revolution, with recommendations to boost federal funding and private sector incentives for AI development, and ideas for containing China's meddling in the U.S. AI infrastructure.

The Center's references to international cooperation focus on building AI "alliances and partnerships with like-minded countries" such as South Korea and the Netherlands.[82] A report titled *Artificial Intelligence and International Security* touches lightly on the problem of giving machines excessive power over military decisions. The prospect of autonomous weapons, CNAS writes, "raises profound questions about humanity's relationship to war and even the nature of war itself," questions it neither explores nor tries to answer. It concludes blandly that "the U.S. will need to adopt a national strategy for how to take advantage of the benefits of AI while mitigating its disruptive effects."

This is inadequate, since those disruptive effects include the potential to slide us all into nuclear war. First and foremost, the hypersonics and artificial intelligence arms races need to be slowed down. Even Mac Thornberry (D-TX), the former chair of the House Armed Services Committee, who seemed never to encounter a weapons system he didn't like, said, "It seems to me that we're always a lot better at developing technologies than we are the policies on how to use them."[83] The countries doing the developing need to be talking.

As Michael Klare points out, all these countries have reason to avoid this arms race, knowing full well that they are vulnerable to attack by their rivals. After decades of effort and billions of dollars spent on missile defense systems to make themselves invulnerable, it should be clear that this is a distant dream, one that these new technologies render even more unrealistic.

Instead of talking, however, they are all feverishly developing their offensive weapons for the new frontiers. In September of 2017 the United States and Russia did convene strategic stability talks in Helsinki. A second round was scheduled for the following March, but increasing bilateral tensions, and then war, derailed it. A long-term strategy to avoid nuclear catastrophe must involve this pursuit of strategic stability, involving China as well as the United States and Russia. And developing a framework for controlling the new dangers introduced by hypersonic, space-based, and autonomous weapons needs to be included in the discussions.

Klare suggests that while the negotiations are underway, the parties could build confidence by sharing information on the range and capabilities of these weapons and develop protocols enabling each country to differentiate between conventional and nuclear-armed hypersonics. A moratorium on testing of hypersonics could build a pause into this arms race, giving the negotiations time to proceed.[84]

As the existing frameworks of strategic arms control are being rebuilt, they should be extended to include both China and the new weapons that all three countries are currently pursuing, either prohibiting all weapons of a certain type or limiting their numbers. The parties should also begin consulting about the dangers that increased nuclear command-and-control automation could lead to inadvertent or accidental war, and the technical steps that could reduce this risk.

The three countries' preparations for war in space complicates and therefore exacerbates these risks. No enforceable rules over this domain exist. Though the Outer Space Treaty of 1967—signed by 100 countries, including the United States, China, and the former Soviet Union—prohibits the installation of nuclear weapons in space, its overbroad language does not restrict warfare over the satellites that now help to target these weapons.

The United States has so far rejected proposals by China and Russia to ban the installation of any weapon in space, arguing that such a ban would be unverifiable and would favor the Russian and Chinese positions. By failing to propose any alternative framework or even to signal openness to negotiations around an alternative, the United States has thrown in its lot with preparation for war in this new domain.

Conclusion

Thinking Beyond the Box

Outside actors, ranging from academic institutes like the Monterey Institute for International Studies to non-governmental organizations—like the Arms Control Association and the Union of Concerned Scientists to activist groups such as the Global Network Against Weapons and Nuclear Power in Space and the Campaign to Stop Killer Robots—seek to convince the world that our survival depends on finding another way. In a world of competing, unprecedented challenges, this one struggles for public attention.

These challenges may provide the answer though.

A broader perspective on how to make Americans safer came from an unlikely source, who gets the last word here. Max Boot, a military historian and columnist for the *Washington Post* and the *Wall Street Journal*, is a self-described defense "hawk" who has "always been a strong supporter of the U.S. armed forces." In a March 2020 piece, Boot runs through the major crises of the twenty-first century—the 9/11 attacks and the Afghan and Iraq wars that followed; the 2008 financial crisis; the 2016 Russian attack on the U.S. presidential election, global warming, and the coronavirus—observing how many of them "fall outside our traditional 'national security' parameters." The wars "could not bring lasting peace or stability to Iraq and Afghanistan…. Global warming is an even bigger crisis, yet it, too, has no military solution." Nor does the pandemic. These facts have made him "question whether we are spending our $738 billion defense budget on the right priorities."

Though the military professes to be open to new strategies, he says, they are always "safely in the realm of conventional military operations."

> What we really need is a more radical rethink of the whole concept of "national security." It never made any sense, as Trump's 2021 budget had initially proposed, to increase spending on nuclear weapons by $7 billion while cutting Centers for Disease Control and Prevention funding by $1.2 billion. Or to create an unnecessary Space Force out of the U.S. Air Force while eliminating the vitally important directorate of global health by folding it into another office within the National Security Council. Instead of simply pouring more money into the Pentagon, we need to develop new capacities to combat foreign disinformation, transition away from carbon fuels and stop the spread of pandemics. Those are more pressing priorities than a military attack from China, Russia, Iran or North Korea.[85]

Notes

1 Editorial, "The President Takes a Campaign Donation from the Pentagon," *The New York Times*, February 16, 2020, www.nytimes.com/2020/02/14/opinion/editorials/trump-wall-cuts.html.

2 Todd Miller, "More Than a Wall: Corporate Profiteering and the Militarization of US Borders," *Transnational Institute*, September 2019, p. 25, www.toddmillerwriter.com/more-than-a-wall/.

3 Transcript: "Media Roundtable Background Briefing on DHS Request for DOD Assistance in Blocking Drug-Smuggling Corridors Along the Southern US Border," Department of Defense, January 16, 2020, www.defense.gov/Newsroom/Transcripts/Transcript/Article/2060432/media-roundtable-background-briefing-on-dhs-request-for-dod-assistance-in-block/source/GovDelivery/.

4 Jonathan Stevenson, "A Different Kind of Emergency," *New York Review of Books*, April 24, 2019, pp. 24–26, www.nybooks.com/articles/2019/05/23/trump-different-emergency/.
5 Nick Miroff, "People are sawing through and climbing over Trump's border wall. Now contractors are being asked for ideas to make it less vulnerable," *Washington Post*, June 4, 2020, www.washingtonpost.com/immigration/trump-border-wall-vulnerable/2020/06/04/ccd40e5e-a66e-11ea-8681-7d471bf20207_story.html.
6 Miller, "More Than a Wall."
7 John W. Whitehead, "Has the Dept. of Homeland Security become America's standing army?" chron.com, June 16, 2014 (www.chron.com/neighborhood/friendswood/opinion/article/WHITEHEAD-Has-the-Dept-of-HomelandSecurity-9677926.php).
8 Quoted in Seymour Melman, *Pentagon Capitalism* (New York: McGraw Hill, 1970) pp. 231–234.
9 Robert Krinsky, "Swords and Sheepskins," in eds. Lloyd Dumas and Marek Thee, *Making Peace Possible* (Oxford: Pergamon Press, 1989) pp. 89–98.
10 AAAS, "Trends in Federal R&D, FY 1976–2020," www.aaas.org/sites/default/files/2020-10/DefNon.png.
11 Jean E. Jackson, "Anthropologists Express Concern over Government Plan to Support Military-Related Research," MIT Faculty Newsletter, web.mit.edu/fnl/volume/205/jackson.html.
12 Krinsky, p. 105.
13 Hugh Gusterson, *Nuclear Rites* (Berkeley: University of California Press, 1996) pp. 1989–1990.
14 International Campaign to Abolish Nuclear Weapons (ICAN), "Schools of Mass Destruction: American Universities in the U.S. Nuclear Weapons Complex" (Geneva, Switzerland: ICAN, November 2019) www.icanw.org/schools_of_mass_destruction.
15 "LA County Economic Development Strategy," p. 279.
16 Miller p. 65.
17 Miller p. 31.
18 Miller p. 20.
19 Miller p. 21.
20 Christopher Witco, "Campaign contributions, access and government contracting," *Journal of Public Administration Research and Theory 21*, 2011, pp. 761–778, https://academic.oup.com/jpart/article/21/4/761/955742?login=true.
21 Miller p. 65.
22 Miller p. 32.
23 Tim Fernholz, "US defense contractors profit from child detention—and you might, too," *Quartz*, June 19, 2018. https://qz.com/1309460/defense-contractors-like-general-dynamics-are-profiting-from-child-detention-and-you-might-too/.
24 Press release, "General Atomics Aeronautical Systems awarded DHS-CBP UAS contract," September 1, 2005, www.ga.com/general-atomics-aeronautical-systems-awarded-dhscbp-uas-contract.
25 "Investigate: Elbit Systems Ltd.," American Friends Service Committee, https://investigate.afsc.org/company/elbit-systems#:~:text=Elbit%20Systems%20Ltd%20is%20the,drone%20and%20military%20surveillance%20technologies.
26 Miller pp. 36, 50.
27 "Federal Contractor Misconduct Database," Project on Government Oversight, www.contractormisconduct.org/about-fcmd.

28 Miller pp. 32.
29 Aaron Mehta, Valerie Insinna, David Larter and Joe Gould, "Pentagon seeks to cut F-35s, other equipment to pay for Trump's border wall," *Defense News*, February 13, 2020, www.defensenews.com/breaking-news/2020/02/13/pentagon-seeks-to-cut-f-35s-other-equipment-to-pay-for-trumps-border-wall/.
30 Dan Lamothe, "Pentagon will pull money from ballistic missile and surveillance plane programs to fund border wall," *Washington Post*, May 12, 2019, www.washingtonpost.com/national-security/2019/05/12/pentagon-will-pull-money-ballistic-missile-surveillance-plane-programs-fund-border-wall/.
31 "Defense Primer: Department of Defense Contractors," Congressional Research Service, Updated February 3, 2021, https://fas.org/sgp/crs/natsec/IF10600.pdf.
32 Mijente, "The War Against Immigrants: Powered by Palantir," *notechforice.com*, https://notechforice.com/palantir/.
33 Mijente, p. 31.
34 Sam Dean, "A 26-year-old billionaire is building virtual border walls—and the federal government is buying," *Los Angeles Times*, July 26, 2019, www.latimes.com/business/story/2019-07-25/anduril-profile-palmer-luckey-border-controversy.
35 Mijente, p. 31.
36 Mijente, p. 31.
37 Mijente, p. 19.
38 Mijente, p. 4.
39 Miller, p. 79.
40 Department of Defense, "Summary of the 2018 National Defense Strategy of The United States of America," p. 3, https://dod.defense.gov/Portals/1/Documents/pubs/2018-National-Defense-Strategy-Summary.pdf.
41 Sydney J. Freedberg Jr., "Hypersonics: 5 More Army-Navy Flight Tests by 2023," Breaking Defense, 4-15-2020, https://breakingdefense.com/2020/04/hypersonics-5-more-army-navy-flight-tests-by-2023/.
42 Paul McCleary, "Pentagon Sounds Alarm Over Sub-Hunting Tech Shortage, Hypersonic Funding," *Breaking Defense*, July 23, 2018, https://breakingdefense.com/2018/07/pentagon-sounds-alarm-over-sub-hunting-tech-shortage-hypersonic-funding/.
43 United Nations Office of Disarmament Affairs, "Hypersonic Weapons: A Challenge and Opportunity for Strategic Arms Control," February 2019, www.un.org/disarmament/publications/more/hypersonic-weapons-a-challengeand-opportunity-for-strategic-arms-control/.
44 Paul Bernstein and Dain Hancock, "China's Hypersonic Weapons," *Georgetown Journal of International Affairs*, January 27, 2021, https://gjia.georgetown.edu/2021/01/27/chinas-hypersonic-weapons/.
45 Theresa Hitchens and Sydney J. Freedberg Jr., "Exclusive: DoD Seeks $2.9B for Hypersonics in 2021," *Breaking Defense*, 4/14/20, https://breakingdefense.com/2020/04/exclusive-dod-asks-2-9b-for-hypersonics-in-2021/.
46 https://breakingdefense.com/2019/03/army-sets-2023-hypersonic-flight-test-strategic-cannon-advances/.
47 Congressional Research Service, "Conventional Prompt Global Strike and Long-Range Ballistic Missiles: Background and Issues," updated February 14, 2020, p. 46, https://sgp.fas.org/crs/nuke/R41464.pdf.

48 Sydney J. Freedberg Jr., "Hypersonics: DoD Wants 'Hundreds of Weapons ASAP,'" *Breaking Defense*, April 24, 2020,https://breakingdefense.com/2020/04/hypersonics-dod-wants-hundreds-of-weapons-asap/.

49 Congressional Research Service, "Hypersonic Weapons: Background and Issues for Congress," Updated August 25, 2021, https://sgp.fas.org/crs/weapons/R45811.pdf.

50 Aaron Gregg, "Military-Industrial Complex Finds a Growth Market in Hypersonic Weaponry," *The Washington Post*, December 31, 2018, www.washingtonpost.com/business/2018/12/21/military-industrial-complex-finds-growth-market-hypersonic-weaponry/.

51 Vikram Mittal, "U.S. Military Strives to Take the Lead in a Hypersonic Weapon Arms Race," *Forbes*, February 15, 2021, www.forbes.com/sites/vikrammittal/2021/02/15/us-military-awards-contracts-striving-to-take-lead-in-the-hypersonic-arms-race/?sh=774c3b537df9.

52 Joseph Trevithick, "Here's How Hypersonic Weapons Could Completely Change the Face of Warfare," *The War Zone*, June 6, 2017, www.thedrive.com/the-war-zone/11177/heres-how-hypersonic-weapons-could-completely-change-the-face-of-warfare.

53 Joseph Trevithick, "Northrop and Raytheon Have Been Secretly Working on Scramjet Powered by Hypersonic Missile," *The War Zone*, June 18, 2019, www.thedrive.com/the-war-zone/28580/northrop-and-raytheon-have-been-secretly-working-on-scamjet-powered-hypersonic-missile.

54 CRS, "Conventional Prompt Global Strike and Long-Range Ballistic Missiles: Background and Issues," p. 47.

55 James M. Acton, "Hypersonic Weapons Explainer," Carnegie Endowment for International Peace, April 2, 2018, https://carnegieendowment.org/2018/04/02/hypersonic-weapons-explainer-pub-75957.

56 "Contracts for March 23, 2021, Department of Defense, www.defense.gov/Newsroom/Contracts/Contract/Article/2547591/source/GovDelivery/.

57 Congressional Budget Office, "Costs of Implementing Recommendations of the 2019 Missile Defense Review," January 2021, www.cbo.gov/publication/56960#_idTextAnchor038.

58 Quoted in Mark Thompson, "The Bunker," Project on Government Oversight, August 18, 2021, www.pogo.org/analysis/2021/08/the-bunker-afghanistan-down-the-drain/.

59 Michael Klare, "An 'Arms Race in Speed': Hypersonic Weapons and the Changing Calculus of Battle," *Arms Control Today*, June 2019, www.armscontrol.org/act/2019-06/features/arms-race-speed-hypersonic-weapons-changing-calculus-battle.

60 Department of Defense, Directive 3000.09, *Autonomy in Weapon Systems*, www.esd.whs.mil/Portals/54/ Documents/DD/issuances/DODd/300009p.pdf., cited in "Artificial Intelligence and National Security," Congressional Research Service, Updated November 21, 2019, p. 3.

61 CRS, "Artificial Intelligence and National Security," pp. 20–25.

62 Troy Rummler, "Future hypersonics could be artificially intelligent," *Sandia Lab News*, April 25, 2019, www.sandia.gov/labnews/2019/04/25/hypersonics/.

63 Marcus Roth, "Artificial Intelligence at the Top 5 US Defense Contractors," Emerj, The AI Research and Advisory Company, updated January 3, 2019, https://emerj.com/ai-sector-overviews/artificial-intelligence-at-the-top-5-us-defense-contractors/.

64 CRS, "Artificial Intelligence and National Security," p. 2.

65 CRS, "Artificial Intelligence," p. 6.

66 National Security Commission on Artificial Intelligence, Interim Report, November 2019, p. 35, https://drive.google.com/file/d/153OrxnuGEjsUvlxWsFYauslwNeCEk vUb/view.

67 CRS, "Artificial Intelligence and National Security," p. 18.

68 Scott Shane and Daisuke Wakabayashi, "'The Business of War': Google Employees Protest Work for the Pentagon," *New York Times*, April 4, 2018, www.nytimes.com/ 2018/04/04/technology/google-letter-ceo-pentagon-project.html.

69 Nick Statt and James Vincent, "Google pledges not to develop AI weapons, but says it will still work with the military," *The Verge*, June 7, 2018. www.theverge.com/2018/6/ 7/17439310/google-ai-ethics-principles-warfare-weapons-military-project-maven.

70 Dean, *Los Angeles Times*, 2019.

71 CRS, "Artificial Intelligence and National Security," p. 14.

72 Paul Scharre, *Autonomous Weapons and Operational Risk*, Center for a New American Security, February 2016, p. 23, www.cnas.org/publications/reports/ autonomous-weapons-and-operational-risk.

73 The MITRE Corporation, "Perspectives on Research in Artificial Intelligence and Artificial General Intelligence Relevant to DOD," Office of the Assistant Secretary of Defense for Research and Engineering, January 2017, p. 32, https://irp.fas.org/age ncy/dod/jason/ai-dod.pdf.

74 Michael T. Klare, "Autonomous Weapons Systems and the Laws of War," Arms Control Today, March 19, 2019, www.armscontrol.org/act/2019-03/features/ autonomous-weapons-systems-laws-war.

75 U.S. Congressional Budget Office, "Projected Costs of U.S. Nuclear Forces, 2019 to 2028," January 2019, www.cbo.gov/system/files/2019-01/54914-NuclearForces.pdf.

76 James Johnson, "Artificial Intelligence, Autonomy, and the Risk of Catalytic Nuclear War," Modern War Institute, March 18, 2021, https://mwi.usma.edu/artificial-intellige nce-autonomy-and-the-risk-of-catalytic-nuclear-war/.

77 Adam Lowther and Curtis McGiffin, "America Needs a 'Dead Hand,'" War on the Rocks, August 16, 2019, https://warontherocks.com/2019/08/america-needs-a- dead-hand/.

78 Quoted in W.J. Hennigan, "America Really Does Have a Space Force. We Went Inside to See What It Does," *Time*, July 23, 2020, https://time.com/5869987/spaceforce/.

79 Hennigan.

80 Hennigan, *Time*, July 23, 2020.

81 "SPACE ACQUISITIONS: DOD Faces Significant Challenges as It Seeks to Accelerate Space Programs and Address Threats," General Accounting Office, March 27, 2019, www.gao.gov/assets/700/697998.pdf.

82 "The American AI Century: A Blueprint for Action," December 17, 2019, www.cnas. org/publications/reports/the-american-ai-century-a-blueprint-for-action.

83 Morgan Chalfant, "Congress told to brace for 'robotic soldiers,'" *The Hill*, March 1, 2017, https://thehill.com/policy/cybersecurity/321825-congress-told-to-brace-for- robotic-soldiers.

84 Klare, "An Arms Race in Speed," 2019.

85 Max Boot, "Covid-19 is killing off our traditional notions of national defense," *Washington Post*, March 31, 2020, www.washingtonpost.com/opinions/2020/03/31/ covid-19-is-killing-off-our-traditional-notions-national-defense/?arc404=true.

8
GREATER BINGHAMTON, NY

Swords into Plowshares

The last stop on our tour brings us back to the Rust Belt, four hours by car north of Johnstown, to the banks of the Susquehanna River flowing between the Appalachians and the Adirondacks.

We're back to one of the minor locations on the Pentagon's contracting map. New York State's dependency on the military economy has been on a long slide. It now ranks 15th among the states in total Pentagon contract amounts, but dead last in the proportion of the state's economy coming from this source.[1]

Contrary to the prosperity gospel of military contracting, Greater Binghamton (population about 250,000) is, like Johnstown, one of its state's more economically depressed *and* defense-dependent spots. In the concluding chapter we'll take a broader look at how far from unusual this combination can be.

In addition to the two top-ten prime contractors with major operations in the area, comprehensive sources list more than 140 other companies with tiny pieces of the military pie.[2] The vast majority of these contracts are under two million dollars, most of them under $100,000, many under $100. There's Ametek, supplying electronic instruments globally from operations in Binghamton, Kansas, and Pennsylvania. PB Industries got $1.9 million from the Pentagon in 2019 to manage shipping logistics. There's Virtusphere that got $252,000 that year for some of its virtual reality software, and Enviren Services, which got $179,935 for environmental testing equipment.

Except for the two big primes, the connections of these companies to the Pentagon are largely invisible to most local residents. Joshua Reno, an anthropology professor at the State University of New York (SUNY) Binghamton, who has studied these connections, notes that the military industrial complex "weaves its way into our lives" without announcing itself.[3]

DOI: 10.4324/9781003293705-9

We are here for only one reason. Current examples of military contractors that have successfully and sustainably converted their "swords into plowshares" are hard to come by. When the defense budget fell sharply after the Cold War, many of them started to try. But as the budget began to rise again in the late 1990s, most of these conversion efforts were dropped. The Pentagon's surging fiscal incentives underwrote a retreat to the comfort zone of the market they knew best.

It wasn't the absence of a Pentagon-sized replacement funding stream alone that defeated many contractors' efforts to make it in commercial manufacturing. It also came down to thinking they could simply apply the practices of military manufacturing to making commercial products, rather than facing the challenges of adapting their practices to new conditions.

We're here because in Binghamton one contractor overcame these challenges and showed that it can be done, and how. What they made, and still make, not only employs people and makes a profit, but is providing one piece of the solution to the looming national security challenge—climate change—that, as bears repeating, no military force, or military budget of any size, can contain.

An Economic Evolution

Like Johnstown, Binghamton set down its roots in a river valley and then powered its industrial development with a rail link and waves of immigrants from Eastern Europe and elsewhere. Its claims to manufacturing repute initially came after the Civil War from the second-largest cigar-producing operation in the country, and a shoe company turning out 52 million pairs a year.[4] The outbreak of the Civil War turned portions of the city's industrial capacity toward guns and other munitions.

During much of the twentieth century Binghamton tagged itself "The Birthplace of IBM." In the suburb of Endicott, a group of nineteenth-century inventors tinkering with things like early adding machines and employee time clocks joined forces. By 1924 their enterprise had evolved into International Business Machines (IBM), the Binghamton area's largest employer and economic mainstay. After the turn of the next century, as we'll see, the nickname, if used at all, often came with a side of bitterness.

The New Deal made IBM into a corporate powerhouse, as its pioneering computing capabilities turned out to be invaluable in organizing the massive operations of the Social Security Administration, among other programs. Then World War II pulled it into military contracting. IBM supplied everything from punch-card machines used by the Manhattan Project, to the first large-scale electromechanical calculator for the Navy and precision devices for weapons, including the Browning and M1 Carbine rifles. New production sites sprouted in Greater Binghamton to accommodate wartime production.

Then, while taking the lead on the postwar revolution in civilian computing, IBM also shifted into servicing such Cold War projects as the military's nascent efforts to build early-detection air defense systems.

The other major player in Binghamton's military economy was General Electric (GE). This sprawling twentieth-century corporate giant with its fingers, at one time or another, in everything from dishwashers to computers to radio and TV, had gotten a jump on military contracting during World War I, by inventing a "turbo supercharger" that increased an airplane engine's power at altitude, and its rate of climb. GE installed 300,000 of them in World War II fighters and bombers, and was chosen to develop the Army's first jet engine for the war effort.[5]

Like many of the companies whose normal route back to civilian manufacturing was partially short-circuited by the Cold War, GE stayed put in the lucrative market for military jet engines, as well as satellites and other apparati of military communications. By 1948 the company had set up shop on the banks of the river on the 30-acre Air Force Base 59, in Johnson City, another Binghamton suburb. At this "government-owned contractor-operated" (GOCO) facility, they made flight controls and navigation systems for a series of military aircraft. By the 1980s these included the F-15 and F-18 fighter jets as well as the B-1 bomber and the V-22 helicopter/plane combo.[6]

GE also took on a major role in the Cold War's new growth industry, nuclear weapons. As protests of industrial complicity in the nuclear terror grew during the 1980s, the company became the focus of a multi-year boycott of its commercial light bulbs, refrigerators and so on—a boycott that claimed 4 million adherents and 450 supporting organizations, including religious organizations and labor unions.[7] In 1993 GE exited the nuclear weapons business.[8]

By then the Cold War had, miraculously, ended without bloodshed between the United States and the Soviet Union, and what the *New York Times* referred to as "the wrenching new era for the military-industrial complex" was underway.[9] The two-thirds cut in the Pentagon procurement budget sent its contractors scrambling in one of two opposite directions (with many variations): hunkering down and laying off workers to cast their lot with "pure play" in military contracting, or reducing that dependency on a shrinking pile of Pentagon contracts by redirecting their businesses more toward the civilian world. Sales, mergers, acquisitions, and new ventures by contractors groping to accomplish these goals churned defense market waters at a rate not seen before or since.

With the confidence that came from having feet well-planted in both the commercial and military worlds, GE became the first major contractor to take the plunge toward demilitarizing its portfolio. Beyond ending its work on nuclear weapons, it announced in November 1992 that it was selling off its military electronics businesses. These businesses, based in Binghamton as well as Syracuse and Utica, New York, and locations in Pennsylvania, New Jersey, Massachusetts, Vermont, and Florida, would now be the property of defense giant Martin Marietta.

Swords into Plowshares: How to, and How Not to

Bob Devine took his first job out of engineering school in 1985 with GE in Johnson City. He worked first on the flight controls of the exotic new $2 billion-a-copy B-2 bomber (assembled in Palmdale) and then on the old warhorse A-10 Warthog. The 1993 acquisition by Martin Marietta changed the name on the building, but most of the work that went on there, and the people doing it, stayed the same. This remained true two years later when Martin Marietta merged with Lockheed to become Lockheed Martin.

Yet while focusing primarily on dominating the defense-oriented mergers and acquisitions party, Lockheed was also looking to hedge its bets by allowing a team to explore what commercial products they might be able to make within their own walls. Devine found himself on Lockheed's "What else could we do?" team.

In standard thinking on new product development, Devine says, the goal is to look at where your current product lines fit on a grid and find "the one-box move."

> You try to find these market adjacencies [between the military and com-
> mercial markets] which are also business adjacencies…. A one-box move
> might be new technology into the same market. Or new market, same tech-
> nology. But trying to jump to commercial in a new market with new tech-
> nology or a different approach to the business altogether is kind of a move
> on both those axes…. So it's a stretch for the business to be able to adapt.[10]

So, Devine's engineering team looked for technology adjacencies. They had been working on a contract with McDonnell Douglas (which would be swallowed up by Boeing in 1997) to convert the F-15 fighter jet to lighter and more reliable electronic hydraulic flight controls, replacing heavy and less-reliable mechanical versions.

At the same time, they had a contract to build an electronic fuel injection control for a new freight locomotive, which made them conversant in how their diesel electric motors convert mechanical to electric power.

> And we said, this is really interesting—if you have a set of batteries you
> have a hybrid. And you'll be able to capture regeneration—taking the heat
> energy that would normally be lost in braking and putting that back in the
> batteries. And thus was born the idea of a hybrid. Locomotives had been
> doing that for years, but we applied it to rubber tire vehicles—buses and
> trucks.

Toyota was figuring out regenerative braking around the same time, for its Priuses, but Devine claims his shop got there first! They like to bring this up with Toyota from time to time, he says laughing.

Though their work on the airplanes involved power levels that were orders of magnitude lower than what's required to push a bus, "the power processing and the control knowledge to do it is very similar." They asked themselves why they couldn't take the light, compact, high-reliability power controls from the aircraft and apply them to the diesel-electric power train of the locomotive, and add battery storage to it, "and voila, we have a hybrid [power train] to put on a transit bus." They assembled a team including the variety of mechanical, electrical, power design and software engineers required to build a complex military system, and got to work on a prototype for the system they called HybriDrive. Their system pulled together the bus's entire power propulsion system, including battery packs, motors and generators.

Navigating the Move(s)

But the idea of the technological one-box move doesn't really get you very far in figuring out this challenge, says Devine, because a successful move from the military to the commercial box requires a lot of other moves.

> Let's say you're building flight controls for the F-18 Super Hornet. You've got to build as many of those flight controls as there are Super Hornets coming off the Boeing production line, and there are only going to be maybe 50 a year, or 100 would be a lot. So you go from a quantity of 100 to a quantity of 1000, 3000, depending on what commercial business you're in. A 10-fold, maybe an order of magnitude, change in production. That's difficult.

What are the keys to getting there? Topping the list is bringing on people who understand the demands of higher-volume commercial manufacturing. The GE acquisition gave Martin Marietta, and then Lockheed, access to that know-how in-house. Devine singles out the contributions of one project leader, Tom Arseneault, who worked with him on GE's military contracts and then did a stint with GE Appliances in Louisville before returning to the Johnson City plant. So Arseneault came to the project with refined skills at managing commercial supply chains, and familiarity with how cost-conscious, high-volume manufacturing is done.

Also, he says, the team was not trying to switch gears from fighter jets to toasters. It's less of a reach, he says, to move from one market to another when both of them require "high maneuverability, well-engineered, heavy duty-type systems." The team also hired people out of the automotive industry who knew all about automating production for high volumes. And they teamed up with an established bus company, Orion Industries.

They knew they were entering a market poised for growth. In Chapter 4 we looked at California's pioneering work to grow the infrastructure of a clean transportation transition. Beyond California, big-city mayors were also beginning to focus on fixing the poor air quality on their streets. Hybrid electric buses would not only reduce pollutants, but save fuel costs, and, without a transmission, maintenance costs as well. Hybrids are also quieter. And the news was beginning to filter down from climate scientists to the general public that reducing fossil fuel emissions was necessary to keep global warming's dangerous effects at bay.

The inertial force most responsible for keeping Pentagon contractors from venturing beyond the defense market is almost surely the reliable low-risk funding stream they usually enjoy by staying put: R&D paid for, and frequently, despite the temptations to cost-padding, the cost-plus contract.

More common is the cost-padding mechanism of the cost overrun. The Pentagon has never solved the problem of awarding a contract to the low bidders (low on the basis of cost estimates they won't be held to), who "discover"—when it's too late for the Pentagon to switch contractors—that they can't deliver without more time (often measured in years) and much more money. In the commercial world, which operates almost exclusively with fixed-price contracts, this strategy goes away.

To finance their project, the Lockheed team saw the chance to make more of a one-box move. Rather than having to make the leap to sell their wares on an unpredictable open market, they would be shifting from one federal funding source to another. City transit agencies are subsidized by the Federal Transit Administration (FTA) to help fund their transit solutions, in transportation spending plans that are usually five years long. So, the funding level is, like DoD's, fairly predictable—though a tiny fraction of what DoD has to offer.

Finding "adjacencies" hardly means you've cleared your path to civilian manufacturing success. As far back as the 1970s, researchers of industrial change had been analyzing the failures of managers who thought they could apply the practices of military contracting wholesale to the commercial arena. Beyond identifying the pitfalls of concurrency, Columbia industrial engineering professor Seymour Melman argued that moving from low-volume, high-performance, cost-no-object military production to cost-conscious mass production was not just a matter of retooling some machines and reorganizing the production line, but required restructuring management itself.[11]

Devine and the team experienced this first-hand as they started trying to invent a hybrid electric bus. "It's a culture shift," he says. "Engineers who've been in military work for a long time are tough. They want perfection. It's 100 percent mission success, everything has to work, all the time." Those standards take a lot of time and money. And whereas the military design cycles "tend to be up to 36 months, in the commercial world you have to keep up with competitors who are spinning out new designs in a 12-month cycle."

So if you're organizing commercial production according to a military timetable, you're falling behind. If there aren't many complaints about your commercial product, "and they only seem to crop up in Bismarck, North Dakota in the winter, you say 'Let's extend the warranty on that.' The military wouldn't go for that," he says laughing.

A commercial customer is able to say, "Oh, you gotta make a change?" Or "You can't get that part? But this part will work? Put it in." In military manufacturing, such changes set elaborate bureaucratic sequences in motion. Every part has to be traceable to its source, for example, and no part can be altered without government approval, adding time and money to the whole process.

Efforts to make commercial products using machines built for military production have frequently foundered because the extreme high-performance standards demanded by the military calibrate the machines with such extremely tight tolerances that they increase costs beyond what the commercial marketplace will bear. Standing up a production line to install components for hybrid buses required some retooling, particularly to scale operations for higher volumes. But, Devine says, while circuit boards for military and commercial production will need to be built according to different requirements, "the little machine that puts the parts on the board and solders them down? That can be exactly the same."

Production was set up as what they called a "Factory Within a Factory" inside the military division. Setting up a separate cost-accounting structure that prioritized cost savings was a big, and necessary, challenge. They liberated themselves as much as possible from the world of MILSPECS (extremely precise military specifications), and all the extra paperwork required by the FAR (Federal Acquisition Regulations). "One great way to destroy value is choke the business with requirements it doesn't really need," Devine says. "Like we're going to force you to buy your parts from these top suppliers that mostly do military." They also needed a separate IT system that allowed them to work more freely with international partners.

"I used to have all sorts of conversations with our president about this. 'What about ditching all of this stuff? Let's write our own policies, do our own payroll.' But once you're doing your own payroll, human resources, IT, you're almost better off getting sold to a commercial company. It's the old 'Play me or trade me!'"

On the other hand, there were definite advantages to staying put. In addition to the reliable financial underwriting, says Devine:

> You have an operations base to get the parts built that doesn't have to be part of your core team. You can just go out and say "Here's a project, go build it out on the floor." Let's say you're beyond the mechanical design phase, the ink is dry on your drawings and you're cutting metal now. You don't need so many mechanical people so you can give them back to the business and they get assigned to a new project.

How did they overcome the challenges of building a commercial product within a military business?

He's honest: "We didn't, completely." Since management insisted on retaining some residual military practices, "The product definitely carries a bit more cost [than its all-commercial competitors]."

> The way to overcome that is through very high reliability hardware, and very good customer service and support. You make the total value proposition of working with you through the life cycle of that product worthwhile, rather than just buying it from a company that knocked out 1000 of these things in China and then doesn't support you.

Getting a Business Up and Running (literally)

Examples of failure were there to show them what to avoid. Devine cites the foray of Long Island-based Grumman (before it was taken over by Northrop) into the bus business. Using the military model of concurrency—go into mass production before you've worked the bugs out—Grumman's buses began breaking down on New York streets. "There was something in the paper about it every day," Devine says. NYC's Metropolitan Transit Authority (MTA) sued the company.

So, Devine's team took it slow. First, they did as much testing off road as they could and then avoided Grumman's public-relations disaster by initially putting only ten buses on the street. "We got our pinkie toe in the door…. And we didn't do that well at first … [But] the best way to avoid getting sued is you are responsive and fix everything you can for them at your cost," Devine says.

In addition to the internal funding from Lockheed, and the subsidies from the Federal Transit Administration, they got R&D money and technical assistance from the New York State Energy Research and Development Authority, the public benefit corporation set up to increase the state's energy efficiency and reliance on fossil fuels.

And they joined CALSTART, the green transition consortium we met in Chapter 4 focused on linking government agencies setting stringent emissions standards with the industrial infrastructure to meet them. Bill Van Amburg, CALSTART's executive vice president, cites the HybriDrive project's incremental approach as key to its success:

> They didn't try to do everything at once. They focused on what can we do really well that would add value right now? So they added hybridization to the power train. At the start it could be dropped into an existing bus, made to work effectively and add some value.

The corollary is that being patient about developing a new product, for a new market, requires patient capital. This has been in short supply ever since economist Milton Friedman decreed that the point of a business was to make profits for its shareholders, and that profitability was to be measured by the quarterly report.[12]

FIGURE 8.1 Bob Devine in front of a HybriDrive bus bound for San Francisco
Photo courtesy of Mark Kammerer, used with permission.

Devine thinks Lockheed executives "tolerated us through some of the loss years" because those were the years of military budget cuts, and they were on the lookout for ways to "help soften the blow of a bad cycle." But, he says, "You gotta show payback. Nobody's going to allow you to spend money and not pay it back," adding, "We have."

For all the stress headaches, "It was very exciting to do something that was definitely out of the mold. Putting together systems we'd never put together before. Fast moving, dynamic, challenging." Fortunately, he says, engineers tend to be "intellectually curious people."

While fixing the bugs in their ten buses out on the streets of New York City, they also had to contend with the human resistance to change.

> New technology is shunned a lot of times by the old guard. At places like transit agencies. They love their big diesel engines and they like hydraulic systems—mechanical, not electronic. Even up and down the chain. You can have the head of MTA [New York's Metropolitan Transit Agency] say we want to do this but then have the maintenance supervisors say "We're not bought in." What happens then is your buses get parked. Sometimes for silly reasons.

After what seemed like a protracted time fixing and negotiating over the ten buses built with Orion Industries, they got an order for 100 more. "That was pivotal. It meant the business could actually compete and stay alive." Other large-city transit agencies, including Boston's, became interested. As they began placing orders for these hybrid electric buses, these cities were beginning the process of converting to a fleet that would cut both fuel consumption and greenhouse gas emissions in half.

Sold

In January of 1999, Lockheed Martin Control Systems announced another small order from New York City, this time putting HybriDrive systems on buses built by Nova Bus, the most popular bus fleet in the city. James Scanlon, president of Lockheed's Control Systems division, touted this order as proof that the technology worked, and New York City was committed to it. Nova added: "We are excited to join Lockheed Martin at the forefront of this significant advance in transit bus technology."[13]

At the end of the year, Lockheed's Control Systems announced two new contracts. One was another New York City order, for 125 more buses. The other: to design and build a hybrid electric propulsion system for an Army line-haul tractor.[14] This latter contract was both a move in the box matrix back toward its comfort zone of military contracting, and a harbinger of another big move in that direction.

Five months later, just as HybriDrive bus sales were beginning to multiply, Lockheed Martin announced it was selling the Control Systems division, including the HybriDrive project, to BAE Systems, another defense contractor.

Why sell? Lockheed Martin's then-CEO, Vance Coffman, explained that "This proposed transaction is consistent with Lockheed Martin's strategic initiative to focus on business and technical competencies that will strengthen our position … in core aerospace and defense markets."[15] Since by then defense budget cuts seemed to be a thing of the past, straying from one's familiar "core competencies" seemed, to Lockheed and numerous other contractors, no longer necessary.

The BAE Era Begins

BAE began life as British Aerospace. It clocks in at 7th among military contractors, right after the top five plus the Aviation Industry Corporation of China.[16]

The U.S. military used to restrict itself to "buying American"; it has relaxed these rules in recent years as the leading military corporations have been acting more and more like multinationals, and as our military allies have insisted on a piece of the action. But to become a major player in the U.S. defense market, BAE had to set up a separate U.S. subsidiary, incorporated in Delaware to, in its words, "mitigate our foreign ownership through a Special Security Agreement between the U.S. Government, BAE Systems, Inc. and BAE Systems plc." The agreement requires outside directors on a government security committee certifying the company's compliance with U.S. security and export rules.[17] The BAE subsidiary is the top foreign arms seller to the U.S. military.[18]

BAE gets 95 percent of its revenue from military contracting. This is a slightly lower percentage than Lockheed Martin (96%), and higher than Northrop Grumman (85%) and General Dynamics (79%); Raytheon Technologies's merger has brought its military balance down to 65 percent. Boeing's troubles with its commercial aircraft line has boosted its military balance slightly, to 56 percent. Between 2020 and 2021 BAE increased its defense revenue by 12 percent, a higher percentage than any of the others, including Lockheed.[19]

BAE's products include armored combat vehicles, artillery and missile launching systems, and precision strike munitions, as well as flight and engine controls and electronic warfare systems in its Electronic Systems division. While most of what it got from the sale expanded its military portfolio, it also got HybriDrive.

And the business really began to take off. New York City bought another 200 buses, "And after," Devine says, "you turned on the TV, and anything that's filmed on location in NYC, one of our hybrids is usually driving in the background."

"And then [in 2005] we picked up Toronto. We were hummin'. Then it was time … to go overseas." Because BAE is a British company, it was natural to start selling their buses in Europe, beginning in the UK and France.

> Going to Europe was a one-box move for us: We changed the geography, not the technology.… Plus it was home turf. If [something on the bus] wasn't right we could send people right out of Kent [County, in the south of England] to solve it. So we had boots on the ground there, to keep the customers happy.

Under New Management

A lot stayed the same: existing on-site leadership, and contracts, and teams. But the team "had to learn the BAE way of doing things," based on a British "process-oriented" model, a change from Lockheed's "performance-driven," style.

> The cultures of Lockheed and BAE are a little bit different.… Not saying one is better than the other.… Every company is focused on core financial performance.… But Lockheed was *really* focused on never having a red program, one that they knew was risky and you had difficulty performing. And if they did they would really really bear down on that program hard.… You could expect to be literally riding the elevator on Sunday with the CEO or president if you had a red program, and everybody just *felt* it.
>
> BAE would do the same things but expected that they'd have a red program once in a while. The expectation wasn't that you live here 24-7 until this program wasn't red anymore. They had processes to take these programs and return them to green. It was more like we're going to plan our way out of this problem. And give you guys some time to do it, and do it right.

In establishing a new commercial product within a military firm, they were up against the perception that this was a short-term strategy to ride out a trough in defense spending.

> The biggest fear for our customers was that as soon as the defense budget goes back up you guys are going to just leave us high and dry. And we had to assure them that that was not gonna happen.

While turning up the pressure to turn a profit all along the way, Lockheed did give the project several years to succeed: The first HybriDrive buses didn't roll onto New York City streets until 1998.

They basically left it up to the local leadership to decide how they were going to fund it and invest in it, and as long as they could show they had a good case for return, they'd let them continue it.

But just as this tolerance was beginning to pay off—while, as their customers feared, the defense budget was surging—Lockheed bailed.

Multi-year internal funding without a return is "kind of a foreign idea to some military businesses," Devine explains. Military R&D on a new product` can take far longer—look at the unfinished 30-year process on the F-35—but mostly it is funded by DoD,

> on cost-plus or cost-plus-fixed-fee programs, so the risks are so much lower.… So a lot has to be said for the top executive leadership at BAE. To be able to stomach what it takes to do this.… They gave us latitude on things like hard financials provided there was a path for a good financial return.

As their buses were reducing transit fuel consumption and greenhouse gas emissions in places like Chicago, Paris, and Tokyo, Devine and his team were rolling out one improvement to the product after another. The first buses used lead acid batteries. The team pioneered a redesign of the power propulsion system to run on cleaner and much lighter lithium ion batteries. And, using their experience in converting mechanical systems on military aircraft to operate electronically, they began electrifying more and more systems on the bus, including air conditioning, steering, and braking. And they began branching out beyond the bus market, for example putting HybriDrive systems into marine applications such as towboats.

The Setback that Wasn't

As mentioned, Greater Binghamton and Johnstown share a lot beyond a heavy stake in the military economy. They are both officially designated "Distressed Communities," according to measures including poverty, unemployment, and housing vacancy rates.[20]

And they share one other thing that most Rust Belt communities now don't (though more of them will): they are flood prone.

The Susquehanna flows west through Binghamton before turning back toward its endpoint in the Chesapeake Bay. The river that put Binghamton on the map also becomes from time to time its greatest threat, or at least a threat more dramatic than the slow decline of U.S. manufacturing.

Unusually heavy rains fell on the city during August of 2011, which became the prelude to Hurricane Irene, followed by the tail end of Tropical Storm Lee. This all climaxed on September 7 when, within a 24-hour period, up to 12 additional inches sent water pouring over the retaining walls built during the forties to keep the Susquehanna River within its banks.[21]

As a resident named Stacey Gould watched muddy water pour through her house, she told the *New York Times* that "In 2005, we had the 100-year flood, and in 2006, we had the 500-year flood. What-year flood is this?"[22] A hundred thousand people had to be evacuated from the Susquehanna watershed area, and more than 7,300 buildings in Greater Binghamton were damaged or destroyed.[23]

The mayor of Johnson City, Dennis Hannon, told the local *Press & Sun* newspaper, "This is going to be a long recovery." It was, or more accurately, it still is. But for BAE, it wasn't.

The Flood Plain

In 1942 the U.S. Defense Plant Corporation built Air Force Plant 59 for war manufacturing on the riverbank in Johnson City. During the war Remington Rand produced aluminum aircraft propellers there. Following a postwar fallow period, GE's Aeronautics and Ordnance Systems Division began building other parts for Cold War aircraft at the plant, especially flight controls. Activity ebbed and flowed with the tides of U.S. wars in Korea and Vietnam and the Reagan military buildup.[24]

Twice—in 1958 and 1986—the military tried to dispose of AFB 59, but the usual political forces aligned to keep it off the closure list, and under the successive management of GE, Lockheed, and BAE.

In May of 2011, BAE announced that more than 3,500 buses powered by Hybridrive were carrying nearly 2 million passengers a day in cities like Houston, Manchester (UK), Seattle, Atlanta, and Chicago. These trips, the company claimed, had eliminated 280,000 tons of CO_2 emissions and saved 25 million gallons of diesel fuel.[25]

By September, the BAE plant and the flood plain it sat on were swamped.

Steve Trichka, who was then general manager of power and energy management at the plant, describes a remarkably quick recovery, reminiscent of the steel mills after Johnstown's flood. They set up tents on slightly higher ground where the engineering team began taking apart, cleaning, reassembling and testing all their waterlogged equipment. Eighty percent, he says, turned out to be reusable.

They set up temporary workspaces in several locations and, "in a short time, pretty much all the workforce was back to work. We didn't really miss a shipment. It's pretty amazing."[26]

Less than a month after the flood, Trichka was in New Orleans, at the American Public Transportation Association Annual Meeting, unveiling the new HybriDrive design for BAE's higher-capacity articulated bus.

Endicott

BAE focused its search for a new home in Greater Binghamton, because as he says, "There's a technical base of capability and experience that you can't really duplicate very easily by picking up and moving." In a matter of days, they found that home, a building capable of accommodating the contents of a 620,000-square-foot manufacturing operation, in the adjoining village of Endicott. It was the old IBM site.

BAE took possession of the site within days of the flood because it had been largely vacant since 2002. Why?

Most of us think of computer companies as "clean" and heavy industry as "dirty." This is not necessarily so.

More than 20 years before, IBM had reported a 4,100-gallon spill of a commonly used industrial solvent on the property. As with the previous year's notorious disaster at Love Canal near Niagara, years passed before anyone started getting to the bottom of what the IBM spill had done to its environment. As Endicott Mayor John Bertoni saw it, "no one really knew the risk until it was too late. We didn't realize the magnitude to which it would seep and seek its own path and have ramifications."[27] According to the federal Environmental Protection Agency, IBM's hydrological study eventually determined that chemicals, including trichloroethene (TCE) and benzene, had leaked into the groundwater beyond the site, and into the river.

Environmental scientists then began to discover that vapor plumes from groundwater contamination could rise from soil into people's homes. In 2002 the New York State Department of Environmental Conservation (NYSDEC) required IBM to investigate whether this had happened in Endicott. It had.

That was the year IBM began drastically reducing its workforce of 4,000 in Endicott.

Two years later NYSDEC reclassified the former IBM property as a Class 2 Superfund site, that is, "one where hazardous waste constitutes a significant threat to the public health or environment." They ordered IBM to begin "appropriate cleanup measures."[28] By 2019, NYSDEC said a portion of the site still had contaminants underground, but that "the plume has shrunk significantly since remediation efforts started."[29] In 2011, BAE needed a place to set up shop, and Endicott needed new enterprise to take IBM's place. So, with remarkable speed, the move was done. How do BAE's managers feel about being there? Steve Trichka thinks it's safe to work there: "We've had it all tested through the state DEC. We monitor on regular intervals."

Devine adds,

> They remediated all the ground underneath…. It's a legendary environ-
> mental issue that's studied worldwide … and unfortunately those plumes
> reach for miles. But it's not sitting right under the building that we're
> working in…. We are in the buildings that aren't contaminated.

People have reacted to industry's toll on their environment in one of three ways: leaving the spoiled territory behind them to light out for cleaner pastures; living in denial; or staying to clean up the mess and keep the community intact. (Occasionally, the contamination is of such proportions, as at Love Canal and Chernobyl, for example, that there is no choice.) Planners call the second choice "infilling," and it is what BAE chose. The fallout for BAE workers, and the broader Binghamton community, is yet to be known.

Industrial Policy for the Next Level

Climate science in the new century has made it ever clearer that reducing emissions by half, as BAE's diesel electric hybrids do, is not enough. Bob Devine was put in charge of the "Advanced Applications" team assigned to figure out how BAE buses could "Get to Zero." After spending several years elsewhere, he came back to the clean bus business in 2007 "because I loved it so much. I was always really happy there."

The question of whether the future of all-electric transport runs best through electric batteries or hydrogen fuel cells has been an open debate for decades. The BAE team is working on both.

Barely two months after the 2011 flood, Trichka announced that they had delivered a demonstrator fuel cell-powered bus to a Southern California regional transit agency called Sunline Transit. Sunline's manager called it "the closest to a commercially available fuel cell bus that has been developed so far" by an American manufacturer. It actually combined a fuel cell module as the power plant with a lithium ion battery for storage and a HybriDrive system for propulsion.[30]

They developed the bus as part of a partnership with the Federal Transit Administration, CALSTART, the California Air Resources Board, and the California South Coast Air Quality Management District. While other defense contractors are CALSTART members, only Trichka now sits on its board.

With 260 member companies, utilities, research labs, and other "agency innovators" in the United States and beyond, CALSTART, as noted, has had successes helping to push zero emission, long-range technology into a wide range of vehicles, from heavy trucks to tractors to package delivery vans, along with the carrots (incentives) and sticks (regulatory frameworks) to accelerate their use. Its integrative approach to achieving a clean transport transition sketches some of the outlines of a national industrial policy dedicated to this goal.

The Biden administration's Clean Energy Revolution plan would push the United States further in this direction than ever before. Political pressures keep pushing back.

And we are getting a very late start. Despite major advances in both batteries and fuel cells, problems of storage, range, waste streams, and affordability remain with both products. CALSTART, among many others, started their search for solutions nearly three decades ago. One more time: It's safe to say that had we adopted a moon-shot style national industrial policy to solve these problems, we would be there by now. And we could be bending the curve of accelerating climate change in a less terrifying direction. We instead sent the defense budget soaring to heights not seen since World War II. And with a patchwork of clean transition programs perpetually scrambling for funding, we're still groping to solve our emissions problem and prevent climate catastrophe.

Devine is an industrial policy advocate. Speaking of his hydrogen fuel cell bus design, he "hope[s] that someday we'll see it take off and we see that there's a willingness to develop national policy to do it, to develop a hydrogen economy." As it is, his zero emission initiatives form a small fraction of BAE's hybrid business, and its hybrid business forms a similarly small fraction of what the factory in Endicott does. (The exact proportions are guarded as proprietary secrets. Trichka and Devine estimate the clean bus portion of BAE's business in Greater Binghamton at about 5%.) The financial incentives driven by the defense budget, against the meager amounts for mass transit, are still stacked up to keep it that way.

Devine spent numerous summer vacations writing grant proposals to fund his R&D. States like California are doing their best to subsidize cutting-edge green technologies. But Devine describes the process this way:

> They say, "We're going to put $10 million this year into this technology and we're going to go for three bidders," and everyone goes yeah yeah yeah and produces it, but you end up with a business that's not sustainable because … the program by definition has a start and end date that helps fund, test out and prove the technology … and then the subsidy goes away.

For years BAE was able to stay ahead in the hybrid electric market they pioneered. But their competitive advantage has lost some of its value recent years. Like the other big prime defense contractors, BAE is an experienced hand at "systems integration," that is, at making systems work that require harmonizing complex technologies and managing a complex supply chain. Applying this expertise to the clean bus market, they developed integrated designs connecting power plant to propulsion to electric accessories to energy storage.

Building an all-electric bus by dropping a battery or a fuel cell into it is a simpler proposition, however, and more and companies are deciding to do it themselves. Devine says,

> You could think of a purely electrified bus as a glorified golf cart. There's no blending of energy from a generator anymore. It's just basically charging batteries and then draining them, through a motor. So the controls problem solving is simpler.
>
> So for a company that's used to selling a smaller battery pack, a motor, and generator, all the cables connecting it together, that's a lot more content than [you need in] a pure electric. So one of the challenges as the technology changes is how do you maintain your content, and your profitability.
>
> This is where national policy comes in. Things like Buy American help. We can't obviously skew the cards so that we go completely nationalistic. But the Chinese come in with cheap designs that nobody can compete with. And they're willing to invest. Some of these companies have 20 percent government ownership.... There are Chinese battery bus companies [like BYD, in the next town over from Palmdale] that are doing this.

The United States isn't investing at that level. Without a whole national policy, he says, the transition won't happen on its own. "Because it doesn't solve a business case where you want to see a return every quarter."

Devine turns philosophical when he contemplates the pioneering work of his team. When New Flyer, one of the major North American bus manufacturers, decided to compete with BAE's fuel cell bus design, "Since they're so big and have so many customers, they can basically outsell us 10 to 1. That might not have been a win for BAE Systems but it was definitely a win for the environment."

In the Game

The HybriDrive team at BAE is still having its own wins, though. Between the time of the flood and six months later, when New York Senator Chuck Schumer unveiled the new BAE sign on the old IBM building, they had increased their tally of HybriDrive buses on the road from 3,500 to 4,000. There are now three times that many. In the course of two years, Tom Arseneault, the manager who started with Devine at GE, has engineered a fourfold increase in production, from about 500 buses a year to about 2,000. In June 2020 New York City placed another order for 435 more.

And their "Get to Zero" program has rolled out several alternative all-electric designs, including one that combines lithium ion batteries and hydrogen fuel cells, and another—with fewer, lighter and more-compact components—that uses only batteries. Their battery-only models have been hooked into the Bay Area Rapid Transit (BART) system where they are recharged wirelessly during layovers.

FIGURE 8.2 BAE in the old IBM building

Photo courtesy of Margaret E. Reynolds, used with permission.

"BAE's leadership has really stood by the business," says Devine.

> They've had a lot of drive to see it happen…. I think it's a point of pride for Steve [Trichka] and the business that they've built it to a point where 350 people have steady employment … which is damn good. Being able to turn around and say, "Hey, there's a business that got created, out of nowhere, employing all those people."

It is a good sign that Tom Arseneault, one of HybriDrive's architects, took over as CEO of BAE Systems, in April of 2020.

Binghamton's Military Economy and Its Other Ambitions

Mostly, though, Arseneault is in charge of a company that makes weapons systems. Electronic warfare systems for the F-35. Armored vehicles including mortar carriers for the Army. Ship-amounted guns for the Navy. And so on. And BAE is joined, 20 miles west down the river in Owego, by a larger piece of the region's military economy: Lockheed Martin's "Rotary and Mission Systems" division. It supplies helicopters to all five branches of the U.S. military.

"The commercial business is liked by the CEOs," Devine says. "They're kind of intrigued by it. But at the end of the day the decisions are made around the military business. They have to position themselves for that."

Because that's where the money is. So, changing that fact—tilting the balance of the federal budget toward other priorities—is the key to steering them toward manufacturing for the civilian world. Devine talks about working with BAE's legislative affairs (lobbying) people, with all their relationships with staff on the key committees governing military spending.

We say "Hey, we'd really like you guys to get into the Department of Transportation for me." And they'd say "Whaa?" They don't even know what street it's on. They would do it for us, but it's not really their day job.... But then the military budget curves down, and they say "Hey, this is a really good way to diversify the business."

That is not, to repeat, what's happening now. The last quarter of 2020 was Lockheed Martin's most lucrative ever.[31]

The mass-transit business, on the other hand, needs help. In recent years only about $10 billion a year has been allotted to the Federal Transit Administration's Transit Formula Grants, which are supposed to fund mass-transit systems across the country.[32] And in the world of the pandemic, Trichka says, "Transit is down, budgets are down." BAE Systems' 2020 10K half-year report to the SEC mentioned covid-19 challenges while citing increased production volumes for the F-35 and amphibious combat vehicle programs "off-setting the shortfall in commercial business." Most of the blueprints for federal infrastructure investment include substantial sums for mass transit that we haven't seen in years.

Devine thinks BAE is in the clean bus business "for the long haul. And there's a good future in it for them." But beyond the threat that their company might abandon the bus business, every employee of a major defense corporation lives with the possibility that its employer will abandon the community itself and go elsewhere. The most common denominator of such uprootings in recent decades, as we saw in Connecticut, has been the move to non-union southern states. Devine thinks (hopes) that "BAE's got so many sunk costs … in things like labs, business and program-specific wiring that it's hard to believe they would walk away."

But they could. New thinking in the field of economic development focuses on building an economic strategy around enterprises—anchors—that a community can be reasonably sure *won't* move away. One of the more celebrated examples is Cleveland, where purchasing and procurement agreements with the renowned Cleveland Clinic to buy locally has created a network of new businesses, supplying, for example, the hospitals' laundry services.[33]

Binghamton's primary anchor institution is the university there, one of four flagship University Centers within SUNY's expansive higher-education network. Beyond Binghamton University Hospital, the university is building a Health Sciences Campus in Johnson City, near the old Air Force Base/BAE site, including a nursing school taking up residence in the old, abandoned shoe factory. The new pharmacy school being built nearby, the anthropology professor Joshua Reno says, is "the biggest thing to happen in Johnson City in a long time."

But such economic engines have a long way to go to power Binghamton beyond its status as one of the two most distressed communities—as measured by job growth—in the state. Looking for those power engines is Stacey Duncan, executive director of the Broome County Industrial Development Agency, known around town as "The Agency." And one of the steep challenges on her plate is finding job-creating enterprises to move onto the empty flood plain in Johnson City that BAE had to vacate in a hurry back in 2011. The site has, like most closed military bases, and like BAE's current home, a toxics legacy, which the Air Force has been cleaning up to an industrial standard. Though they've "had inquiries," she says in 2021, it's pretty much "a blank slate."

Across town in Endicott, at the former IBM plant where BAE is now, the scars of IBM's toxic legacy fueled enough community opposition to prevent a lithium battery recycling plant from locating on the site. But now BAE has another new neighbor. In 2021 a company called Imperium3 New York (iM3NY) began standing up its first lithium-ion electric vehicle battery "Gigafactory." It is a locally grown enterprise, building on the work of Binghamton University professor Stanley Whittingham, Nobel Prize laureate for his work on lithium-ion battery development. Finance is coming from a combination of private equity and public incentives, including a grant from the Upstate Revitalization Initiative and New State tax credits dependent on job creation. The plan is to start with 150 employees, and then to expand to as many as 2,500 people over eight years, plus supply chain partners it is hoped will relocate near the factory.

We've seen on this tour the Pentagon's Office of Economic Adjustment fund a variety of local efforts at economic development. The key idea is that communities should get together to decide what they want to replace what they've had. Duncan, the Agency director, has transplanted that idea from Johnson City to Endicott. Following the defeat of the battery recycling proposal, she said "We need to have a collective community conversation of what we want to see in Endicott."

And she saw the coming of Imperium as reason for optimism "about clean technology coming to New York State. We're seeing the advancement of battery technology connected to university research, and growth not just on the research side but with commercialization as well."[34] Endicott's Mayor Linda Jackson imagines a "clean energy ecosystem" that keeps Binghamton University grads in the area and new subcontractors moving in. "We want Endicott to be known as the clean energy hub," she says.[35] This identity took another step toward fulfillment when, in the fall of 2021, Ubiquity Solar announced it would manufacture solar panels at the site.[36]

As the Imperium plan solidified, BAE announced a significant step forward in putting hydrogen fuel cells into the mix of power options for zero-emission buses. It is entering into an "all-inclusive partnership" with Plug Power Inc., which claims to be the "foremost provider of hydrogen fuel cell engines in the world" and to have "built more hydrogen refueling stations than any other company" as "the largest buyer of liquid hydrogen globally." Plug Power fuel cell engines will be integrated with BAE electric drive train systems in heavy-duty transit buses, and hydrogen and refueling infrastructure will be built for "end-customers use points."[37]

Conclusion

Norman Augustine is one of the most renowned names in defense contracting. He engineered the merger that created Lockheed Martin and got the federal government to underwrite his acquisitions of other military businesses during the post-Cold War shakeup. This put his company on top of the military contracting pile, where it has remained ever since. Augustine and Kenneth Adelman, in a spring 1992 *Foreign Affairs* article, coined the phrase that ever since has dogged the efforts of defense companies to turn their swords into plowshares: This transition, they said, has a record "unblemished by success."[38]

Though Augustine and Adelman were mostly referring to "massive" defense conversion, of the kind then being attempted in Eastern Europe, they also called conversion in the West "largely a failure." Just as the big cuts in the U.S. defense budget were beginning to bite, and contractors were beginning to examine non-military work, "unblemished by success," unqualified, became the catchphrase telling them not to try. It gave unknown numbers of them permission to retreat to the comfort zone of remaining defense contracts, and worker layoffs.

Within his own company, Augustine tolerated the HybriDrive business while it struggled but then, just after he retired, and before the business started to take off, his successor let it go. Under new more flexible management it then succeeded in doing what most defense contractors failed to do: apply and adapt the skills, processes, and technology learned in military production to meet the demands of the civilian marketplace. Proving Augustine's elegant turn of phrase wrong, its struggle revealed the challenges and pitfalls of the process, and the ways around them. In doing so, the HybriDrive team's products also pushed the technological frontier on the larger struggle to prevent climate catastrophe.

It has not turned BAE's ship many degrees from its course as a military contractor. Only a significant budgetary shift, complementing a strong civilian industrial policy, will do that.

Notes

1 Office of Local Defense Community Cooperation, "Defense Spending by State, FY 2020."
2 governmentcontractswon.com.
3 Phone interview, October 6, 2020. Reno is the author of *Military Waste: The Unexpected Consequences of Permanent War Readiness*, University of California Press, 2019.
4 The shoe factory is now a rusting hulk just outside of town, behind the Walmart.
5 Austin Weber, "General Electric Pioneers Jet Engine Manufacturing," *Assembly Magazine*, March 28, 2017, www.assemblymag.com/articles/93760-general-electric-pioneers-jet-engine-manufacturing.
6 "Air Force Plant 59: Johnson City, NY," *GlobalSecurity.org*, www.globalsecurity.org/military/facility/afp-59.htm#.
7 Matthew L. Wald, "G.E. Boycott is working, Group Says," June 13, 1991, www.nytimes.com/1991/06/13/business/company-news-ge-boycott-is-working-group-says.html.

8   Corporate Accountability International, "Boycott steps GE's nuclear weapons business," April 2, 1993, www.corporateaccountability.org/blog/boycott-stops-ges-nuclear-weapons-business/. .

9   Adam Bryant, "G.E. Will Sell Aerospace Unit for $3 Billion," November 24, 1992, www.nytimes.com/1992/11/24/business/ge-will-sell-aerospace-unit-for-3-billion.html.

10 Phone interviews with Devine were conducted on October 22 and November 11 of 2020, and April 29 and August 18 of 2021.

11 See for example *Profits Without Production* (Philadelphia: University of Pennsylvania Press, 1987).

12 Milton Friedman, "A Friedman Doctrine: The Social Responsibility of Business Is to Increase Its Profits," *New York Times*, September 13, 1970, www.nytimes.com/1970/09/13/archives/a-friedman-doctrine-the-social-responsibility-of-business-is-to.html.

13 "Lockheed Martin to deliver more diesel electric propulsion systems for New York City buses," *DieselNet*, January 13, 1999, https://dieselnet.com/news/1999/01lmco2.php.

14 "Lockheed Martin to build hybrid electric propulsion system for Army line-haul tractor," *DieselNet*, November 11, 1999, https://dieselnet.com/news/1999/11lmco.php.

15 "BAE Systems Agrees to Acquire Control Systems Business from Lockheed Martin for $510 Million," *defense-aerospace.com*, April 27, 2000, www.defense-aerospace.com/article-view/release/2147/bae-buys-lockheed-unit-for-.

16 "Top 100 for 2021," Defense News, https://people.defensenews.com/top-100/.

17 "BAE Systems, Inc.," www.baesystems.com/en-us/our-company.

18 "Top-100 defense contractors 2020," *AeroWeb: Forecast International's Aerospace Portal*, www.fi-aeroweb.com/Top-100-Defense-Contractors.html.

19 "Top 100 Defense Contractors," *Defense News*, https://people.defensenews.com/top-100/.

20 Ben Axelson, "Most distressed places in Upstate NY: 53 communities struggling to get by, ranked," NYupstate.com, May 21, 2019, www.newyorkupstate.com/news/2017/10/most_distressed_places_in_upstate_new_york.html.

21 Jeff Platsky, "Former BAE site in Johnson City ready for development after 2011 flood ravaged facility," Binghamton Press & Sun-Bulletin, February 20, 2019, www.pressconnects.com/story/news/local/2019/02/20/johnson-city-bae-site-ready-redevelopment/2929331002/.

22 Corey Kilgannon, "Flooding Persists in Southern Tier of New York," September 9, 2011, www.nytimes.com/2011/09/10/nyregion/ny-region-in-triage-mode-as-flooding-persists.html.

23 "100,000 Forced to Evacuate as Flood Waters Rise," *PBS NewsHour*, September 8, 2011, www.pbs.org/newshour/show/100-000-in-pa-n-y-forced-to-evacuate-as-floodwaters-rise

24 "Air Force Plant 59," Global Security.org, www.globalsecurity.org/military/facility/afp-59.htm.

25 Jeff Platsky, "Former BAE site in Johnson City ready for development after 2011 flood ravaged facility," pressconnects.com, February 20, 2019.

26 Phone interview, September 30, 2020.

27 Chloe Vincente, "40 years after spill, former IBM Endicott Campus still toxic," WBNG.com, November 21, 2019, https://wbng.com/2019/11/21/40-years-after-spill-former-ibm-endicott-campus-still-toxic/.

28 "Hazardous Waste Cleanup: IBM Corporation in Endicott, NY," Environmental Protection Agency, Last updated September 14, 2017, www.epa.gov/hwcorrectiveactionsites/hazardous-waste-cleanup-ibm-corporation-endicott-new-york#.

29 WBNG.com, ibid.

30 "BAE Systems Delivers Hydrogen Fuel Cell Bus for Sunline Transit," baesystems.com, November 15, 2011, www.baesystems.com/en-us/article/bae-systems-delivers-hydrogen-fuel-cell-bus-for-sunline-transit.

31 Aaron Gregg, "Pandemic opens a stark divide in America's aerospace industry," *Washington Post*, November 4, 2020, www.washingtonpost.com/business/2020/11/03/defense-industry-earnings/.

32 "Budgetary Resources: Federal Transit Administration," "FY 2021 Budget Highlights," U.S. Department of Transportation, www.transportation.gov/sites/dot.gov/files/2021-05/Budget-Highlights2022_052721_FINAL.PDF.

33 "Leveraging Anchor Institutions," Democracy Collaborative, February 3, 2020, https://democracycollaborative.org/learn/collections/leveraging-anchor-institutions.

34 Chris Potter, "How Endicott's industrial past impacts its economic future," *Binghamton Press & Sun-Bulletin*, April 29, 2021, www.pressconnects.com/story/news/local/2021/04/29/endicott-ny-looks-traces-ibm-past-economic-future/4734105001/.

35 Chris Potter, "Nearly 2 decades after IBM's departure, Endicott is hopeful for economic renaissance," *Binghamton Press & Sun-Bulletin*, May 3, 2021, www.pressconnects.com/story/news/local/2021/05/03/endicott-ny-looking-economic-turnaround-years-after-ibm-left/6980177002/.

36 Tom Passmore, "Huron Campus in Endicott, home to IBM for decades, sold to real estate company," *Binghamton Press & Sun-Bulletin*, October 1, 2021, www.pressconnects.com/story/money/2021/10/01/former-ibm-campus-endicott-sold-phoenix-investors/5951940001/.

37 Press release, "Plug Power and BAE Systems Partner on Hydrogen-Powered Electric Buses," Plug Power, Inc., April 29, 2021, www.ir.plugpower.com/Press-Releases/Press-Release-Details/2021/Plug-Power-and-BAE-Systems-Partner-on-Hydrogen-Powered-Electric-Buses/.

38 Kenneth Adelman and Norman Augustine, "Defense Conversion: Bulldozing the Management," *Foreign Affairs*, Spring 1992, www.foreignaffairs.com/articles/russia-fsu/1992-03-01/defense-conversion-bulldozing-management; William Hartung, "Stormin' Norman," *Washington Post*, July 28, 1996, www.washingtonpost.com/archive/opinions/1996/07/28/stormin-norman/df52d264-9643-4da4-aaee-586e8cc432a8/.

9
CONCLUSION

As this book went to press, a dictator launched a hot war with dreams of reconstituting his country's Cold War geopolitical status. As the United States formulated a response based primarily at first on non-military economic measures—targeting Russian elites rather than ordinary citizens—on humanitarian relief, and on avoiding escalation to a wider war, the pressure turned immediately to raising military spending. In the short term, this is where we are headed—the question no longer whether, but how much and for how long.

In this climate of uncertainty, one thing is certain: The Military Industrial Complex will capitalize (literally) on the crisis by pushing for more. This creature of the Cold War will continue to employ its repertoire of tactics to that end, Cold War, or hot war, or no.

It is in all of our interests to oppose them. Among the reasons: The United States' military budget is already more than ten times the size of Russia's. As noted, our budget exceeds the military spending of the next 11 countries put together, most of them our allies. It is higher now, in inflation-adjusted terms, than it ever was during the Cold War. Adding to it is not the answer. And, in spending decades building national security around military dominance, we have neglected the task of avoiding climate catastrophe, and we are running out of time. The war in Ukraine puts the spotlight on the need for investing in clean-energy economies to curb the reliance of democracies on oil from autocrats.

In the short term, the prospects for demilitarization have gotten tougher. The question is whether in the years ahead the world can find ways to build peace or become even more militarized. And in the long term there is no path to a livable, demilitarized planet that doesn't address the economic interests propelling war. This book has tried to be a resource for that task.

DOI: 10.4324/9781003293705-10

The Military Dominance Doctrine

Following World War II, U.S. geopoliticians chose permanent military mobilization to undergird the country's self-image as container of Communism and defender of the Free World. When this rationale dissolved along with the Soviet Union, here was a new one: America, the Sole Remaining Superpower, would use its military forces to secure itself and the world by "shaping the international environment" with "full-spectrum dominance."

Successive National Defense Strategy documents since then have preserved this line, while ratcheting up the budget to pay for it by simply adding new weapons for new missions on top of the old ones. The latest one (2018) leaned more heavily on one theme: Great Power Competition—in other words a return to Cold War geopolitics. Following a decade of strategic drift after the first Cold War ended, the 9/11 attacks birthed the Global War on Terror (GWOT). But as previously noted, while military spending soared to cover the two wars that were started in GWOT's name, the anti-terrorist mission was a poor fit both for Cold War weapons systems and the exotic new versions on the drawing board. Great Power Competition (GPC) had to return.

China has been its focus. In April of 2021, journalist Fareed Zakaria put it this way:

> Having spent two decades fighting wars in the Middle East without much success, the Pentagon will now revert to its favorite kind of conflict, a cold war with a nuclear power. It can raise endless amounts of money to 'outpace' China, even if nuclear deterrence makes it unlikely there will be an actual fighting war in Asia.[1]

And even if, as we saw in Chapter 7, the hair triggers of hypersonics and AI make inadvertent plunges into nuclear war *more* likely. The Russian invasion brought these dangers back into the spotlight, along with the dangers of a politics grounded in the quest for military supremacy.

The contractors are using Great Power Competition as one justification for increasing their own market power even further over the others. In 2020, for example, Lockheed Martin announced its intent to spend $4.4 billion acquiring rocket engine manufacturer Aerojet Rocketdyne, thus increasing its dominion over military aircraft manufacturing. Lockheed made the case that since China's military operations are "vertically integrated," competing with them means we have to do the same.[2] Traditional American scruples against adopting the practices of state-owned "socialist" enterprises can apparently go by the wayside. To its credit, the Biden administration cited the dangers of defense industry anti-competitive consolidation in disallowing the sale.

GPC—its currency now endowing it with acronym status—sustained decades of rising military spending and threatens to do so again. The Biden administration framed its decision to pull out of Afghanistan as necessary so that the military's attention and resources could be redirected toward China. And now toward Russia.

The long-term alternative is a strategic framework of military restraint, one that finally abandons the idea that U.S. security depends on a global military presence. It focuses on building structures of regional security led by regional actors. With respect to China, this would include scaling back the U.S. military presence in the South China Sea and promoting inclusive multilateralism among countries in the region around shared interests and dispute resolution.[3]

The day the United States ended its military operations in Afghanistan, historian Jeremi Suri made the case that the counterproductive force undermining U.S. national security was the military dominance doctrine itself. The "peril of creating such a large force," he wrote, was that the larger the military budget has grown, the more likely we are to use it, and less likely to invest in better substitutes. "American leaders have depended on our armed forces so much because they are so vast and easy to deploy.... We send soldiers where we need civilians because the soldiers get the resources." Reviewing the history of failed postwar interventions—Vietnam, Lebanon, Iraq, Afghanistan, among others—he argued that we would be better off with a smaller military and a doctrine of strategic restraint.[4]

Economic Interests

As we've seen, the Military Industrial Complex (MIC) embeds military contracts in as many communities as possible to sustain political support for ever higher military budgets.

Pumping millions of military dollars into a community is an obvious way to secure its dependency, and loyalty, and it usually does. But, on this tour, we kept encountering defects in the prosperity gospel that preaches high military spending as the ticket to community affluence. Connecticut's economy hangs on the boom-and-bust cycles of military procurement (including its potentially-endangered species called F-35), as well as on the veiled threats from its contractors to go where unions aren't. And the poverty rate in East Hartford, with the highest concentration of those contractors in an affluent state, is well above the national average.[5] As is the poverty rate in Palmdale, hosting three of the Big Five primes and a cornucopia of new military contracts.[6]

Then there is Los Alamos, where the people at the top of the mountain make among the highest incomes per capita in the nation, and the people at the bottom make among the lowest. And Johnstown's, Binghamton's, and Pine Bluff's buy-ins to the military economy have failed to lift them off lists of the most distressed places in America. And a clear majority of the states with the most military contracts have poverty rates above the national average.

Here are the poverty rates of the top three military contracting locations in each of the top 20 military contracting states, compared to that average:

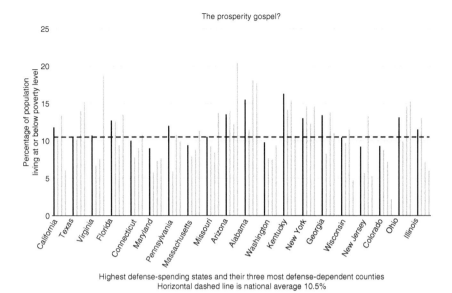

The prosperity gospel?

Highest defense-spending states and their three most defense-dependent counties
Horizontal dashed line is national average 10.5%

FIGURE 9.1   Percentage of U.S. population living at or below poverty level

Without question, all those taxpayer-funded Pentagon dollars flowing into favored places in each state do make a few people extremely rich[7] and create well-paying jobs for a lot more—although as noted, not as many jobs as if those dollars were invested in, for example, education, health care, clean energy, or even tax cuts.

But this financial lift does not reliably extend to the community as a whole: in nearly half of these locations bathed in military money, and more than half of the most defense-dependent states, the poverty rate remains stuck above the national average.

We found some of these communities looking elsewhere for sources of economic dynamism: to infotech in Johnstown for example, or in Arkansas's case biotech and more recently, casinos, or clean energy and transport (California, Connecticut, New Mexico, New York). It's hardly surprising that they have tried their hardest to diversify beyond the defense market when that market is down. As we've seen, the end of the Cold War provided the most significant catalyst to this effort, propelling creative work in California, Connecticut, New Mexico, and New York. The more modest decline in the Pentagon's budget precipitated by reduced spending on the Afghan and Iraq wars also produced initiatives we can learn from in Pennsylvania, Connecticut, and Arkansas.

None, though, have significantly managed to disengage their economies from Pentagon dependency. The overall pull of rising military budgets has been too strong, and the countervailing pulls too weak.

So how to build new sources of prosperity for these communities? It comes down to two requirements: Cut the bloat out of the military budget and reinvest those dollars into civilian national missions critical to our well-being and our national security.

After 80 years, can we finally break the stranglehold of military-industrial interests on our national and local economies? Since it's clear that this cannot be done without cutting the Pentagon budget, we'll begin there, acknowledging that in 2022 the task got harder.

The Fate of U.S. Military Spending

During the first two decades of the twenty-first century, U.S. military spending more than doubled. In one of the last president's many whipsawing moves, he pushed military spending levels to near-postwar historic highs while complaining periodically about the Military Industrial Complex's drain on the Treasury and the excessive profiteering of its contractors. Helping along those profits, though, was his policy of vigorously promoting U.S. arms sales—for some contractors, making up as much as a fifth of their revenues—thus spreading the catalysts of war around the world and creating new arms races—not to mention new rationales for "next generation" U.S. weapons, at the expense of other national priorities. And when in 2020 the pandemic squeezed most of the rest of the national economy, U.S. military contractors did fine, becoming a port-in-a-storm, go-to recommendation to stock market investors looking to protect their portfolios.[8] After the Russian invasion, their fortunes improved even more.

One key indicator of future U.S. military expenditures suggests the fix has been baked in to send them higher. The 2020 annual GAO assessment of the Pentagon's major defense acquisition programs (MDAP) found 85 of those programs already underway, and 8 more soon to be, budgeted to cost $1.8 trillion before they're done. History nearly screams that the actual cost will be much more: The current programs have accumulated more than $628 billion in cost growth, amounting to 54 percent more than the projected cost when programs began.[9]

Will this history continue to repeat itself? Budgeteers faced with military programming that outstrips the money allocated to it *could* focus on living within their means: by prioritizing programs and getting rid of others, adjusting strategy and instituting reforms to curb cost overruns. The contractors are employing strategies of their own, some traditional, some novel, to ensure that, instead, the solution is more money. Beyond the traditional devices we have surveyed, such as strategic campaign contributions and revolving-door insider job placements, are the updated-but-perennial appeals to national security needs. These include the expressions of alarm that Pentagon spending takes a smaller slice of GDP than it used to—as if when the national hoard of public and private wealth expands, national security requires the Pentagon to take a bigger slice.

Then there are the efforts to add money for military projects outside the regular budget, like the Overseas Contingency Operations (OCO) account and the National Sea-Based Deterrent fund. In 2020 DoD redirected most of the $1 billion intended for pandemic relief to military contractors for jet engine parts, body armor, and dress uniforms.[10] In 2021 came the pitch to give the Navy extra procurement money by applying $25 billion in infrastructure funds to the repair of naval shipyards.[11] New funding triggered by the Russian invasion threatens to become a blank check.

Taking office, the Biden administration sent a good signal by elevating the role of diplomacy in U.S. foreign policy over military power as its foreign policy signature. According to a "source close to Biden," introducing the members of its National Security team before a DoD secretary had been chosen was a way of signaling "that this is not an administration that is going to put the Pentagon at the center of things."[12] And its budget increased spending on non-military foreign engagement by nearly 20 percent. This budget remains 3 percent of federal discretionary spending, though, compared to 50 percent for DoD.

By September of 2021 the defense spending authorizers in Congress on the armed services committees declared that even preserving Trump-era increases wasn't enough. Both the House and Senate committees, dominated by members whose careers are tied up in a web of military interests, added approximately $25 billion *more* to the defense budget.

In the Senate, there was only one dissenter. In the House, all Republicans and a slight minority of Democrats voted in favor. Among them were Joe Courtney (D-CT) and Rob Wittman (R-VA), the team still in charge of submarine funding, whose alliance for this cause in 2018, in the same hearing room, kicked off our tour. The cause in 2021 added more than $500 million to, once again, accelerate production of the *Virginia*-class sub.

By March of 2022 the Biden administration had added $15 billion on top. And Congressman Adam Smith, the chair of the House Armed Services Committee who had spent years complaining of Pentagon bloat, was talking about the bigger military budget that would be needed in the coming year.

If Congress succeeds in building in increases like these every year, they will add in excess of $1.2 trillion over the next decade to the currently-projected military budget.[13] For context, these things were also happening outside the room: Climate change was engulfing the West in fires, and the East and South in floods; and the United States was ending the longest war in its history.

While Congress wrangled through the year over spending $350 billion on priorities including health care, child care, and climate change prevention, it had no trouble agreeing on a military budget more than twice as large.

Ways to Cut

Honest assessors, including one long-term secretary of defense, acknowledge that this military budget hides plenty of waste. Robert Gates served as defense secretary—in both the Bush II and Obama administrations. In 2009 he declared this:

If the Department of Defense can't figure out a way to defend the United States on half a trillion dollars a year ($613 billion in today's dollars, and we have since then added close to $200 billion more) then our problems are much bigger than anything that can be cured by buying a few more ships and planes.

There is no scarcity of obvious places to cut. In 2016 the *Washington Post* uncovered an internal Pentagon study showing that the Defense Department could save $125 billion over five years simply by reducing its bloated workforce, which currently includes 200,000 people working in property-management alone. Evidently fearing this tip of the iceberg might inspire more scrutiny underneath, the Pentagon then imposed security restrictions on the data, "ensuring," the *Post* said, that "no one could replicate the findings."[14]

Digging deeper, in 2019 a Sustainable Defense Task Force made up of former White House and Congressional budget experts, retired military officers and former Pentagon officials and think tank analysts from across the political spectrum (I was a member), outlined a plan to reduce Pentagon spending by $1.2 trillion over ten years—a decrease of more than 15 percent—and explaining how each cut enhanced rather than threatened U.S. security.[15]

Other more ambitious frameworks include the "Moral Budget" of the Poor People's Campaign, which laid out $350 billion in cuts per year targeting for example unneeded military bases and the Foreign Military Financing (FMF) program; and the work of the People Over Pentagon coalition, led by the Project on Government Oversight and Public Citizen. This coalition outlined $199 billion in one-year cuts with such targets as specific procurement reforms and weapons system cancellations including the B-1B bomber, the F-22 fighter and the Long-Range Standoff Weapon.[16] On the right of the political spectrum, the Cato Institute's list of cuts includes many of the same items.[17] And in the middle, the Congressional Budget Office's annual report, "Options for Reducing the Deficit," includes billions in military budget cuts; their overlaps with these other lists suggest the beginnings of common ground.[18]

Cutting Isn't Enough

On this tour we've encountered communities struggling to replace defense dependency with new economic foundations. The results have been underwhelming, again, mostly because the federal budget incentives overwhelmingly push in the opposite direction. The engineers at BAE Binghamton, for example, struggle to cobble together the finances for their bus project with a grab bag of state, federal, and private sources—crumbs relative to the military procurement money readily available to fund the rest of BAE's operations in the buildings around them. To research scientific questions beyond the purview of nuclear weapons, Los Alamos scientists likewise have to put in considerable work to fund them—work that their nuclear weapons projects do not require.

This book has made the case for changing those incentives with a new industrial policy. It would abandon the charade that state planning is not the "American Way," since Congress votes every year to devote most of our federal money to a state-planned military economy. A new policy would also jettison the idea that the nation can't and shouldn't organize its resources around any national mission besides war. The book has made no secret of its convictions about what a new industrial policy's primary mission should be. Drastically reducing our greenhouse gas emissions to prevent the worst ravages of climate change is an all-hands-on-deck project that can't wait. The International Energy Agency provided the most authoritative recent portrait of urgency in its 2021 "Net Zero by 2050: A Roadmap for the Global Energy Sector." Limiting climate change by keeping global temperature rise to 1.5 degrees Celsius by 2030 will require, for example, tripling the rate of energy efficiency improvements of the past two decades, quadrupling the amount of solar and wind power every year, and moving adoption of electric vehicles from its current 5 percent of global sales to 60 percent. While most of the technology to do this is readily available, the transition will require technological innovations, to solve—for example, the problem of the deleterious effects of mining for the metals electric batteries currently require.[19]

Climate change is also, as the U.S. military itself warns, an "urgent and growing" national security problem. As the largest institutional emitter of greenhouse gases, the military must be part of the solution. But it is not a national security project the military can lead. To date the military's climate-change policy response focuses mostly on protecting its own military capabilities (against bases under water, for example, and troops running out of power in the field). And where a transition to new power sources saves money, the military has envisioned plowing those savings into new weapons.

The path to success requires transforming our transportation, energy systems, housing, and agricultural systems. The Biden administration outlined a climate industrial policy whose scope and magnitude make a plausible beginning on its overall goals of cutting U.S. emissions in half by 2030 and getting to net zero by 2050. It combines spending to transform our infrastructure to run on clean power, including grants and incentives to build a national network of electric-vehicle charging stations, with investments in home energy efficiency, R&D funding for new clean energy technology, tax credits for electric vehicles, and the elimination of fossil-fuel subsidies, plus a regulatory framework pushing all of this along in both the private and public sectors.[20] The gauntlet of the legislative process has in the short term blocked most of this from getting underway.

Do Military Contractors Have a Role?

Do they need to have one? Why not do as the Biden administration has done so far, and provide them with near-record levels of military spending, while simultaneously boosting spending on the civilian side of the ledger? Rather than shifting *from* a militarized industrial policy *toward* a civilian industrial policy, the policy so far just adds one on top of the other.

Our soaring national debt provides one reason why this difference matters. Many economists now recognize that deficit spending on the national level can be necessary and useful, particularly when the costs of borrowing are so low. But they emphasize that this spending needs to concentrate on investments that pay off by improving the productivity of the economy as a whole. The Biden administration's infrastructure plans qualify, because they focus on repairing the economy's choke points, including its channels of transportation and communication, and its failures of support for a healthy and educated workforce, in addition to the mounting disruptions of climate change. Increasing the layers of advantage between U.S. weapon stockpiles and everybody else's—to spend 13 times as much as everybody else put together? Spending 14 times?—does not qualify. That kind of debt we can't afford.

Secondly, this all-hands-on-deck emergency requires recouping and reapplying to it what we can of the trillions spent on military technology since the end of World War II. The key to pulling this off is, again, to both reduce military spending and reinvest the savings to create new civilian markets. With a big enough shift, many military contractors will follow the money, as they always have. At the height of the post-Cold War downturn, in 1993, even Lockheed (now 96% defense dependent) publicly predicted that "the growth in Lockheed's forecast will come from our nondefense sector," and that in five years just 55 percent of its revenue would come from DoD.[21] As we've seen, they found ways to avoid this scenario.

The last time we had the chance to redirect our economy substantially toward productive non-military investment—after the Cold War—deficit fears prevented the shift of enough resources to create demand-pull to civilian markets sufficient to overcome 50 years of militarized industrial policy. We have another chance now. We need to acknowledge two things: First, how much further along we would be in slowing climate change if we had made this shift back then and, second, that today we have no more time to fail.

There is a third reason for looking at military contractors as potential contributors to this industrial transition, and it has to do with the powerful strategies documented here that the contractors have used to keep the MIC's interests front and center in national policy. How to challenge that power? Part of the answer is to give them a stake in this new focus of investment. One crucial caveat though: Their expertise in promoting exotic, high-tech, expensive technologies must not be allowed to crowd out companies who know how to produce civilian products the people and the planet need and can afford. Requests for proposals (RFPs) need to prioritize, not the well-connected, but those with demonstrated expertise in civilian, green manufacturing.

As we've seen, military contractors have a way of botching their attempted moves into civilian manufacturing by sticking with the military manufacturing practices they know. Here is one more example from my own home. Among

Lockheed Martin's efforts at diversification, the most successful are generally considered to be the company's forays into information services, airport management, and commercial satellites. During the entire first week of my daughter's senior year in high school, though, she didn't have a class schedule. Lockheed had won the contract to put her school district's scheduling system online. True to its record with military contracts, Lockheed's effort was overbudget and overdue.

If some of the military contractors' work is to be repurposed for the sake of the planet, it must be clear that they have to put in the work to adapt their operations for new conditions. In Binghamton we found one willing to grapple with this task. It remains to be seen how many others are both equipped and inclined to do so.

As already noted, the federal government created several programs during the post-Cold War period to help them, focusing mostly, and appropriately, away from the big primes and toward small and medium manufacturers. For example, the Commerce Department's Manufacturing Extension Centers developed an expertise in helping small- and medium-sized companies make the transition to civilian manufacturing. This capability could be revived and further targeted to green manufacturing.

Let's turn now to the local communities we've been touring that need help finding their way to non-military production. Several have worked with the Pentagon's Office of Economic Adjustment (OEA). This embattled agency has now changed its name, underscoring that its mission was never a good fit at the Pentagon. Now called the Office of Local Defense Community Cooperation, it has thus officially left behind the mission of reducing defense dependency. If we are to shift national attention and resources toward climate change, local defense-dependent economies will need an alternative to OEA helping them move in this direction. A good candidate exists: the Commerce Department's chronically underfunded Economic Development Administration (EDA) has economic transition planning assistance in its mandate. Part of the country's shift toward a green industrial policy could be strengthening EDA's capacity to help local defense-dependent communities become part of it.

We have seen on the tour how, on the ground, our military industrial policy has gotten in the way. President Biden declared in his first address to a joint session of Congress, "There's simply no reason why the blades for wind turbines can't be built in Pittsburgh instead of Beijing!" The key reason they haven't been until now is that for decades U.S. industrial policy has prioritized military production over civilian manufacturing—with a massively subsidized, guaranteed market, as well as subsidized foreign arms sales and R&D funds. In numerous places we have come across foreign companies providing the expertise in green manufacturing that our homegrown manufacturers, left mostly hanging by their own bootstraps, lack.

In Palmdale for example, next door to one of the most intense concentrations of U.S. military contractors in the country, we found a Korean company building rail cars for Los Angeles and, down the road, a Chinese company making electric buses. And outside of Johnstown—a few mountain ridges over from

Pittsburgh—Chinese manufacturer Talesun has constructed one of Pennsylvania's largest solar farms on top of the remains of a coal mine; the panels are manufactured in China and Thailand.[22] A green industrial policy would turn this around.

But Can the U.S. Addiction to Excessive Military Spending Be Curbed?

Here are some of the forces pushing in that direction:

Congress

While boosting military spending is a cause usually identified with the political right, as we've seen, it attracts much more bipartisanship than most (remember, for example, the comradeship of Representatives Courtney and Wittman). There have always been congressional dissenters to this cause.

But for the first time there is a Defense Spending Reductions Caucus, a core group prepared to press for a shift of Pentagon funds toward non-military priorities. Its membership is so far dwarfed by the Congressional Progressive Caucus (CPC), which formally opposed the fiscal year 2021 defense budget as needing to be "meaningfully reduced and reallocated to programs that serve the needs of the American public." Of the plethora of congressional caucuses, the CPC is the third largest, after the New Democrat Coalition and the Republican Study Committee. The CPC supported bicameral amendments to the 2021 defense bill authorizing a 10 percent cut in the budget and reallocating the cut to priorities including infrastructure, sustainable energy, community health centers, and hiring more teachers.

Although many in Congress have responded to the Ukraine crisis with calls to add billions to the military budget, the larger point still holds: In the context of a mounting list of neglected national priorities, a strategy designed to win wars against Russia and China while maintaining the capability to win regional conflicts and wage a global counterterrorism campaign is both misguided and unaffordable in the context of other neglected national priorities. In April of 2020, the chair of the House Armed Services Committee, Adam Smith, discussed a strategic rationale for cuts in the military budget. When the U.S. builds its national security strategy around preserving its global military dominance, Smith said, it is committing to a goal no longer attainable, and thus making the country less safe. He cited the proliferation of cheap drones available to all as ending the "era of unipolarity."

"Swarms of these drones … [costing] next to nothing can deliver more firepower than an F-35, which can't get into the zone because of the surface-to-air missiles that are guarding it." Beyond switching to a strategy that is "a lot more nimble, a lot smarter, and a lot more diversified," he prescribed replacing one seeking to dominate all adversaries with one that looks for ways to make it clear that conflict was not in their interests: "Deterrence, not dominance."[23] While

Smith more recently committed to a higher budget, his rationale for altering the goal of military superiority remains convincing.

In addition to the debate over the Pentagon's top line, there are bicameral bills to close the revolving door, improve defense lobbying transparency and, yet again, reform some procurement practices to reduce waste.[24]

And during most of the Cold War the government had an important tool for Pentagon waste reduction it now lacks. In 1951 Congress created a Renegotiation Board that had specific criteria for reviewing defense contracts for excess profits. Where it found them, it could renegotiate the contract and return the excess to the U.S. Treasury. In 1976 Congress let the program die. It needs to come back.[25]

The Administration

Before taking office, the Biden administration made gestures of intent toward restraining military spending. In 2020 the now-Deputy Defense Secretary Kathleen Hicks wrote an article in *Foreign Affairs* titled "Getting to Less." Once installed, the administration adopted the mainstream consensus favoring increases to both the military and domestic spending, and rough parity between them. By 2022, with their most important domestic-spending goals stalled, this parity was endangered, as spending to "provide for the national defense" was taking precedence over the need to "promote the general welfare." The administration's commitments to address the struggles of the citizenry at home and to protect them from the worst ravages of climate change depend on reversing these priorities.

Civil Society

Non-governmental critics of U.S. military spending have been around since postwar turned into Cold War; quotations of Eisenhower's Military Industrial Complex speech keep on coming. In the climate of new possibilities for this cause, they have adopted two different ways of breaching the silos that have held them back. One focuses on building trans-partisan alliances, uniting groups on the right, who want to rein in government spending in general, with groups on the center and left who want to shift spending from military forces to domestic needs. The key effort here is called the Pentagon Budget Campaign.

The other principal strategy works to link the military spending issue to other issues and movements—among them climate, public health to fight pandemics, and immigration. The Poor People's Campaign, for example, is picking up where Martin Luther King left off in connecting the "three evils" of racism, economic exploitation, and militarism. The People Over Pentagon Campaign links environmental groups like 350.org, Greenpeace, and Friends of the Earth with public-interest advocacy groups like Public Citizen with foreign policy groups, including Just Foreign Policy and the Center for International Policy, with immigrant rights groups like United We Dream with political advocacy groups like MoveOn and Indivisible with Social Security Works. To name a few.

Corporations

Beyond Boeing, whose business is split down the middle between military and commercial aerospace, the major contractors are still playing around the edges of civilian manufacturing, including in the field of low-emissions technologies. Without a major shift of federal resources in that direction, this is unlikely to change.

In 2019 the Business Roundtable, a group of 181 CEOs, including four of the big five military contractors, signed a statement in response to growing suspicion of corporate behavior. This statement purported to redefine the purpose of a corporation beyond producing a fat quarterly earnings report for the shareholders (and obese compensation for its CEO). Some see this as the beginnings of "stakeholder capitalism," responsible to customers, workers, and communities as well as shareholders, and deemphasizing quarterly profits in favor of long-term investment. Unfortunately, a year later a Ford Foundation study found little evidence that much beyond public relations had actually changed.[26]

There are movements looking to follow the lead of climate activism in applying shareholder pressure, including divestment strategies, on military contractors, though without the urgency of a climate crisis to propel them, these movements are smaller. In April of 2021 an activist shareholder broached a dialogue with the CEO of General Dynamics at its annual meeting, forcing the attendees, for that moment, to see the company's work in the context of its effects on the ground in Yemen.[27]

Pressure for change is also coming from within some companies, as for example the Google employees, discussed in Chapter 7, who managed to stop their company from completing a DoD contract enabling drones to better pinpoint their targets using AI. (They didn't succeed in their goal of steering the company away from all military contracts.)

Public Opinion

Mangled political arrangements in Washington have widened the gap between what majorities of the public say they want and what their elected representatives do in their name. But to the extent that public opinion can be made to drive policy, polling prior to the Russia invasion of Ukraine found support for a demilitarized foreign and industrial policy. For example, a 2018 survey by the Chicago Council on Global Affairs found successive generations progressively less in favor of military interventions than their parents.[28] A year later Data for Progress polled voters from across the political spectrum on their conception of top security threats, and found significant majorities putting the climate crisis, the rise of authoritarianism and white nationalism, and global economic competition above the risk of foreign attack from a hostile nation or terror group.[29]

A 2021 survey of American foreign policy attitudes found twice as many respondents favoring decreasing as increasing. military spending; Americans 18 to 29 favored a decrease by a factor of five to one.[30] And large majorities have favored major investment in infrastructure centered on a transition to a low-emissions economy.[31] Following the invasion, as mentioned above, majorities favored prioritizing economic and humanitarian measures over military confrontation. The long-term effect of the crisis on public opinion toward increased military spending remained uncertain.

The Last Word Is a Question

Since its founding, the United States has based its commitment to "provide for the common defense" squarely on its military force, and, by the measure of our federal budget allocations, it still does. But accelerating climate change is creating a constellation of security problems that these forces cannot solve. Just after the world experienced the hottest month in recorded history, the scientists constituting the International Panel on Climate Change concluded that our failure to act so far now ensures that continued warming over the next 30 years is inevitable.[32] Earlier in the year the same group concluded that the world's current pledges to curb emissions are vastly insufficient to avoid the most catastrophic effects of climate change.[33]

If National Security is really about identifying our greatest security threats and prioritizing our resources to meet them, then it's time—and past time—to seriously reallocate our security resources toward this existential threat. Doing so will allow the communities we've visited to find ways to join an economy built around the climate security imperative. Will the U.S. economy, steeped in the structures and self-serving mechanisms of its Military Industrial Complex, be able to adjust before it's too late?

Notes

1 "The Pentagon is using China as an excuse for huge new budgets," *Washington Post*, March 18, 2021, www.washingtonpost.com/opinions/the-pentagon-is-using-china-as-an-excuse-for-huge-new-budgets/2021/03/18/.
2 Eli Clifton, "Lockheed cites 'great power competition' with China in bid to consolidate engine market," *Responsible Statecraft*, March 29, 2021, https://responsiblestatecraft.org/2021/03/29/lockheed-cites-great-power-competition-with-china-in-bid-to-consolidate-engine-market/.
3 See Michael D. Swaine, Jessica J. Lee and Rachel Esplin Odell, "Toward an Inclusive & Balanced Regional order: A New U.S. Strategy in East Asia, Quincy Institute, January 2021, www.defenseone.com/ideas/2021/04/us-armys-plan-needlessly-duplicates-air-force-strike-capabilities/173118/.
4 "History is Clear. America's Military is Way too Big," *New York Times*, August 30, 2021, www.nytimes.com/2021/08/30/opinion/american-military-afghanistan.html.

5 U.S. Census Bureau QuickFacts, "East Hartford town, Hartford County, Connecticut," July 1, 2019, www.census.gov/quickfacts/fact/table/easthartfordtownhartfordcountyconnecticut/PST045219.

6 U.S. Census Bureau QuickFacts, "Palmdale city, California," July 1, 2019, www.census.gov/quickfacts/palmdalecitycalifornia.

7 Sarah Anderson, "Defense contractors and the joys of war profiteering," *New England Diary*, January 7, 2020, https://newenglanddiary.com/home/sarah-anderson-defense-contractors-and-the-joys-of-war-profiteering/1/7/2020.

8 Tim Gray, "How to Invest in the Military-Industrial Complex, *New York Times*, April 20, 2020, www.nytimes.com/2020/04/15/business/how-invest-military-industrial-complex.html.

9 U.S. Census Bureau QuickFacts, "Palmdale city, California," July 1, 2019, www.census.gov/quickfacts/palmdalecitycalifornia.

10 Aaron Gregg and Yeganeh Torbati, "Pentagon used taxpayer money meant for masks and swabs to make jet engine parts and body armor," *Washington Post*, September 22, 2020, www.washingtonpost.com/business/2020/09/22/covid-funds-pentagon/.

11 Joe Gould, "Sea power backers propose $25 billion to fix US shipyards," *Defense News*, April 28, 2021, www.yahoo.com/now/seapower-backers-propose-25b-fix-093000037.html.

12 Hans Nichols and Jonathan Swan, "Scoop: Biden weighs retired General Lloyd Austin for Pentagon chief," November 27, 2020, www.axios.com/biden-defense-secretary-lloyd-austin-1af4a702-aaf2-4e9e-9f5f-3ece6a9ff362.html.

13 Andrew Lautz, "Lawmakers pave way for $1.2 trillion in new military spending over next 10 years," *Responsible Statecraft*, September 2, 2021, https://responsiblestatecraft.org/2021/09/02/lawmakers-pave-way-for-1-2-trillion-in-new-military-spending-over-next-10-years/.

14 Bob Woodward and Craig Whitlock, "Pentagon buries evidence of $125 billion in bureaucratic waste," December 5, 2016, www.washingtonpost.com/investigations/pentagon-buries-evidence-of-125-billion-in-bureaucratic-waste/2016/12/05.

15 William D. Hartung and Ben Freeman, "SUSTAINABLE DEFENSE: A Pentagon Spending Plan for December 2020 and Beyond," Center for International Policy, December 2020, www.internationalpolicy.org/program/Sustainable-Defense-Task-Force.

16 Shailly Gupta Barnes, Lindsay Koshgarian and Ashik Siddique eds., "Poor People's Moral Budget," Institute for Policy Studies, June 2019, https://ips-dc.org/wp-content/uploads/2019/07/PPC-Moral-Budget-2019-report-FULL-FINAL-1.pdf; Project on Government Oversight, "Guide to Cuts," May 2019, https://peopleoverpentagon.org/guidetocuts/.

17 Benjamin H. Friedman, "How the U.S. Military Can Save $1 Trillion," November 6, 2016, www.cato.org/commentary/how-us-military-can-save-1-trillion.

18 www.cbo.gov/system/files/2020-12/56783-budget-options.pdf.

19 International Energy Agency, "Net Zero by 2050," May 2021, www.iea.org/reports/net-zero-by-2050.

20 Rachel Siegel, "What's in Biden's $2 trillion jobs and infrastructure plan?" *Washington Post*, March 31, 2021, www.washingtonpost.com/us-policy/2021/03/31/what-is-in-biden-infrastructure-plan/.

21 Patrice Apodaca, "Lockheed Looks Beyond Defense: Conglomerate: The company is calling its current strategy to diversify a big part of its future," *Los Angeles Times*, June 29, 1993, www.latimes.com/archives/la-xpm-1993-06-29-fi-8299-story.html.

22 Randy Griffith, "Solar power farm construction begins," *Tribune-Democrat*, May 28, 2021, www.tribdem.com/news/local_news/capturing-the-sun-solar-power-farm-construction-begins/article.

23 Shaun Waterman, "HASC's Smith: U.S. Should Abandon Quest for Military Preeminence," *Air Force Magazine*, April 22, 2021, www.airforcemag.com/hascs-smith-u-s-should-abandon-quest-for-military-preeminence/.

24 See, for example, Tara Golshan, "Elizabeth Warren's new policy rollout targets Pentagon corruption," *vox.com*, www.vox.com/2019/5/16/18627204/elizabeth-warren-2020-anti-corruption-pentagon.

25 "Renegotiation Act," *CQ Almanac 1976*, 32nd ed. (Washington, DC: Congressional Quarterly, 1977) 1976, pp. 510–512, http://library.cqpress.com/cqalmanac/cqal76-1187035.

26 Peter S. Goodman, "Stakeholder Capitalism Gets a Report Card. It's Not Good," *New York Times*, September 22, 2020, www.nytimes.com/2020/09/22/business/business-roundtable-stakeholder-capitalism.html.

27 Benjamin Novakic, "Transcript," *Responsible Statecraft*, May 2021, https://responsiblestatecraft.org/wp-content/uploads/2021/05/Benjamin-Novakovic-Transcript.pdf.

28 Chicago Council on Global Affairs, "The Clash of Generations? Intergenerational Change and American Foreign Policy Views," June 25, 2018, www.thechicagocouncil.org/research/public-opinion-survey/clash-generations-intergenerational-change-and-american-foreign.

29 Elizabeth Beavers, Alexander McCoy and Sean McElwee, "Memo: Americans want a progressive overhaul of American Foreign Policy," October 17, 2019, www.filesforprogress.org/memos/progressive-foreign-policy.pdf.

30 Eurasia Group Foundation, "Vox Populi," September 28, 2021, https://egfound.org/2021/09/inflection-point/#full-report.

31 Hart Research, "New poll: Three in Four Voters Support Build Back Better Reconciliation Package," August 11, 2021, https://climatepower.us/resources/new-poll-three-in-four-voters-support-build-back-better-reconciliation-package/.

32 "IPCC: Climate Change 2021: The Physical Science Basis: Summary for Policymakers," August 7, 2021, www.ipcc.ch/report/ar6/wg1/downloads/report/IPCC_AR6_WGI_SPM.pdf.

33 "NDC Synthesis Report," United Nations Climate Change, February 26, 2021, https://unfccc.int/process-and-meetings/the-paris-agreement/nationally-determined-contributions-ndcs/nationally-determined-contributions-ndcs/ndc-synthesis-report.

APPENDIX

Poverty and military spending data for the three highest military spending counties in the twenty highest military spending states.

State	State Poverty Rate	1st Contracting County	1st County rate	2nd Contracting county	2d County rate	3rd Contracting county	3rd County rate
California	11.8	San Diego	10.3	Los Angeles	13.4	Santa Clara	6.1
Texas	10.5	Tarrant	10.2	Dallas	14	Bexar	15.2
Virginia	10.7	Fairfax	6.7	Arlington	7.6	Norfolk	18.7
Florida	12.7	Orange	12.6	Brevard	9.4	Duval	13.5
Connecticut	10	New London	7.8	Fairfield	9	Hartford	10.8
Maryland	9	Anne Arundel	5.8	Montgomery	7.3	St. Mary's	7.7
Pennsylvania	12	Chester	5.9	Allegheny	10.8	Delaware	9.9
Massachusetts	9.4	Middlesex	7.9	Essex	8.8	Bristol	11.3
Missouri	10.5	St. Louis	9.3	Jefferson	8.4	Jackson	13.7
Arizona	13.5	Pima	14	Maricopa	12.2	Yuma	20.4
Alabama	15.5	Madison	11.5	Dale	18.1	Mobile	17.7
Washington	9.8	King	7.7	Kitsap	7.5	Pierce	9.4
Kentucky	16.3	Jefferson	14.2	Fayette	15.4	Hardin	10.7
New York	13	Jefferson	14.6	Orange	12.3	Oneida	14.6
Georgia	13.4	Cobb	8.3	Fulton	13.8	Houston	11
Wisconsin	10.4	Winnebago	9.7	Marinette	11.5	Waukesha	4.7
New Jersey	9.2	Burlington		Passaic	13.3	Morris	5.3
Colorado	9.3	El Paso	8.8	Arapahoe	7.2	Douglas	2.2
Ohio	13.1	Greene	9.9	Hamilton	14.6	Montgomery	15.3
Illinois	11.5	Cook	13	Lake	7.2	DuPage	6

Sources: DoD, "Defense Spending by State—FY 2020, https://oldcc.gov/dsbs-fy2020; U.S. Census Bureau QuickFacts, 2019, www.census.gov/quickfacts/fact/table/US.

INDEX

For Product Safety Concerns and Information please contact our EU
representative GPSR@taylorandfrancis.com
Taylor & Francis Verlag GmbH, Kaufingerstraße 24, 80331 München, Germany

www.ingramcontent.com/pod-product-compliance
Ingram Content Group UK Ltd.
Pitfield, Milton Keynes, MK11 3LW, UK
UKHW021448080625
459435UK00012B/419

* 9 7 8 0 3 6 7 2 5 7 6 7 5 *